THE MAN OF SIN

*UNCOVERING THE TRUTH
ABOUT THE ANTICHRIST*

KIM RIDDLEBARGER

BakerBooks
Grand Rapids, Michigan

APRIL 2008

© 2006 by Kim Riddlebarger

Published by Baker Books
a division of Baker Publishing Group
P.O. Box 6287, Grand Rapids, MI 49516-6287
www.bakerbooks.com

Printed in the United States of America

Library of Congress Cataloging-in-Publication Data
Riddlebarger, Kim, 1954–
    The man of sin : uncovering the truth about the Antichrist / Kim Riddlebarger.
      p. cm.
    Includes bibliographical references.
    ISBN-10: 0-8010-6606-9 (pbk.)
    ISBN 978-0-8010-6606-1 (pbk.)
    1. Antichrist. I. Title.
  BT985.R53 2006
  236—dc22
                                           2005036431

THE MAN OF SIN

CONTENTS

A WORD OF THANKS

While I have been thinking about this topic for many years, the idea for this book was conceived during a church-planting conference in Reno, Nevada, when Dr. Robert Godfrey, president of Westminster Seminary California, gave a fascinating lecture on the millennial views of the seventeenth century. Not only did Dr. Godfrey suggest helpful ways to resolve some of the issues in the amil-postmil debate: he briefly touched on some of the Antichrist speculation of the English Puritans. Godfrey's lecture led me to Christopher Hill's book *Antichrist in Seventeenth Century England*,[1] and I was off and running.

A word of thanks goes to those of you who endured my lectures and public musings on this topic, as well as to the consistory of Christ Reformed Church for giving me the time to complete my research. Thanks, as always, go to the White Horse Inn crew, Michael Horton, Rod Rosenbladt, and Ken Jones, for all of the stimulating discussion. Thanks also to our producer, Shane Rosenthal, for his helpful suggestions and corrections with the manuscript. Thanks to my wife, Micki, for managing to put up with all the "creepy" books lying around the house while I was doing my research. Thanks also to our church administrator, Winona Taylor (the "church lady"), for all of her help and proofreading of the manuscript.

Thanks also to Don Stephenson, my editors Chad Allen and Paul Brinkerhoff, and the rest of the kind folks at Baker for letting me do this!

INTRODUCTION

We live in an age when far too many Christians learn their doctrine from Christian novels and from American popular culture. This is a sad situation because Christians are supposed to learn their doctrine from the pages of Holy Scripture. One doctrine where far too much Christian thinking is informed by Christian fiction and popular culture than by Holy Scripture is the doctrine of the Antichrist. *The Man of Sin: Uncovering the Truth about the Antichrist* seeks to be a corrective to this unfortunate situation.

In those circles where Christians are especially interested in Bible prophecy and the relationship between current events and end times, it is common to hear people engaging in speculation about the dreaded archenemy of Jesus Christ. Is the Antichrist already alive? How will he deceive Israel into making a peace treaty with the nations of a revived Roman Empire? Will Christians be around to face this dreaded foe? Or will they be removed from the earth by the rapture before the seven-year tribulation begins, leaving only those "left behind" to face the wrath of Antichrist?[1] What is the "mark of the beast"? Is it tied to some current form of technology? How will this mark be applied to all those who serve the Antichrist and do his bidding? And what about the mysterious number 666? Can we "crack the code" and use this number to identify the Antichrist before he shows himself in public? These are all common, interesting, and important questions.

Much of this kind of speculation is promoted by adherents of dispensational premillennialism, which is the system of understanding the end times set forth in the hugely successful *Left Behind* novels written by Tim LaHaye and Jerry Jenkins. Sadly, the dispensational approach to biblical prophecy generally, and to the doctrine of Antichrist specifically, has drifted far afield from the teaching of Scripture and from the way in which Christians throughout the ages have understood this doctrine.

The church fathers, by and large, believed that the Antichrist would be an apostate Jew who would appear after the fall of the Roman Empire and who would claim to be the Messiah in a rebuilt temple in Jerusalem. The medieval church was rife with speculation regarding the Antichrist. After the time of Constantine and the rise of the Holy Roman Empire, any foe who attacked Christendom was labeled "Antichrist"—from the marauding Vandals and Huns, who threatened to sack the city of Rome, to the armies of Muhammad from the east, sweeping throughout the Mediterranean and threatening Christendom with conquest and subjugation. But as Christendom suffered repeated military and political setbacks and needed almost constant reform from internal corruption and apathy, there were those who actually dared to think it possible that the Antichrist might arise from within. Perhaps Antichrist would be a pope who would somehow manage to deceive the faithful before truth finally prevailed.

The Reformers and their theological descendants were of one mind on this subject: the Antichrist is the pope—the so-called "historicist" interpretation. Since the pope claimed to be the Vicar of Christ and promulgated doctrines Protestants did not believe to be biblical, the pope was considered the Man of Sin foretold by Paul in his second letter to the Thessalonians (2 Thess. 2:3). In response, Roman Catholic theologians argued that the pope could not be the Antichrist because the manifestation of the Antichrist was yet future. It was Protestantism, Rome argued, with its undermining of church authority and sacred tradition that was actually preparing the way for Antichrist's appearance.

While the majority of popular Christian writers today who address the subject believe that there is an Antichrist yet to be revealed, as do I, an increasing number of writers (preterists of various sorts) contend that the Antichrist has already been revealed at the time of the cataclysmic events associated with the destruction of the Jerusalem temple by the Roman legions in AD 70. Preterists (those who believe most of the prophecies of the New Testament have already been fulfilled and who thus see all the NT, not just Revelation, through this lens) are quite correct to take seriously the "time is near" language throughout the New Testament (e.g., Rev. 1:3), unlike the dispensational-ists, who push most prophetic fulfillment off into the distant future. But preterists are quite wrong to assert that the events of AD 70 exhaust those prophecies related to our Lord's second advent. Rather, these prophecies speak of events that precede our Lord's coming at the end of the age or are directly tied to it, including those prophecies that deal with Antichrist. Many preterists believe that Nero was the Antichrist (the beast). This would mean that the Antichrist is not a future foe; he is a relic of history. The Antichrist has already made his appearance on the scene and has been defeated by the power of Christ and his kingdom.

A word of clarification about preterism is in order, since we shall be referring to the "preterist" interpretation throughout this study. So-called "full" or "hyper" preterists believe that the Lord returned in AD 70, ending the curse and bringing about a nonbodily resurrection and the final judgment—a position too extreme for so-called "partial" preterists, who believe that while Christ returned in judgment upon Israel in AD 70, he will nevertheless return again bodily at the last day to raise the dead and judge the world. Since hyper-preterism denies both the bodily resurrection of believers and the bodily advent of our Lord at his second coming, hyper-preterism is heretical. Partial preterism, however, is not heretical and is held by many Reformed and evangelical Christians.[2] Throughout this study I speak of preterism in the generic sense of those who tie the fulfillment of the prophecies regarding Antichrist directly to the events of AD 70.

Given the nature of this topic—always controversial and often prone to wild speculation—my goal is to examine the biblical data regarding the Antichrist and the way in which Christians have understood this doctrine across the ages. To best accomplish this, *The Man of Sin* is organized as follows: Chapter 1 introduces the subject, attempts to explain our fascination with the Antichrist, examines the consequences of our understanding of this doctrine, and then sets out the manner in which we should approach this doctrine so as to treat it with due seriousness and avoid unbiblical speculation. Chapter 2 deals with the forerunners of Antichrist in the Old Testament, giving us the backdrop against which the writers of the New Testament speak of the archfoe of the Messiah. Chapter 3 deals with a number of preliminary considerations regarding the doctrine as it is found in the New Testament, including the two-age model, Jesus's teaching regarding the abomination of desolation, and the phenomena of "double fulfillment" in which biblical prophecies have more than one fulfillment. This gives us a biblical foundation to look at the complex New Testament teaching about this individual and his predecessors.

There are three distinct strands of teaching about the Antichrist in the New Testament. These three strands will be discussed separately before we attempt the difficult task of tying the three strands together while at the same time attempting to keep each particular emphasis distinct. Chapter 4 deals with the first strand of teaching, the discussion in John's Epistles about the presence of many antichrists in the apostolic church along with John's declaration that the appearance of these antichrists is the indication that it is now the last hour. Chapter 5 deals with the second strand of teaching, which is found in the Book of Revelation (especially chapters 13 and 17), regarding the mysterious figures of the dragon, the beast, and the false prophet, all of which likely refer to the Roman Empire of the first century and to future anti-Christian governments and their leaders until the time of the end. Chapter 6 discusses the third and final strand of teaching, which is Paul's reference in 2 Thessalonians 2:1–12 to the Man of Lawlessness, who sets himself up in the temple of God and then demands to be worshiped. Is Paul referring to events of AD 70? Or is he using the word *temple* as a metaphor for the church? If it is the latter, is Paul referring to the papacy or to an end-times Antichrist?

Having looked at these individual strands of biblical teaching, in chapter 7 we will then briefly survey the church's teaching on this subject, concentrating on issues and personalities discussed throughout the earlier chapters. In chapter 8 we will offer a summation of the ground previously covered and set forth a series of conclusions about the Man of Sin developed in light of the three strands of teaching regarding Antichrist and set forth against the backdrop of the Old Testament.

I write this book as a Reformed Christian committed to an amillennial eschatology.[3] I believe that the church has faced a series of antichrists from the time of the apostles and that this series of antichrists will culminate in the appearance of the Antichrist immediately before the return of Jesus Christ at the end of the age. This future appearance of Antichrist reflects the fact that he is a false Messiah *par excellence* who mimics the work of Christ. As Christ died, was raised from the dead, and will return, so too Antichrist has his own death, resurrection, and second coming, all designed to imitate the redemption secured by Christ so as to direct worship unto his master, the dragon.

The final manifestation of Antichrist will amount to an unholy marriage between the bride of heresy and blasphemy against Christ and his kingdom and a groom that takes the form of a satanically energized state (government), which pours out its wrath upon the people of God. The appearance of this individual—commonly called the Antichrist—in whom these two powers merge (heresy and the worship of state) is the supreme and final harbinger of the coming of Jesus Christ at the end of the age to judge the world, raise the dead, and make all things new.

Throughout this study I will draw heavily from a number of theologians, such as Meredith Kline, G. K. Beale, Geerhardus Vos, B. B. Warfield, Richard Bauckham, and F. F. Bruce, whose brilliant insights and perceptive exegesis of key biblical texts have remained hidden from many because these writers do not write to a broad evangelical audience. It is my hope that my efforts will bring some of their insight and learned understanding of the biblical text to a much wider audience.

Unlike a number of historians, such as Bernard McGinn, who have written otherwise outstanding treatments of the history of this subject, I write with the conviction that Christian theologians must treat this subject as part of God's self-revelation in Holy Scripture. The subject matter is a revealed doctrine and not a mere legend. The doctrine of Antichrist is not merely the fruit of a Christian people's fearful response to the hostile and unbelieving world around them, as certain writers contend.[4] It is important to survey the history of the Christian interpretation of the doctrine of Antichrist before attempting to reach final conclusions because this doctrine has so often been framed by Christian writers through a contemporary historical lens, which colored how they framed this doctrine. But the Bible presents this doctrine in a particular theological context with the expectation that even as Jesus Christ died on a Roman cross and was raised from the dead in ordinary human history (leaving a rich man's tomb quite empty), so too the Antichrist is (or will be) a figure of history. He is not merely a figment of the Christian imagination.[5] He will have a name and a face, and he will be cast into the lake of fire by none other than Jesus Christ (see Rev. 19:20; 20:10).

Different Perspectives on the Doctrine of Antichrist

	Time of Antichrist Appearing	Distinctive Emphases
Church Fathers (Irenaeus, Hippolytus)	Many antichrists (false teachers) will appear, but the Antichrist is yet future.	Antichrist will be an apostate Jew and false Messiah. He will appear after the fall of the Roman Empire in a rebuilt temple in Jerusalem.
Dispensationalism (John Walvoord, Hal Lindsey, Tim LaHaye)	Many antichrists (false teachers) will appear, but the Antichrist is yet future.	Antichrist appears during the seventieth week of Daniel after the rapture (see Dan. 9:24–27) and makes a peace treaty with Israel at the beginning of the seven-year tribulation period. He reveals his true identity in a rebuilt temple in Jerusalem by betraying Israel.
Historicism (Reformers, Westminster Confession of Faith)	Antichrist is identified with the papacy.	The temple mentioned by Paul in 2 Thessalonians 2:4 is a reference to the church, not the Jerusalem temple. The harlot Babylon (Revelation 17) is a reference to the Roman Catholic Church.
Preterism (B. B. Warfield, Ken Gentry)	Many antichrists (false teachers) present throughout the course of this age. The beast of Revelation 13 was Nero and the Book of Revelation depicts events of the first century that are already largely fulfilled.	Jesus Christ returned in judgment upon Israel in AD 70, closing out the end of the Jewish age. When Paul refers to the temple in 2 Thessalonians 2:4, he is referring to the Jerusalem temple, which was destroyed in AD 70.
Reformed Amillennialism (Geerhardus Vos, Anthony Hoekema)	Many antichrists (false teachers) appear throughout the course of this age. A final Antichrist is yet to come in the form of state-sponsored heresy and the persecution of the church.	The temple mentioned by Paul in 2 Thessalonians 2:4 is a reference to the church, not the Jerusalem temple. Antichrist's appearance is tied to a time of great apostasy (cf. Rev. 20:1–10).

1

A Morbid Curiosity

Misconceptions about Antichrist

The Antichrist in Evangelical Film and Fiction

None of us want to die as a martyr. None of us want to look down the barrel of a gun and hear the demand that if we want to live, we must deny our allegiance to Jesus Christ and bow the knee to Satan and his henchmen. We do not want to be persecuted by the state or forced to live in abject poverty. None of us want to be imprisoned because we are followers of Jesus Christ. But this is exactly how the rise of the Antichrist is depicted in much of popular Christian literature. When the Antichrist appears, we are told, it will be a time of unprecedented tribulation when what I have just described will be the fate of many. Renounce Jesus Christ and take the "mark of the beast" or else die as a martyr.

The 1972 movie *Thief in the Night* opens with the rapture having just taken place. It then goes on to depict the fate of those who have been left behind. Who can forget the scene in which a man's razor buzzes in the sink while his unbelieving wife looks for him in a panic? Forced to run for her life from the forces of Antichrist (easily identified as those thuggish types driving vans with "Unite" stenciled on the side), the movie's heroine must either be willing to die as a martyr or else forfeit her soul. Many who saw the movie recall how *Thief in the Night* terrified them. But that is what this movie was designed to do—scare people into accepting Jesus as their Savior before it is too late. Wait too long to come to Christ and you may find yourself missing out on the rapture and facing the Antichrist. We might quibble with the message but not with the motive.

Thief in the Night may reveal more about the 1970s "Jesus people" subculture than it does about what the Bible actually teaches about the Antichrist. Larry Norman's haunting ballad, *I Wish We'd All Been Ready,* with the last words of the refrain, "You've been left behind," sums up the message of this movie. In rather sensational and vivid terms, *Thief in the Night* lays out the dispensational interpretation of end times through which many American Christians continue to understand the end times and the doctrine of Antichrist.[1]

The dispensational understanding of end times underlying *Thief in the Night* had already been made accessible to millions through Hal Lindsey's 1970 best-selling book, *The Late Great Planet Earth*, which, according to the *New York Times*, sold more copies in America than any other single book during the 1970s.[2] As Lindsey explains to his readers, the reestablishment of the nation of Israel in the land of Palestine in 1948 is the critical sign that the end is at hand. Because of the remarkable fact that the Jews are back in their ancient homeland, God's prophetic stopwatch has been restarted so that the rapture can occur at any moment. The rapture is Christ's invisible coming "like a thief in the night" (cf. 1 Thess. 5:4) when all Christian believers are instantaneously snatched from the earth, marking the beginning of the seven-year tribulation when Antichrist comes to power and seduces the world's inhabitants. All of this, supposedly, was foretold by Daniel in the famous prophecy of the seventy weeks (see Dan. 9:24–27).[3]

When the rapture occurs and Christians are removed from the earth, the long-dreaded Antichrist takes his place on the stage of world history. Described by Lindsey as the "Future Fuehrer," this man will be able to explain the disappearance of countless people suddenly missing after the rapture.[4] The leader of a revived Roman Empire, the Antichrist first appears as a problem solver and beloved world leader who amazingly brings the nations of the earth together in an unprecedented time of peace. In dramatic fashion he survives an assassination attempt and begins to perform miraculous signs and wonders—his primary means of deception. Even the nation of Israel is taken in by his cunning. The Antichrist is able to negotiate a seven-year peace treaty between Israel and her hostile neighbors—something no one else has ever been able to accomplish.

But this man's benign appearance is deceiving. He's not *really* solving the world's problems. He's plotting and scheming to betray Israel and to set himself up as the object of the world's worship. Using the latest technological innovations, he will set up a lifelike image of himself and demand to be worshiped. He will seek to place his mysterious mark (666) on the forehead or the back of the hand of those whom he is beginning to enslave. Empowered by Satan himself, the Antichrist's intentions will slowly but surely be revealed to all, before three and a half years of world peace give way to an unprecedented time of warfare, persecution, and just plain evil. At some point the Antichrist will enter the rebuilt Jewish temple in Jerusalem and demand to be worshiped as God. This act of unspeakable blasphemy is the supreme revelation of the Antichrist's true character.

The Antichrist's horrific deeds set in motion the geopolitical events that lead to the final battle of Armageddon, when Jesus Christ bodily returns to earth and not only destroys those armies allied against Israel but also casts Antichrist and all his henchmen into the lake of fire. Only after Antichrist and his followers have been overcome by Christ does the millennial age begin (the thousand years of Rev. 20:1–10). As lions lie down with lambs, God's people now rule the earth with Jesus Christ, who will sit upon David's royal throne in the city of Jerusalem. This is the dispensational grid in a nutshell.

One reason the *Left Behind* novels and films are so successful—they have sold millions of units—is because they are written for people who already believe and embrace this dispensational understanding of end times, which is now thoroughly established among American evangelicals. Tim LaHaye and Jerry Jenkins have sown in the fertile soil prepared by *The Late Great Planet Earth* and *Thief in the Night*. While LaHaye and Jenkins give Antichrist a name (Nicolae Carpathia)—and in the *Left Behind* movies he's given a face (he's short, blond, and, since he is Romanian, has a noticeable Eastern European accent)[5]—many of those who read these novels are scarcely aware of how speculative all of this is. The reason these books are so compelling and packed with interesting detail is precisely because they are fictional. But compelling stories about a fictional Antichrist are easily confused with the biblical teaching about the Antichrist, especially when people are familiar with the former and far too ill-informed about the latter.

While the recently developed dispensational variety of Antichrist speculation dominates our age, we are not the first generation of Christians who lived when "pin the tail on the Antichrist" was a popular Christian pastime. Throughout the history of the church, Christians have resorted to calling political threats and theological rivals "Antichrist." The Middle Ages were filled with Antichrist speculation. Seventeenth-century England was not only a tumultuous time politically but was also a time when Antichrist speculation among the otherwise cautious Puritans was surprisingly commonplace.[6] How many American evangelicals are even aware of the fact that their own Protestant forebears were adamant that the Antichrist had already appeared and also possessed a name and a face—the sitting pope of Rome?

Because we live in an age when Christians are not well-informed about either biblical teaching or the reflection of the church, many professing Christians fear an enemy of which Scripture does not speak (a slick, young world leader, such as a Nicolae Carpathia), and they ignore those enemies of which

Scripture repeatedly warns—purveyors of false doctrine within our own churches and tyrannical governments that persecute God's people. The Bible teaches that the antichrist is anyone who denies the doctrine that Jesus Christ is God in human flesh and that many antichrists were already present in the first century (1 John 4:3). Yet some may find this latter statement disconcerting because they have not heard it before, although it is found in Scripture.

It is understandable that Christians would fear the archenemy of Jesus Christ. They should. Jesus himself told us that if we love him, the world will hate us (Matt. 10:22). The very thought of a personal manifestation of a satanically empowered individual who wages war upon the people of God is a frightening thing. Images of persecution and martyrdom are found throughout the Book of Revelation. Jesus warned his own disciples that this would be their fate (Matt. 24:9). When divorced from their biblical context and the prior theological reflection of the church, these themes can be easily mutated through the lens of fiction and film. In today's evangelical church, novels are often read as though they were systematic theology—a most unfortunate circumstance since the power of a good novel and the importance of systematic theology are both undermined. If people can easily create alternative realities due to the power of images conveyed through film,[7] then surely devotees of biblical prophecy are prone to allowing what they've seen portrayed in a fictional story on a DVD to become what they assume the Bible teaches, even if it teaches no such thing.

Obviously, ours is a difficult context in which to examine afresh the biblical teaching on the subject of the Antichrist, but it is nevertheless something I will attempt to do throughout *The Man of Sin*. I would ask the reader to be willing to evaluate what follows in the light of Scripture. My guess is that you will be amazed at how little of what many people—Christians included—assume to be the biblical teaching regarding the Antichrist is actually taught in Holy Scripture.

When many people think of the Antichrist, they often think of things they have seen in *Thief in the Night* or in the *Left Behind* movies, which have little basis in Scripture. But Christian fiction is not the only negative influence upon the way in which people form their views on this subject. Antichrist has also had a starring role in American pop culture.

The Antichrist as the Personification of Evil

There is a reason this topic has garnered so much interest across the centuries.[8] Evil is much more frightening to us when it is manifest in the concrete actions of a particular person. We can speak of the "evils" of communism and fascism, but it is not until a Joseph Stalin or an Adolf Hitler appears on the world scene that such evil is no longer theoretical; it is now personified. These men act out on the stage of world history the kind of evil most of us can scarcely conceive. While the neighborhood drug dealer, rapist, or burglar is capable of great harm to our property and our person, the local authorities are able to keep criminals like these in check. Such people will be punished and put in jail. But when the Antichrist comes, all this will be turned upside down. The good guys will become the bad guys.

When men such as Hitler or Stalin come to power, entire national economies are devoted to building the implements of war. Armies march. Navies wage war on the seas. Conflict extends to the ends of the earth. Daily life is turned on its head. Normal commerce ceases. Vast amounts of treasured belongings and personal property are destroyed. The victims of this upheaval are countless individuals, each with a personal horror story. In what is the greatest of ironies, those who are supposed to protect us instead perpetrate the worst crimes—think of Hitler's Gestapo or Stalin's KGB. Evil flourishes. The suffering such leaders and their henchmen inflict upon those they rule is inconceivable. It is nevertheless real and impacts every area of life.

Hitler and Stalin were not the first to do this. But they are the closest to us in time. We read of Alexander the Great's heartless conquest of the peoples from Macedonia to the Indus River, simply because he could.[9] We read of despots such as Nero, who defy all societal norms in an insatiable pursuit of personal pleasure. We read of an Attila the Hun or of Islamic armies of the East led by a Saladin, who ruthlessly conquer and enslave. These men are legendary because of their mercilessness.

The point is that evil is most frightening when it is realized in a head of state who is able to exercise economic control and use national military power for his own ends. Surely that is why the doctrine of Antichrist is such a frightening and yet fascinating topic. This individual is thought to be evil personified—the supreme manifestation in human history of Satan's relentless war to overcome all that is good. While Christians have always faced the temptation to speak of the evil in their own age as a manifestation of the Antichrist, most everyone understands that what is meant by the term *Antichrist* is not just any manifestation of evil but the supreme and final manifestation of Satan's rage at the end of time through the agency of a particular individual.

The Antichrist is expected to conquer with the insatiable craving of an Alexander. He will possess the lust for pleasure and the desire to be worshiped like Nero. He will possess a hatred for God's people like that of Hitler. He will betray and kill his own as did Stalin. He will be these things and more. The roster of the tyrants of history amounts to but a series of dress rehearsals for the final personification of evil in the person of the Antichrist. We fear this man like no other.

As God incarnate, Christians believe that Jesus Christ is the supreme manifestation of good. One thinks of Jesus's words to Philip, "Anyone who has seen me has seen the Father" (John 14:9). The Antichrist, on the other hand, is the supreme manifestation of all that is evil. As a human agent of Satan, Antichrist is either a counterfeit Christ or else the very antithesis of the incarnation of our Lord. If Jesus is God in human flesh, the Antichrist is Satan with a human face.

While not taught anywhere in the Bible, the notion of the incarnation of Satan is taken up in several films such as *Rosemary's Baby* (1968).[10] In this disturbing film, a lapsed Roman Catholic couple (played by Mia Farrow and John Cassavetes) make a deal with the devil. As a result, Mia Farrow's character eventually gives birth to a child who is Satan incarnate. Another film that is very loosely based on the beast of the Book of Revelation is *The Omen* (1976). When the newborn son of a "well to do" couple (played by Gregory Peck and Lee Remick) dies, he is secretly replaced with a diabolical substitute, the infamous Damien. Damien was born of a jackal in Rome on the sixth day of the sixth month in the year 1966. His scalp bears the mysterious mark of the beast (the number 666). The exercise of his mysterious powers (always accompanied by an evil smirk) brings about the death of both his mother and his father—ensuring that in the sequel (*Damien—Omen II*), he is well on his way to world domination.[11] These and similar movies have helped to popularize the idea that Antichrist is Satan incarnate.

Rosemary's Baby and *The Omen* are very dark. They were produced at the time when the "God is dead" movement had reached its zenith and when Hal Lindsey and others were making apocalyptic drama popular well beyond the relatively small circle of dispensationalists.[12] These terrifying films placed in the minds of many viewers a series of unbiblical images about Satan, the Book of Revelation, and the Antichrist—images that even years later continue to influence the thinking of many Christians and much of popular culture.[13] Ask someone about the Antichrist, and many times the answer is connected to these or similar films. If people are unfamiliar with the content of the Bible, it is easy to fall back on the images they have gleaned from nonbiblical sources such as these. It is not much of an intellectual leap from thinking of Antichrist as a human agent of Satan to thinking of him as Satan incarnate—an altogether unbiblical idea.

If the Antichrist is the personification or incarnation of evil, then once he bursts upon the scene he will begin a ruthless persecution of God's people. Not only is this a theme in much of evangelical literature and film (such as *Thief in the Night*), but secular movies graphically depict the horrible fate of all those who seek to oppose the archenemy of God. In *The Omen*, Lee Remick's character is thrown to her death from an upperstory hospital window after surviving a terrible fall from a second-story landing in her home, which just happened to be arranged by Damien and his satanic nanny. The Catholic priest who figured out Damien's true origin is impaled by a piece of a cross. Likewise, the investigative reporter is beheaded by a sheet of glass in a mysterious accident just when he put things together. And then at the end of the film, Gregory Peck is mistakenly killed by police as he seeks to put Damien to death on the altar in the same church that Damien had earlier refused to enter. These vignettes convey the imagery that the Antichrist figure is supremely powerful and cannot be overcome by mere mortals. Members of the clergy, Christian symbols, and Christian places of worship may disrupt his progress, but they cannot stop him nor thwart his ultimate purpose. The viewer is left with the message that people are helpless against him since at the least the Antichrist is empowered by the devil if he's not the devil himself.

Since the Antichrist cannot be overcome by human effort, it will take the direct intervention of God to keep evil from conquering in the end—the thought of evil triumphing over good is a conclusion that neither Christians nor popular culture, apparently, can accept.[14] Therefore, the appearance of the Antichrist is the harbinger of the end of the world and the day of final judgment. When the Antichrist finally appears, the second coming of Jesus Christ cannot be far behind. Drawn rather loosely from the biblical text and Christian tradition, the Antichrist of film and fiction is finally overcome by the same Jesus (also loosely drawn from Scripture) he so militantly opposes. What story could be any more compelling than one in which we have both the ultimate protagonist and the ultimate antagonist and in which the antagonist gets what he deserves in the end?

Some Implications of Antichrist Expectation

An image as powerful as that of Antichrist can exercise a tremendous influence upon a society far beyond the confines of popular culture. As Bernard McGinn has pointed out, "The whole history of Western Civilization can be read through the prism of John's apocalypse."[15] Not only has John given us a linear view of history that culminates in a final judgment, but the anticipation of this final judgment by Christians, coupled with the role that Jesus Christ and the forces of evil will play in bringing history to an end, means that Antichrist speculation is inevitable. We cannot escape it.

If McGinn is correct about the extent of the influence of John's Apocalypse on the history of Western civilization (and I think he is), then certainly Robert Fuller's judgment about America is also true. In his book, *Naming the Antichrist: The History of an American Obsession*, Fuller writes, "The history of the Antichrist reveals Americans' historical obsession with understanding themselves—and their enemies—in the mythic context of the struggle between absolute good and evil."[16] Fuller sees Antichrist speculation as part of the uniquely American ability to mythologize all of life through the lens of biblical metaphor and the apocalyptic beliefs handed down to us by the apostle John. While I reject Fuller's attempt to explain the Antichrist doctrine in purely psychological terms, I do think the American experience, especially since the beginning of the Cold War, has lent itself to the kind of Antichrist speculation Fuller describes. The success of films such as *Rosemary's Baby* and *The Omen* and the phenomenal success of the *Left Behind* novels bear this out.

There are a number of reasons why this is the case—most of them related to the course of world history of the past generation. The most important historical event fueling this current wave of Antichrist speculation is the fact that the Jews are back in the land promised to Abraham, giving powerful weight to the idea that ancient prophecies in the Bible accurately explain (and predict) current events. This fact by itself creates tremendous political intrigue and keeps wars and rumors of wars on the front page of the morning paper and in the evening news. Every Israeli leader and his Arab counterpart may be bringing about those events that will lead to the final battle of Armageddon and the end of the age.

With the rise of world communism and threat of world domination at the hands of a militarist atheistic ideology, an atomic conflagration was also a real possibility. Now that communism has fallen, the nuclear threat has been transferred to shadowy Islamic terrorists who might be the beneficiaries of the states of the former Soviet Union failing to keep their weapons of mass destruction secure. How does the fall of the Soviet Union, the rise of Islamic fascism, and a revitalized and aggressive People's Republic of China fit into the prophetic scene? Prophecy experts assert that the unfolding of current events can be interpreted by the Bible to tell us, or at least give us important clues regarding, the way in which end-times events will come to pass as predicted in the Bible millennia earlier.

The formation of the United Nations after World War II gives us a plausible scenario in which a coalition of nations might be able to surpass the economic might and military power of the United States. Here is an explanation for why the United States is not mentioned anywhere in biblical prophecy, while also providing the kind of potential "Big Brother" that every freedom-loving American quite naturally fears. Those black helicopters have to come from somewhere! Since America will not be defeated militarily anytime soon, the only way America can be eclipsed is by a worldwide alliance like the U.N.

Then there is the advent of the European Union, which looked to many American evangelicals like the kind of revived Roman Empire predicted by John in the Book of Revelation (see chapters 13, 17, 18).[17] In the minds of dispensationalists, the rise of a new European confederacy in conjunction with the restoration of Israel cannot be coincidental. The Bible does indeed foretell all of these events, they reason, so the appearance of Antichrist cannot be far behind. In fact, according to Dave Hunt, "Somewhere, at this very moment, on planet Earth, the Antichrist is certainly alive—biding his time, awaiting his cue."[18] Hal Lindsey agrees, adding, "There is a potential dictator waiting in the wings somewhere in Europe who will make Adolf Hitler and Joseph Stalin look like choir boys. Right now he is preparing to take his throne."[19]

In a climate fueled by the prophetic speculation of dispensationalists and the images popularized throughout our culture, the appearance of Antichrist as a world leader is now a frightening possibility in the minds of many. People like Mikhail Gorbachev (the birthmark on his forehead was too obvious to ignore), Henry Kissinger (a Jew and Secretary of State), and Saddam Hussein, who described himself as the new Saladin bent on restoring the Babylonian Empire to its former greatness, were all objects of Antichrist speculation.[20] But then so was Ronald Wilson Reagan, whose first, middle, and last names each have six letters and who was wounded yet survived![21]

Given all that has transpired on the world stage since World War II, it is no wonder that a cottage industry of sorts was born in the form of various Bible prophecy ministries, in which evangelical pastors and prophecy experts also double as political pundits. Dispensationalist prophecy experts such as Jack Van Impe[22] and Hal Lindsey[23] have devoted much print media and television airtime to correlating current events to biblical prophecies. Not only do these men evaluate the latest political events in the light of Scripture as they understand it; they also attempt to explain how climate change, natural disasters, and disease fit into the prophetic scenario. This is only natural given their assumption that the next event on God's prophetic timetable is the rapture, followed by the advent of Antichrist. After all, understanding world events—the signs of the end of which Jesus so clearly spoke (Matt. 24:4–25)—is the key to understanding our immediate future.

The fascination with signs of the end in the form of world events also has unintended but serious consequences. If the Bible predicts that certain events must come to pass so that everything is in place for the Lord's return, then Christians who see these events through the dispensational grid are open to the charge (fairly or otherwise) that they will implicitly do whatever they can to ensure that political events line up accordingly.[24] Paul Boyer has documented a number of ways the dispensational understanding of end times has influenced the views of American politicians on everything from nuclear war, communism, and the expansionism of "Red China" to events in the Middle East.[25] Timothy Weber has argued in his book *On the Road to Armageddon: How Evangelicals Became Israel's Best Friend* that one of the primary outcomes of dispensational theology is the rise of a Christian Zionism, which aims to see American foreign policy in the Middle East adopt a strongly pro-Israel position, only exacerbating the great tensions that already exist with Islamic states and those who support the Palestinians.[26]

The Christian Zionist view is clearly set forth by Michael D. Evans in his best-selling book, *The American Prophecies: Ancient Scriptures Reveal Our Nation's Future*, which argues that the horrible events of September 11, 2001, came about because "God's hedge of protection was lifted from America" on the basis of what Evans calls an unholy marriage between the United States and the descendants of the two sons of Abraham—Isaac and Ishmael.[27] As Evans sees it, America must side with Israel (Isaac) against the Arab alliance (Ishmael) standing against God's chosen people or be consigned to the ash-heap of history. In Evans's scenario, if America fails to stand with Israel, our nation will become the spiritual Babylon of the end times and, presumably, one of the primary agents of Antichrist's efforts at world dominion.[28]

The primary biblical text that leads dispensationalists to see current events in this manner is Daniel's prophecy of the seventy weeks (Dan. 9:24–27).[29] In Daniel 9:27, the prophet speaks of an individual who "will confirm a covenant with many for one 'seven.' In the middle of the 'seven' he will put an end to sacrifice and offering." According to dispensationalists, the one who confirms the covenant refers back to the previous verse (v. 26) and to the ruler who will come and "destroy the city and the sanctuary." This ruler yet to come is understood to be a prophetic reference made by Daniel, looking ahead to the coming of Titus and the destruction of Jerusalem and its temple by the Roman army in AD 70. This means that verse 27 is a prophecy regarding the Antichrist, who, like Titus, must be connected in some way to a revived Roman Empire and a rebuilt Jerusalem temple. Antichrist will come once the seventieth week of the prophecy begins, and he will make a peace treaty ("confirm a covenant") with the many (Israel) for one seven (seven years). The final "seven" of the seventy weeks is a prophecy of the so-called "seven-year tribulation" period, which begins at or about the time of the rapture. The importance of the dispensational interpretation of this text, not only upon the dispensational understanding of Antichrist but upon the whole dispensationalist chronology of end times, cannot be underestimated.

Alva J. McClain, a noted dispensational theologian, spoke of the prophecy of the seventy weeks as "the indispensable chronological key to all New Testament prophecy."[30] In other words, Daniel's prophecy provides us with the means to interpret the New Testament teaching regarding the Antichrist, among other things.[31] Therefore, it is from this one passage—which I believe dispensationalists seriously misunderstand[32]—that two ideas are developed: the Antichrist will make a peace treaty with Israel, and there will be a future seven-year tribulation period. The revelation of the one (Antichrist) is connected to the other (the tribulation).[33] Given this reading of Daniel 9:24–27, it is only natural that dispensationalists would attempt to tie current events to biblical prophecy. Any event that serves to bring lasting peace to Israel and her Arab neighbors might just be the sign that the end is at hand. This is why so many dispensational prophecy writers fancy themselves to be experts on the political affairs of Europe and the Middle East. They need to be, given their theological presuppositions.

Speculation about the "Mark of the Beast"

There can be no doubt that one of the reasons the Antichrist has been the object of such fear and speculation is that his appearance is connected to a mysterious mark that will be placed on the back of the hand or the forehead of those who serve him. This mark identifies all who take it as servants of the beast and therefore subject to the same horrible and eternal fate as their master. In Revelation 13:16–17, John speaks of the beast who arises out of the earth, "He also forced everyone, small and great, rich and poor, free and slave, to receive a mark on his right hand or on his forehead, so that no one could buy or sell unless he had the mark, which is the name of the beast or the number of his name." John goes on to say of this number, "It is man's number. His number is 666" (v. 18).

The connection between the beast (presumably the Antichrist) and this mark has long been the subject of great speculation. Since John tells us this is man's number and the beast is most often identified with the Roman Empire, the mysterious 666 is usually tied to some evil figure of the past, such as Nero.[34] Not so with the dispensationalists, who believe that the mark is exclusively a future phenomenon.

John Walvoord, in many ways the dean of dispensational interpreters, believes that John's discussion of the beast in Revelation 13 is tied to the still-future great tribulation (the final "seven" of the prophecy of Daniel's seventy weeks) when Satan "will have his way."[35] According to Walvoord, "The Bible predicts a world government that will be an attempt on the part of Satan to imitate Christ's universal rule." The ruler of this world empire "will mark his worshipers . . . as a token of his immense power and worldwide authority."[36] Whatever this mark is, it is tied directly to the appearance of the Antichrist during the seven-year tribulation period. Since this mark has not yet been made manifest, the speculative door is open wide about what this might entail and what as-yet-unknown future technology will be involved. Indeed, such speculation enables popular dispensational writers to tie together their interest in political events and their apprehension about the advent of new technology. It all makes for a great conspiracy between a supremely evil individual (the Antichrist) and his all-encompassing means to control those left behind after the rapture (his mark).

While Walvoord wisely refuses to speculate about what the mark of the beast involves, his disciples have not been as careful. In one of his many sequels to *The Late Great Planet Earth*, Hal Lindsey was already warning Christians in 1973 that the mark of the beast was probably connected to some kind of high-tech identification that may be tied to a government-imposed numbering system—such as a social security number or a driver's license. At the time, Lindsey speculated that this mark might be an invisible tattoo on the back of the hand that can be read with an ultraviolet light.[37]

Lindsey was not alone in this warning about the perils of technology when enlisted in the service of the beast. Like Walvoord and Lindsey, Dave Hunt sees such things necessarily tied to the end of the age because of what Hunt sees as the obvious connection between modern technology and the beast's mysterious mark. Says Hunt, "In the vision of the future given to him by Christ, John saw a world ruler controlling the earth, not only politically and militarily, but economically. . . . While past generations took this threat seriously, there was no way that all commerce and banking on earth could be controlled from a central location. Today there is."[38] The founder of Calvary Chapel, Chuck Smith, once warned the faithful that this mysterious number is probably tied to a cashless society. As proof that this was about to happen, Smith informs his reader that "I've started a collection of items branded 666. I have a little tag from a shirt made in Japan with a 666 trademark. I have a large bag of fertilizer made in West Germany with 666 in big numbers on it."[39] Such comments caused an entire generation to carefully inspect their credit cards, invoices and household goods for the mysterious mark of the beast!

While Hal Lindsey speculated that an ultraviolet light might be involved and Chuck Smith saw the seeds of the beast's future tyranny in electronic product identification, there is now a more obvious means of subversion available to the Antichrist in an age in which every home now possesses a personal computer—the Internet. According to David Webber, "The soul of Internet will be the pulsing powerful entity called the image of the beast. As the living tool of Antichrist, this huge and horrible instrument of death will direct all worship to Antichrist and ultimately to the devil. . . . Consider a world totally dominated by the dark prince—the god of this world who will finally be able to control banking and business, commerce and trade, politics and principalities on high. This will be a world that man has never known before or will ever know again."[40]

Grounded in the very real fear that hackers can access our computers and steal our private data, the fear of an unholy marriage between the Antichrist and some form of cutting-edge technology has become an essential feature of dispensational end-times speculation. So much so that in their book, *Racing Toward the Mark of the Beast*, prophecy pundits and brothers Peter and Paul LaLonde make the leap from speculation to accepted dogma. They boldly assert that the marriage between the Antichrist and technology is the clear teaching of Scripture. "The Bible says the mark of the beast and its accompanying technology will be installed by the Antichrist—not as an end in itself, but as a means of managing the new world order that is even now being created."[41] To dispensationalists, this is not a matter of undue speculation but prudent preparation for what is sure to come.

Keeping the Proper Biblical Tension

Given the picture of Antichrist commonly found in dispensational film and literature as well as that depicted in popular American culture, we should not be surprised that Antichrist speculation is part and parcel of American life. The images of the supreme incarnation of evil, along with that of a cataclysmic final judgment, are very powerful and should not be underestimated. The influence of these images extends far beyond the circle of those who are interested in biblical prophecy and end-times speculation. As McGinn, Fuller, Boyer, and Weber all remind us, not only do these various images of Antichrist have the power to captivate the imagination of popular culture; they even exert a powerful influence upon American foreign policy.

Not only does Antichrist make a good villain for a film or a novel, but preventing or preparing for his inevitable arrival actually influences how many Americans understand the course of world events, especially those in the Middle East. This is no small thing. As Timothy Weber notes, where once dispensationalists were political spectators, after the birth of Israel in

1948 they "believed that it was necessary to leave the bleachers and get onto the playing field to make sure the game ended according to the divine script. As the world edged closer and closer to the end, dispensationalists became important players in their own game plan."[42] As dispensationalists see things, both the rapture of the church and the revelation of the Antichrist are inextricably tied to Israel's future. Because of this, dispensationalists are now avid political participants and critical to the evangelical voting block that keeps one political party in power and the other out.

Not only is Antichrist speculation an interesting topic for many; the uncanny ability of dispensational writers to tie virtually every current event to biblical prophecy makes for a compelling story. Prophecy books and novels sell for a reason: People are afraid in uncertain times. They want to know what the future holds so as to take away the uncertainty. Most often tied to the revival of the ancient Roman Empire in the form of the European Union, the conspiracy theories such books contain attempt to make sense of complex and uncertain events.[43] While I disagree with the dispensationalists' interpretation of the doctrine of Antichrist, they do sincerely strive to come to a biblical understanding of this doctrine—something that cannot be said of those who developed the Antichrist of popular culture, who is purely mythological and designed to sell movie tickets and DVDs rather than faithfully reflect the teaching of Holy Scripture.

Nevertheless, the hard questions must be asked. Were the biblical writers really warning us about what was to them some unknown future technology that would give absolute control to a demonic world leader? Or were they speaking about circumstances facing the apostolic church? Were the authors of the New Testament (along with the prophets of the Old) predicting detailed geopolitical scenarios and conspiracies such as we have just described? We will answer these questions in the coming chapters.

The biblical writers do indeed foretell of Antichrist, but the images found in Scripture are markedly different from those of either *The Omen* or the *Left Behind* novels. The fact that

end-times speculation and sensationalism has trumped sound
biblical exegesis is surely the reason this is the case. Too often
people don't know what's in their Bibles but can recount in great
detail the plot of the most recent Christian novel. Christians are
quite familiar with the frightening images created by Hollywood
but often remain ill-informed about the church's reflection on
this important doctrine. This is most unfortunate and creates
a climate in which Antichrist speculation occurs apart from
serious reflection upon the teaching of the biblical text.

The problematic nature of such speculative notions regarding
Antichrist has created a reaction in the opposite direction. It is
my opinion that the resurgence of various forms of preterism
is due, in part, to the continual overreaching on the part of
dispensationalists. Dispensationalists regard the Antichrist as
purely an end-times foe, neglecting the biblical data that speaks
of Antichrist as a present phenomena when the New Testament
was being written. As Gary DeMar points out, the weakness
of dispensationalism is patently obvious: "One reason stands
above them all: *Fulfilled* prophecy is being interpreted [by dis-
pensationalists] as if it were *unfulfilled* prophecy."[44] DeMar is
quite correct in his assessment, but he unfortunately falls into
the same kind of either-or interpretive error as do the dispensationalists he is criticizing.

While dispensationalists err by not taking the "fulfilled"
prophecy emphasis in the New Testament seriously, preterists
go to the opposite extreme and push all biblical prophecy back
into the past, leaving virtually no place for future eschatology
in the New Testament after the events of AD 70. While it is hard
to find New Testament scholars agreeing about anything these
days, one place where there has been a solid consensus over
the last generation or so is the idea that the key to understanding much of the New Testament correctly is to understand the
relationship between things fulfilled (the already) and things
yet to be fulfilled (the not yet).[45]

It is the failure to acknowledge this eschatological tension,
which pervades the entire New Testament, that leads both dispensationalists and preterists to their respective errors. Both
preterists and dispensationalists find the tension between

the already and the not yet to be intolerable. Both camps cut through this tension just as one would cut through a stretched-out rubber band. When cut, the rubber snaps back in opposite directions, just as dispensationalists push things into the future and preterists push things in the opposite direction, the past. Thus for dispensationalists, Antichrist is yet to come. But for preterists, Antichrist has already come and gone.

There is no doubt that one reason the study of biblical eschatology is so complicated and controversial is the fact that it is difficult at times to know what belongs to the past and what to the future. This holds true for the doctrine of Antichrist. While dispensationalists assign Antichrist to the future and preterists place him in the past, as we will see in the coming chapters, it is not quite that easy. According to the New Testament writers, Antichrist is a past, present, and future foe. As the supreme mimic of Christ, Antichrist will stage his own death, resurrection, and second coming. The apostles faced him. The martyrs faced him. We must face him. And in one final outburst of satanic evil right before the time of the end, Antichrist will make one last dramatic appearance before going to his doom.

Therefore, since Antichrist has already come, remains with us today, and will come again, understanding the tension between the already and the not yet is the key to understanding what the doctrine of Antichrist actually entails, and understanding this tension enables us to know how we are to combat him.

2

FORERUNNERS
OF THE ANTICHRIST

*The Old Testament Background
to the Doctrine of Antichrist*

An Antichrist before a Christ?

Bernard McGinn notes, "While it would be anachronistic to speak of an Antichrist before some Jews in the middle of the first century CE came to identify Jesus of Nazareth as the messiah or Christ . . . earlier Jewish views of apocalyptic adversaries form a necessary part of the background to the Antichrist legend."[1] Just as there is a great deal of messianic prophecy in the Old Testament, there are also the foreshadows of an anti-Messiah: a personal and satanic opponent of God's promised Redeemer who will be made manifest in the last days. And just as many messianic prophecies focus upon the coming Messiah's priestly, prophetic, and kingly offices, so too there are accounts in the Old Testament of various individuals who oppose God's redemptive purposes, demanding worship for themselves, speaking forth blasphemies against the Most High, and using the sword of government to subjugate the people of God.

According to critical scholarship, tracing the history of the doctrine of Antichrist back to its earliest sources is a difficult task.[2] This is due, in part, to the very complex nature of Jewish apocalyptic writings as well as the nature of messianic expectation.[3] Grounded in the expectation that the ongoing struggle between good and evil will culminate in a final judgment, much of Jewish apocalyptic literature develops in a similar way to Near Eastern and Persian combat myths. Throughout these myths, a great battle takes place at the dawn of creation between a powerful God and a monster of chaos, often depicted as a dragon. These myths reflect the struggle of the people of God against Satan after the fall of the human race into sin. In this battle between God and the forces of evil, Yahweh and his people are certain to win. This apocalyptic genre provides an effective structure in which to tell the story of how the righteous must struggle against the powers of evil, who serve the dragon (Satan).

In these apocalypses, the followers of the dragon are sometimes depicted as foreign rulers who persecute the people of God, while other times they take the form of false prophets and teachers who arise and lead the people of God astray.[4] This twofold theme of persecution from without (in the form of a godless state) and error from within (heresies) will resurface again in the New Testament in the form of a series of antichrists (heretics), who arise within the church as well as in the persecuting beast (the Roman Empire), who wages wars on the saints, causing Christians to suffer economic loss as well as to fall by the sword.

One Jewish apocalyptic writing dating from the time of the Maccabean wars (167–163 BC), *Testament of the Twelve Patriarchs*, purports to be the last testament of the twelve sons of Jacob. In the *Testament*, Beliar (Satan), the Prince of Demons, arises from the tribe of Dan. He attempts to deceive Israel into false worship, while a messianic figure from the tribe of Levi will rescue the people of God.[5] At the time of the end, God's people will return to the land from the four corners of the earth. They will face false prophets, and oppressive foreign rulers, all of whom will be overcome by the Messiah (Dan. 11:36; Ezek. 28:2).[6] The righteous will be raised from the dead and will enjoy a new and prosperous life in Jerusalem.

The term "sons of Belial" should also be mentioned at this point, since this too may lie in the background of the New Testament teaching on Antichrist. The background to this may be found in passages such as Judges 19:22 and 20:13, where reference is made to opponents of the people of God (worthless men). It is used in 2 Corinthians 6:15, where Paul contrasts Christ with Belial. In Qumran texts (the Dead Sea Scrolls), Belial is spoken of as the "Prince of Evil."[7] Thus Paul may indeed be contrasting Jesus with some sort of Antichrist figure (Belial), since in the Corinthian passage Paul does not speak of Satan directly as he usually does. Belial clearly seems to be an agent of Satan.[8]

We should not forget that many of the books of the New Testament were written to Jews, who were quite familiar with the Old Testament as well as canonical and noncanonical apocalyptic writings. They were presumably familiar with Jewish messianic expectation. While we may think that the New Testament teaching about Antichrist is altogether a new matter (in some ways it is), many of the images used in connection with this topic are developed directly against the backdrop of a number of the key figures and events in the Old Testament. If the revelation of Jesus Christ as God in human flesh constitutes what Paul calls the "fullness" of time (see Gal. 4:4), we should not be surprised that various New Testament writers would speak of false christs or even of "antichrists" then manifest because the Messiah has come.

When Paul speaks of a Man of Lawlessness, he does so against the backdrop of the prophecies of Daniel that speak of a blasphemous figure (the "little horn") who spoke boastful things against the Most High (Dan. 7:7–12). Likewise, when John speaks of a counterfeit Trinity in the Book of Revelation (the dragon, the beast, and the false prophet), his words are fully intelligible only against the backdrop of a number of Old Testament events and individuals from Israel's history, such as the exodus and conflict with Pharaoh, the Babylonian captivity and King Nebuchadnezzar, along with the Maccabean wars and the desecration of the Jerusalem temple by Antiochus Epiphanes in the years between 167 and 163 BC.

Before we survey the New Testament teaching in John's Epistles regarding Antichrist (chapter 4), the beast (chapter 5), and the Man of Lawlessness (chapter 6), it is important to survey the apocalyptic images, the important people, and critical events in Old Testament history that lie in the background of Antichrist teaching in the New Testament.

Two Seeds, Two Cities

From a redemptive-historical perspective, the origin of the doctrine of Antichrist is quite easy to trace. In fact, his origin can be traced back to the account of the fall of the human race into sin (Gen. 3:1–24). The first promise of redemption from humanity's plight (sin and death) is found in Genesis 3:15. No sooner have Adam and Eve come under God's curse for their act of rebellion in eating from the forbidden tree than God pronounces the covenant curse upon the Serpent: "I will put enmity between you and the woman, and between your offspring and hers; he will crush your head, and you will strike his heel." This curse reveals the great enmity that exists between God and Satan—enmity which began with the fall of Satan and which will not be fully resolved until the final judgment (Rev. 20:10).

The pronouncement of the curse at the beginning of the redemptive drama means that the conflict between two competing seeds is one of the central subplots in the story of redemption.[9] One seed is the promised seed of the woman, who is none other than the coming Messiah, who will crush Satan's head when our Lord dies upon the cross (see Col. 2:15). The other is the seed (or offspring) of the Serpent, whose satanic lineage culminates in an Antichrist at the end of the age.

The stakes in the conflict between these two seeds could not be greater. As Meredith Kline points out, "The enmity between the serpent's seed and the woman's seed was that of rival claimants for the ultimate possession of the world (cf. Matt. 4:8ff.; 1 Peter 1:4; 2 Peter 3:13; Rev. 11:15; 12:10)."[10] Many skirmishes between these two seeds took place throughout the Old Testament. The seed of the woman (the Messiah) can be traced throughout the Old Testament through the line of the patriarchs and the tribe of Judah, while the seed of the Serpent is manifest in a number of different contexts.

One prominent way in which the war between the two seeds can be seen is in the attempted preemptive assassination of the promised seed of the woman to prevent our Lord from taking his place on center stage in redemptive history. This attempted assassination is found in the story of Cain, who murdered his brother Abel (the presumptive seed) under circumstances that transcend tragic disputes between brothers over such things as a father's affection, a woman's love, or who gets the biggest share of the family estate. The murder of Abel occurred because the Lord himself exposed Cain's hypocrisy in worship. Cain's offering, which God rejected, clearly shows Cain to be allied with the Serpent—a fact that lies at the root of Cain's murderous rage against his bother. It is not accidental that the spirit of Cain pervades the City of Man that he began to build (Gen. 4:17), a city that is symbolic of repeated opposition against the people of God throughout redemptive history.[11] When we come to the New Testament teaching regarding the Antichrist, we discover that the City of Man's opposition to the kingdom of God reaches its zenith in the unholy alliance between Babylon the Great and the beast (Revelation 17–18).

There are also attempts to destroy the seed of the woman through the attempted seduction of the people of God. In the account of the rebellion of Korah (Num. 16:1–50), members of the priestly tribe of Levi, as well as 250 men drawn from among the leaders of Israel, directly challenge Moses's authority as covenant mediator, seeking to remove him and replace him with Korah. To vindicate his servant, the Lord causes the ground to open and swallow Korah, his associates, and their families and possessions. The New Testament looks back on Korah's rebellion as a reminder to false teachers about the fate that awaits them (see Jude 11).

A similar satanic attempt to derail redemptive history can also be seen in the efforts of the false prophet Balaam (Numbers 22–25), who is summoned by Balak, king of Moab, who fears the presence of the Israelites in the land. Although Balaam is prevented from speaking a word against Israel, he is able to persuade Moabite women to seduce the Israelites by inviting them to worship their god, Baal of Peor. As a result, God's judgment falls upon all those who participated in the worship of Baal. Both Peter (2 Peter 2:15) and Jude (Jude 11) look upon Balaam as an Old Testament example of the false teachers facing the apostolic church. Peter says that the false prophets working their way into the churches "have left the straight way and wandered off to follow the way of Balaam son of Beor, who loved the wages of wickedness" (2 Peter 2:15). This is very similar to John's assertion that many antichrists have already come (1 John 2:18).

The most prominent way in which the seed of the Serpent opposes the seed of the woman is through the actions of various kings and empires who oppress the people of God through military might and economic deprivation. Prime examples of this manifestation of the wrath of the Serpent against the promised Redeemer and his people can be seen in tyrannical rulers such as Nimrod (Gen. 10:8–12; 11:1–9), Pharaoh (Exod. 1:11, 22; 5:2), and Nebuchadnezzar (2 Kings 24:13–14; Dan. 4:28–30).

Closely tied to the city of Cain is the rise of "the sons of the gods" (the so-called Nephilim) mentioned in Genesis 6:1–7. These men are mighty kings who stand in the lineage of the murderous Lamech, who boasted about taking the life of a man who dared to oppose him (Gen. 4:18–24).[12] These mysterious "sons of the gods" are depicted as men who pervert the creation mandate and its emphasis upon monogamy. The "sons of the gods" not only married any woman they chose (Gen. 6:2), but they blasphemously identified themselves as deities—"sons of the gods." Instead of using their might to administer justice and build a godly society, these men acquired power and began a reign of tyranny upon the earth.[13]

It is not accidental that these same traits will be manifest in the little horn of Daniel 8 and in Paul's Man of Lawlessness, who will "oppose and will exalt himself over everything that is called God or is worshiped, so that he sets himself up in God's temple, proclaiming himself to be God" (2 Thess. 2:4). Sadly, the City of Man had become the temple of man, and this self-professed independence (autonomy) from God's will becomes the ideological basis for the earth's revolt against the Creator, which brought about the great flood as recounted in Genesis 6–9.[14]

Thus when we read in Genesis 10:8–10 of the rise of Nimrod and his prowess as a mighty warrior-hunter, the implication is that Nimrod will build his personal empire in the image of the city of Cain, and Cain's descendants, Lamech and the Nephilim (the "mighty men" or "heroes," Gen. 6:4 NASB and NIV), will be his chosen role models. The organization of a city on the plain of Shinar with a tower that reaches to heaven so that men might make a name for themselves illustrates the satanic ties between Nimrod and the boastful figures swept away by the flood. As Nimrod undertakes the conquest of Babylon and Assyria and then begins the construction project described in Genesis 11:1–9 (the Tower of Babel), we see the dark connection to his predecessors in his boastful claims to divine kingship as evident in the phrase that Nimrod's exploits were performed "before the LORD" (or "in the face" of Yahweh). In this, the spirit of Antichrist is beginning to manifest itself in direct opposition to the purposes of Yahweh.[15] While the seed of the woman can be traced from Adam to Seth to Noah (Gen. 5:3–32), the seed of the Serpent (the theological lineage of Antichrist) can be seen in the autonomous acts of Cain, Lamech, the Nephilim, and Nimrod.

Pharaoh—A Proto-Antichrist

Another proto-Antichrist enters the redemptive drama in the struggle between Moses and the Pharaoh. In the days of Joseph

(Genesis 37–50), the Israelites dwelt safely in Egypt in the region of Goshen as welcomed guests of the Pharaoh. But as the Book of Exodus opens, the situation has changed greatly:

> Then a new king, who did not know about Joseph, came to power in Egypt. "Look," he said to his people, "the Israelites have become much too numerous for us. Come, we must deal shrewdly with them or they will become even more numerous and, if war breaks out, will join our enemies, fight against us and leave the country." So they put slave masters over them to oppress them with forced labor, and they built Pithom and Rameses as store cities for Pharaoh. But the more they were oppressed, the more they multiplied and spread; so the Egyptians came to dread the Israelites.
>
> Exodus 1:8–12

The new king (Pharaoh) began to brutally oppress the Jewish people, but one of his successors witnessed the power of God through the death of his firstborn son on the night of the Passover and in the loss of his elite chariot battalion in the waters of the Red Sea.[16] Thus Pharaoh becomes a type of Antichrist, and the exodus motif will become a major theme throughout subsequent biblical history.[17] Even as God's people were miraculously rescued from the hands of a tyrant (Pharaoh), like Israel, Christians are now undertaking a journey of liberation (from sin and its consequences) through the wilderness of this present evil age en route to the Promised Land (the heavenly city).

The power of Satan is frequently manifest through human agency, especially in those nations and their leaders who worship false gods and seek to force God's people to do the same. Egypt and its Pharaoh at the time of the crackdown (Exod. 1:11) and in the exodus (Exod. 12:31–42) become a striking case of a tyrannical and antichristic ruler and nation. In fact, the sojourn in Egypt is later memorialized through the words of the prophet Joel as a place of "violence done to the people of Judah, in whose land they shed innocent blood" (Joel 3:19). In Revelation 11:8 we read of a great city ("figuratively called

Sodom and Egypt") wherein the two witnesses of God are savagely killed. Like Egypt and its Pharaoh, this city will eventually come under God's judgment because of the murder of the faithful witnesses.[18] It is certainly not a coincidence that the prophet Isaiah describes God's defeat of Egypt and Pharaoh using the imagery of God's mighty strength in cutting the sea monster Rahab (Leviathan) into pieces (Isa. 51:9–11).[19] In oppressing the people of God and keeping them from journeying to the Promised Land (Canaan), Pharaoh is clearly doing the Serpent's bidding.

The Pharaoh not only oppresses the Israelites—viewing them as a source of cheap labor—but when Moses returns to Egypt at the Lord's command and confronts the Pharaoh, declaring, "This is what the LORD, the God of Israel, says: 'Let my people go, so that they may hold a festival to me in the desert,'" Pharaoh's response is to force the Israelites to gather their own straw to make bricks without reducing the quota (Exod. 5:1–10). This begins a series of confrontations between Moses and Pharaoh, which results in the infamous ten plagues.

At first the magicians of Pharaoh's court are apparently able to match Moses and Aaron miracle for miracle. Their miracle-working power in response to God's messengers clearly anticipates the beast coming out of the earth of Revelation 13:11–17, who performs great and miraculous signs to deceive the inhabitants of the earth so that they worship the beast and his image. But Pharaoh's magicians soon realize they are no match for "the finger of God" (Exod. 8:19). Even as they warn Pharaoh that they cannot duplicate the plague of gnats, Pharaoh's heart only grows harder. It is not long before all Egypt lies in waste from plague after plague while Pharaoh's duplicity and double-mindedness only places Egypt in greater and greater peril. We must not overlook the fact that the plagues, which came upon Egypt as a direct result of God's judgment, mirror on a smaller scale the seven trumpet judgments of Revelation 8:6–11:19, which come upon the whole earth.

After Pharaoh finally consents to let the Israelites worship God in the desert only to change his mind yet again (Exod. 10:24–28), one final and devastating plague befalls all Egypt.

Only the region of Goshen, where the Israelites live, is spared. Every firstborn male, man and beast, is struck dead by the Angel of the Lord unless blood from a sacrificial lamb has been smeared upon the doorpost of the home. Even Pharaoh's own firstborn son dies during the night of the first Passover. All Egypt is in a state of panic that quickly gives way to grief as night becomes morning.

At last Pharaoh has had enough and not only permits Moses and the Israelites to leave Egypt, he actually commands them to go and worship their God (Exod. 12:31–32). But once the Israelites have packed up and begun the journey to the Promised Land, Pharaoh soon realizes the loss to the Egyptian economy and to his prestige this mass exodus represents. After the Lord hardens his heart once more, Pharaoh orders his chariots to chase the Israelites and cut them off before they can cross the Red Sea and escape into the wilderness of the Sinai (Exod. 14:5–9). While all Israel passes through the sea on dry ground, that same sea swallows Pharaoh's chariots when they attempt their pursuit.

Throughout the subsequent history of redemption, the Egyptian Pharaoh becomes a symbol of a tyrannical oppressor of the people of God, and his defeat becomes an equally powerful symbol of God's mighty power in procuring the redemption of his people. The Song of Moses—sung in triumph after the Israelites are safely through the sea and have witnessed the destruction of the armies of Pharaoh (Exod. 15:1–18)—is sung again by the saints in heaven as the final seven plagues are poured out by God against the earth's inhabitants who rejected Christ and his gospel (Rev. 15:1–8). If Pharaoh is a type of Antichrist, his defeat is also a vivid picture of the Antichrist's final and ultimate fate (see 2 Thess. 2:8; Rev. 19:20).

Nebuchadnezzar—Image of the Beast

Another tyrant-king who prefigures the Antichrist is Nebuchadnezzar, king of Babylon. In his case, the identification is a bit more obvious. As recounted in 2 Kings 24:13–14, Nebuchadnezzar was an instrument of divine judgment upon disobedient Israel. After besieging the city of Jerusalem and forcing the surrender of Israel's king Jehoiachin, "Nebuchadnezzar removed all the treasures from the temple of the LORD and from the royal palace, and took away all the gold articles that Solomon king of Israel had made for the temple of the LORD. He carried into exile all Jerusalem: all the officers and fighting men, and all the craftsmen and artisans—a total of ten thousand. Only the poorest people of the land were left."

What is striking about this particular conqueror-plunderer is that Nebuchadnezzar is king of the Babylonian Empire, which should immediately call to mind Nimrod and the Tower of Babel built to the heavens on the plains of Shinar. When Nebuchadnezzar declares, "Is not this the great Babylon I have built as the royal residence, by my mighty power and for the glory of my majesty?" (Dan. 4:30), we are harkened back to the blasphemous boasts of Nimrod and the Nephilim. In fact, Nebuchadnezzar's dream (recounted in Dan. 4:10–18) includes a tree rising to heaven, just as the Tower of Babel had done generations earlier. Nebuchadnezzar's self-importance and absolute defiance toward the Lord, which is the root cause of his persecution of the Lord's people, makes him a true forerunner of Antichrist and an archfoe of the promised seed.[20]

In fact, the church father Irenaeus saw more than coincidence in a number of details recorded in chapter 3 of Daniel's prophecy. For one thing, Nebuchadnezzar had erected a golden statue of himself. The statue was sixty cubits high and six cubits wide (Dan. 3:1–7). When taken by themselves, these measurements are not particularly significant. But the king ordered all the people of the city, "As soon as you hear the sound of the horn, flute, zither, lyre, harp, pipes and all kinds of music, you must fall down and worship the image of gold that King Nebuchadnezzar has set up. Whoever does not fall down and worship will immediately be thrown into a blazing furnace" (vv. 5–6). Irenaeus saw this as a clear foreshadowing of the beast and his number 666 (see Rev. 13:11–18). What is especially significant is the fact that the beast from the earth will erect a statue of the beast from the sea and require the earth's inhabitants to worship it (v. 14), just as Nebuchadnezzar had done with his subjects in Babylon.[21] When we add to this the fact that the penalty for failure to worship Nebuchadnezzar's image was to be cast into the fiery furnace, we can see the connection to the beast of Revelation, who causes all those who do not worship the image to be killed (Rev. 13:15).

This brutal treatment of his subjects who would not worship his image explains why Nebuchadnezzar's kingdom is "symbolized by the idol-beasts of the Book of Daniel (chapters 2 and 7)." But Daniel also prophesies that later on there would arise a "little horn from the Seleucids, [an] archenemy of God's holy city and people (Dan. 8:9–13 and 11:21–35). He was a prototype of the antichrist power of the messianic age, the little horn from the fourth beast (Dan. 7:8 and 11:36–45), the dragon-like agent of Satan that issues the final challenge against the city of God, evoking the day of wrath."[22] Thus Nebuchadnezzar not only stands in the line of Cain, he foreshadows the archfoe of Jesus Christ.

Antichrist as Foretold by Daniel

If Nimrod, Pharaoh, and Nebuchadnezzar were representative persecutors of the people of God in Israel's distant past, it was the rise of Antiochus IV Epiphanes of Syria (175–164 BC) that cements the image of a tyrant oppressing the people of God and desecrating the holy place as foretold in the prophecy of Daniel.[23] Most critical scholars would agree with McGinn's assessment that Daniel is "history disguised as prophecy" and was written by an unknown scribe between 167–164 BC, which would make the writing of the Book of Daniel contemporaneous with the rise of Antiochus IV and the period of the Maccabean wars.[24] But a good case can be made for the traditional view that the Book of Daniel was written in the sixth century BC, whereby Daniel's vision of a blasphemous "horn" is indeed a predictive prophecy regarding Antiochus and not "history disguised."[25]

One key prophecy dealing with the coming of Antiochus is that found in Daniel 8:8–13:

> The goat became very great, but at the height of his power his large horn was broken off, and in its place four prominent horns grew up toward the four winds of heaven. Out of one of them came another horn, which started small but grew in power to the south and to the east and toward the Beautiful Land. It grew until it reached the host of the heavens, and it threw some of the starry host down to the earth and trampled on them. It set itself up to be as great as the Prince of the host; it took away the daily sacrifice from him, and the place of his sanctuary was brought low. Because of rebellion, the host of the saints and the daily sacrifice were given over to it. It prospered in everything it did, and truth was thrown to the ground. Then I heard a holy one speaking, and another holy one said to him, "How long will it take for the vision to be fulfilled—the vision concerning the daily sacrifice, the rebellion that causes desolation, and the surrender of the sanctuary and of the host that will be trampled underfoot?"

It was Antiochus IV Epiphanes who desecrated the Jerusalem temple in 167 BC by dedicating the altar to Zeus and then slaughtering a pig.[26] In fact, Antiochus's title (Epiphanes or "manifest") is indicative of his claim to be the earthly manifestation of Zeus.[27] It was his act of blasphemy and desecration of the temple that became the basis for the so-called "abomination of desolation" (NEB) mentioned in Daniel (9:27; 11:31; 12:11), in 1 Maccabees (1:54–64), and in the Gospels (Matt. 24:15; Mark 13:14; Luke 21:20). From the reference to this "abomination" in 1 Maccabees, it is clear that this is a direct reference to Antiochus, who "erected a desolating sacrilege in the altar of burnt offering" (1 Macc. 1:54 NRSV). Because of these despicable acts, Antiochus IV is surely a forerunner of Antichrist. The Gospels see him as such.

While it is clear that the prophecy in Daniel 8:9 of "another horn" refers to Antiochus, this particular prophecy follows the earlier prophecy in Daniel 7:7–12, which similarly speaks of a blasphemous little horn. Daniel writes of this little horn as follows:

> After that, in my vision at night I looked, and there before me was a fourth beast—terrifying and frightening and very powerful. It had large iron teeth; it crushed and devoured its victims and trampled underfoot whatever was left. It was different from all the former beasts, and it had ten horns.
>
> While I was thinking about the horns, there before me was another horn, a little one, which came up among them; and three of the first horns were uprooted before it. This horn had eyes like the eyes of a man and a mouth that spoke boastfully.
>
> As I looked, thrones were set in place, and the Ancient of Days took his seat. His clothing was as white as snow; the hair of his head was white like wool. His throne was flaming with fire, and its wheels were all ablaze. A river of fire was flowing, coming out from before him. Thousands upon thousands attended him; ten thousand times ten thousand stood before him. The court was seated, and the books were opened.
>
> Then I continued to watch because of the boastful words the horn was speaking. I kept looking until the beast was slain and its body destroyed and thrown into the blazing fire. (The other beasts had been stripped of their authority, but were allowed to live for a period of time.)

This prophecy points beyond the evils wrought by Antiochus to someone or something else, far more sinister, especially since the blaspheming horn will be destroyed by the Ancient of Days—Jesus Christ—at the time of the end (v. 11). This is clearly a prophecy of the Roman Empire and perhaps of ten kingdoms that originate from it. The little horn is likely the first direct prophetic reference to the coming Antichrist.[28] Similar prophecies regarding both Antiochus and a blasphemous figure at the time of the end appear again in Daniel 11:21–35, the prophecy of a contemptible person, who is not a legitimate ruler (Antiochus IV), and in Daniel 11:36–45, the prophecy of a king who exalts himself and blasphemes God (the Antichrist).

That this is the case can be seen in how these prophecies of a coming blasphemer were subsequently interpreted by both

Jews and Christians. In AD 40, when the Roman Emperor Caligula announced that he would place a statue of himself in the Jerusalem temple, many Jews believed this to be the act of desolation to which Daniel was referring.[29] This same image of something sacred being profaned is used by Jesus and the Gospel writers in connection to events surrounding the destruction of the Jerusalem temple in AD 70. Quite possibly, it is in the back of Paul's mind when he speaks of a Man of Sin who sets himself up in God's temple, proclaiming himself to be God and demanding worship (2 Thess. 2:4).[30] Since Luke speaks of this event in connection to the Roman siege of Jerusalem when he mentions the city of Jerusalem being surrounded by armies (Luke 21:20), it is clear that Daniel's prophecy was fulfilled when the Romans and the armies of Titus destroyed the temple. But this certainly does not rule out the possibility of this prophecy being fulfilled yet again at the end of the age—a subject to be addressed in chapter 3.[31]

[handwritten margin note: IT IS NOT FULFILLED TWICE. IT IS PARTIALLY FULFILLED HERE.]

Antichrist and Daniel's Seventieth Week

As we have seen, the dispensational interpretation of Daniel 9:24–27 is one of the pillars of the entire system. It is from Daniel 9:24–27 that dispensationalists develop their doctrine of a future seven-year tribulation period, which supposedly commences when the Antichrist signs a peace treaty with the nation of Israel at, or about, the time of the rapture. It is from this passage that dispensationalists set out what they perceive to be the future course of Israel's history and dealings with the Gentile nations. They also teach that a "great parenthesis," known as the church age, results from the supposed gap between the sixty-ninth and seventieth weeks of this prophecy. The passage reads as follows:

> Seventy "sevens" are decreed for your people and your holy city to finish transgression, to put an end to sin, to atone for wickedness, to bring in everlasting righteousness, to seal up vision and prophecy and to anoint the most holy.

Know and understand this: From the issuing of the decree
to restore and rebuild Jerusalem until the Anointed One, the
ruler, comes, there will be seven "sevens," and sixty-two "sevens." It will be rebuilt with streets and a trench, but in times of
trouble. After the sixty-two "sevens," the Anointed One will be
cut off and will have nothing. The people of the ruler who will
come will destroy the city and the sanctuary. The end will come
like a flood: War will continue until the end, and desolations
have been decreed. He will confirm a covenant with many for
one "seven." In the middle of the "seven" he will put an end to
sacrifice and offering. And on a wing of the temple he will set
up an abomination that causes desolation, until the end that is
decreed is poured out on him.

Daniel 9:24–27

When we consider verse 27 and read of a covenant, "there
should be no doubt as to its identity."[32] This is the covenant of
grace, first promised to Adam in Genesis 3:15 and confirmed to
Abraham in Genesis 15:1–21. Dispensationalists insist that the
subjects of Daniel 9:27, "he will confirm a covenant with many
for one seven," must refer back to the preceding "he," that is, the
ruler who will come and destroy the city and the sanctuary of
verse 26 (Titus and the armies of Rome). But they are in error,
confusing the identity of the covenant-maker who is cut off for
his people (Christ), with the Roman prince (i.e., Antichrist).[33]

As we observed in chapter 1, in order to make this fit into
their interpretive scheme, dispensationalists insist that the
Messiah is cut off after the sixty-two sevens and that there is
an indeterminate gap of time between the end of the sixty-nine
sevens and the seventieth seven, when the one who confirms
a covenant with the many (Antichrist) arrives upon the scene
to do his dastardly deed. The insertion of a gap of at least two
thousand years between the sixty-ninth and seventieth week
is a self-contradictory violation of the dispensationalists' pro-
fessed literal hermeneutic. Where is the gap to be found in the
text? The dispensationalists must insert it. It is the failure to
acknowledge the obvious covenantal context of the messianic
covenant-maker of verse 27, who confirms a covenant with the
many, which leads dispensationalists to confuse Christ with

Antichrist. A more serious interpretive error is hard to imagine. In fact, many of the differences between the dispensationalist understanding of Antichrist and that of historic Protestants result from the dispensational misidentification of Christ as Antichrist in this passage.

The failure of dispensationalists to see that it is the Messiah spoken of in verse 27, not Antichrist, stems from a serious interpretive error already made in verse 24, when Daniel speaks of what will be accomplished by the completion of the 490 years. In verse 24 we read, "Seventy 'sevens' are decreed for your people and your holy city to finish transgression, to put an end to sin, to atone for wickedness, to bring in everlasting righteousness, to seal up vision and prophecy and to anoint the most holy." These things must be completed during the 490 years so that the blessings will apply to God's people long after the prophecy is fulfilled (i.e., during the messianic age).

Many Christians will quickly recognize that Daniel is here speaking prophetically of the active and passive obedience of Christ, or as E. J. Young categorizes them, "positive and negative" aspects of the Messiah's work.[34] Christ's death—his so-called passive obedience "finished transgressions" in the sense of breaking sin's power over God's people (Rom. 6:1–2, 14), taking away sin's condemnation (Rom. 5:12–19; 6:23), and atoning for wickedness (Rom. 3:21–26). Through these acts, Jesus Christ will take away all of the consequences of the curse.[35]

Christ's active obedience can be seen here in reference to our Lord's threefold office of prophet, priest, and king—"to bring in everlasting righteousness," which Christ does through his own perfect obedience as the final priest (Rom. 5:19), "to seal up vision and prophecy," which he does in his prophetic office as Peter declares Jesus to be the greater prophet of whom Moses had spoken (Deut. 18:15–16; Acts 3:22), and then finally, "to anoint the most holy," which most likely is a reference to the anointing of the Messiah (Isa. 61:1; Matt. 3:16–17). These things, notes Young, "are all messianic. . . . The termination of the 70 sevens coincides then, not with the time of Antiochus, nor with the end of the present age, the 2nd Advent of our Lord, but with his 1st Advent."[36]

By looking at this passage through the dispensational lens, namely, that Daniel is speaking of Israel, not of the church nor even of Christ, dispensationalists stumble badly in their interpretation of Daniel 9:27. Unlike Reformed Christians, dispensationalists do not see covenant as an overarching redemptive-historical grid, and having inserted a gap between verses 26 and 27—because it is demanded by their hermeneutical presuppositions—they miss what appears to be the obvious meaning. As Meredith Kline points out, "The whole context speaks against the supposition that an altogether different covenant from the divine covenant which is the central theme throughout Daniel 9 is abruptly introduced here at the climax of it all."[37] This has nothing to do with Antichrist but with the coming Messiah.

Indeed, the language throughout Daniel thoroughly supports the identification of the one who makes a covenant with the many as none other than Jesus himself. Not only does verse 25 give us a list of messianic and redemptive accomplishments associated with the coming one, but in verse 26 we read that the Anointed One will be cut off. Daniel uses a verb, *karat*, which is often used to describe the cutting ritual associated with the ratifications of covenants. This connects the "cutting off" of verse 26 with the "confirming" of a covenant in verse 27. The angel certainly informs Daniel of this to assure him that the disturbing word in verse 26 of the cutting off of the Anointed One does not mean the ultimate failure of his mission, hence the words in verse 27 informing Daniel that the one who is cut off nevertheless will make a covenant in the middle of the seventieth week of the prophecy.[38] Daniel could not have understood what these words entailed for New Testament writers centuries later—"Christ died for us while we were yet sinners" (Rom. 5:8 NEB).

It is quite significant that in Daniel 9:27 the angel Gabriel informs Daniel that the Anointed One will "confirm" a covenant with the many. The usual verb used for the making of a covenant, *karat*, is found in verse 26. But in verse 27 the verb *higbir* is used instead, a verb that means to "make strong, cause to prevail."[39] The use of this word is another serious blow to the dispensational interpretation that verse 27 is referring to the Antichrist and an entirely different covenant from that implied by the use of *karat* in verse 26. The use of *higbir* in verse 27 illustrates that the covenant is "made strong" or "to prevail," which means that the covenant is not being made from scratch but is an existing covenant being confirmed or enforced. In other words, the covenant being confirmed in the middle of the seventieth week by the Anointed One is a covenant that already exists! This is a reference to the covenant of grace that God had previously made with Abraham and is now confirming by the Messiah on behalf of the many (cf. the many redeemed by the suffering servant in Isa. 53:12). This would entail all of the blessings promised in verse 24, blessings ultimately secured by the shed blood and perfect righteousness of Jesus Christ. It means that there is no gap between the sixty-ninth and seventieth weeks as dispensationalists argue. It also means that Antichrist is not mentioned in the passage.

This interpretation of Daniel 9:27 raises two immediate questions. The first of these is simply this: if Christ is cut off in the middle of the seventieth week, what happens to the last part (three and one-half years) of the final seven-year period? Here again we can look to see how the New Testament writers interpret the Old Testament. In this case, we find the answer in John's Apocalypse (Rev. 12:14) as John reinterprets this three and one-half years in Daniel, speaking of it as "a time, times and half a time." As Meredith Kline points out,

> The last week is the age of the church in the wilderness of the nations for a time, a times, and half a time (Rev. 12:14). Since the seventy weeks are ten jubilee eras that issue in the last jubilee, the seventieth week closes with angelic trumpeting of the earth's redemption and the glorious liberty of the children of God. The acceptable year of the Lord which came with Christ will then have fully come. Then the new Jerusalem whose temple is the Lord and the Lamb will descend from heaven (Rev. 21:10, 22) and the ark of the covenant will be seen (Rev. 11:19), the covenant the Lamb has made to prevail and the Lord has remembered.[40]

Therefore, Christ has confirmed the covenant God has made, namely, that he is our God and we are his people. Although he has wrought the blessings of the jubilee, including forgiveness of sins and everlasting righteousness, that which has been accomplished by Christ remains yet to be consummated. The final three and one-half years of the seventieth week is, therefore, symbolic of the church on the earth during the entire time of its existence and clearly a reference to the tribulation depicted in Daniel.[41]

The second question has to do with the final two sentences of Daniel 9:27, "In the middle of the 'seven' he will put an end to sacrifice and offering. And on a wing of the temple he will set up an abomination that causes desolation, until the end that is decreed is poured out on him." How can this be fulfilled, since Jewish sacrifices continued on for some years after Christ's crucifixion until the temple was destroyed in AD 70? Several things can be said in response to this. For one thing, the author of Hebrews clearly thought that Christ's death put an end to sacrifice in a religious sense. In Hebrews 9:25–26 we read that Christ appeared at the end of the ages to do away with sin by the sacrifice of himself (see also Heb. 7:11; 8:13; 10:8–9). Though it is true that the sacrifices continued in the temple, once Christ ratified God's covenant on Calvary, the sacrifices that continued in the temple became an abomination to God. When Christ was cut off (crucified) for his own, the temple veil was torn from top to bottom. From that moment forward, the temple became desolate and acceptable sacrifice ceased. The events that transpired in AD 70 with the Roman assault upon Jerusalem and its temple were now assured.

Daniel 9:24–27 is, therefore, a glorious messianic prophecy that does not in any sense support a dispensational belief in a seven-year future tribulation nor that the revelation of Antichrist will be in connection with a peace treaty with Israel. The fact that the passage envisions the ultimate jubilee after the 490 years are completed points forward to the already–not yet distinction—present blessings and future consummation—but also to the fact that once the time, times, and half a time of the great tribulation are complete, the consummation will finally come and the eternal jubilee will dawn.

Gog and Magog (Ezekiel 38–39)

It is fascinating to think prophecy is being fulfilled in world events today, but this fascination can lead to misinterpretation. The famous prophecy of Gog and Magog of Ezekiel 38–39 is one passage that has lent itself to this kind of interpretive manipulation. Even though the passage does not deal with Antichrist directly, it does speak of the Antichrist's confederates and their fate at the time of the end.[42] Since the mysterious Gog and Magog are associated with a persecuting empire depicted in Ezekiel's prophecy as being destroyed at the time of the end—the same holds true in the Book of Revelation (Rev. 20:8)—Gog and Magog have often been tied to the political powers who arise in conjunction with the appearance of Antichrist.[43]

Martin Luther once referred to the Turks, then at the gates of Vienna, as Gog's forces soon to come under the judgment of God.[44] Modern dispensationalists equate the names that appear in this passage (Gog, Magog, Rosh, Meshech, Tubal, and Gomer; Ezek. 38:2–6 NASB) with the nations of modern Europe in some sort of alliance with the Soviet Union (now the nations of the former Soviet Union). According to Hal Lindsey, Gog and Magog are supposedly tied to Russia (Rosh supposedly equals "Russia") while Meshech is identified as "Moscow" and Gomer as "Germany," all of whom will form an alliance with Ethiopia (Cush) and Libya (Put) and invade the modern nation of Israel, now back in the land, sometime toward the end of the great tribulation.[45] This is the so-called "Russian invasion of Israel," long a feature of dispensational prophetic speculation.[46]

Historian-archeologist Edwin Yamauchi has thoroughly refuted the claim that Ezekiel is referring to the modern nation of Russia and the city of Moscow when the prophet uses these names.[47] In addition, this section of Ezekiel's prophecy is "proto-apocalyptic," so it must be seen as a reference not to any specific modern alliance of nations who will invade Israel but as symbolic of those godless powers that arise at the time of the end who persecute the people of God but who are destroyed by Christ at his second coming (cf. Rev. 20:8).[48] This can be seen in a brief look at some of the key elements of the prophecy. The first six verses of Ezekiel's prophecy read as follows:

> The word of the LORD came to me: "Son of man, set your face against Gog, of the land of Magog, the chief prince of Meshech and Tubal; prophesy against him and say: 'This is what the Sovereign LORD says: I am against you, O Gog, chief prince of Meshech and Tubal. I will turn you around, put hooks in your jaws and bring you out with your whole army—your horses, your horsemen fully armed, and a great horde with large and small shields, all of them brandishing their swords. Persia, Cush and Put will be with them, all with shields and helmets, also Gomer with all its troops, and Beth Togarmah from the far north with all its troops—the many nations with you.'"
>
> Ezekiel 38:1–6

Gog is said to be a leader of a group of nations who disrupt the peace of God's people, who are safely living back in the land after a prolonged time of exile. But the essence of the prophecy—which comes in the form of seven oracles[49]—is not that the people of God are judged by an invasion of these nations. Rather, it is God who judges the nations by summoning them to this place for judgment.

> "Therefore, son of man, prophesy and say to Gog: 'This is what the Sovereign LORD says: In that day, when my people Israel are living in safety, will you not take notice of it? You will come from your place in the far north, you and many nations with you, all of them riding on horses, a great horde, a mighty army. You will advance against my people Israel like a cloud that covers the land. In days to come, O Gog, I will bring you against my land, so that the nations may know me when I show myself holy through you before their eyes.'"
>
> Ezekiel 38:14–16

The fate of Gog and his cohorts is also clearly spelled out in verses 19–23:

> "'This is what the Sovereign Lord says: . . . In my zeal and fiery wrath I declare that at that time [when Gog attacks Israel] there shall be a great earthquake in the land of Israel. The fish of the sea, the birds of the air, the beasts of the field, every creature that moves along the ground, and all the people on the face of the earth will tremble at my presence. The mountains will be overturned, the cliffs will crumble and every wall will fall to the ground. I will summon a sword against Gog on all my mountains, declares the Sovereign LORD. Every man's sword will be against his brother. I will execute judgment upon him with plague and bloodshed; I will pour down torrents of rain, hailstones and burning sulfur on him and on his troops and on the many nations with him. And so I will show my greatness and my holiness, and I will make myself known in the sight of many nations. Then they will know that I am the LORD.'"

As we have seen, dispensationalists read this prophecy through their literalistic hermeneutic and believe Ezekiel to be referring to an end-times invasion of Israel after the nation has resettled in the land after being reestablished as a nation in 1948. The invasion takes place after the rapture of the church, some time toward the latter half of the seven-year tribulation.[50] But there are a number of reasons why the dispensational view of this prophecy is untenable. For one thing, the Book of Revelation clearly assigns (and indeed reinterprets) this prophecy as being fulfilled in connection with our Lord's second advent (Rev. 20:7–10). If, as dispensationalists teach, Gog and Magog are involved in an invasion of Israel during the tribulation, only to be destroyed by God, how can they appear again at the end of the millennium when the final judgment takes place? This violates dispensationalists' self-professed literal hermeneutic, for the Gog who supposedly falls on the mountains of Israel (Ezekiel 38–39) has been resurrected by the end of the millennium (Rev. 20:8).

If we go by the basic principle that the New Testament interprets the Old Testament, then it becomes clear that Ezekiel is looking ahead to the future and sees the time of the end. Two things have happened in the meantime. First, God's people have come back from exile and are now dwelling in safety. Second, after a long period of time, Ezekiel sees some type of a divinely orchestrated invasion of the land where God's people dwell, bringing an end to God's enemies once and for all. This is clearly an apocalyptic vision of the messianic age, when Christ's people dwell in safety and will be delivered from their final foe.[51] Although the name "Gog" has some historical connection to Ezekiel, the name is more than likely used in a proverbial sense of an end-times foe—i.e., "another Hitler."[52]

When John sees this same scene from the perspective of the heavenly vision, Gog and Magog have become symbols of all the nations who come from the four corners of the earth to wage war upon the saints. Whereas Ezekiel spoke of the saints involved in terms of the nation of Israel and the city of Jerusalem, John now speaks of the "camp of God's people, the city he loves" (Rev. 20:9). John has already reported the fulfillment of this prophecy in Revelation 16:14–16 and 19:17–21, only now we learn that Gog and Magog suffer the same fate as the beast and false prophet who has deceived them. "Fire came down from heaven and devoured them."[53] Therefore the prophecy of Gog and Magog in Ezekiel 38–39 does not deal with Antichrist *per se*, but at the very least it does depict the fate of those who are allied with him in his futile effort to wage war upon the saints (see Rev. 16:12–16).

3

THE DOCTRINE OF ANTICHRIST IN THE NEW TESTAMENT ERA

Some Preliminary Considerations

The Struggle between the Two Seeds Revisited—Jesus and Satan in the Gospels

If the Messiah belongs to that pivotal period in redemptive history that the apostle Paul calls the "fullness of time" (Gal. 4:4 NRSV), so does the anti-Messiah.[1] In the words of one writer, if all we had regarding the archfoe of the Messiah was the data found in the New Testament, Antichrist "gives the dark background against which [Christ's] victory and his kingdom shine out the more brightly."[2] This will become apparent as we survey the New Testament teaching regarding Antichrist (chapters 4–6) and then survey the history of Christian reflection upon this topic (chapter 7). Antichrist was a foe to be reckoned with in the apostolic age. He has reared his head again and again throughout the centuries that followed, only to be restrained by the power of God through the preaching of the gospel. Antichrist will appear again in his final and most ferocious manifestation at the close of the age.

Before we look at the individual strands of Antichrist teaching, in this chapter we will set out some general considerations regarding the Antichrist. Critical scholars believe the church's identification of Jesus as the Messiah is the fertile soil for the creation of the so-called "Antichrist myth." This Messiah/anti-Messiah structure supposedly serves as the lens through which Christians attempted to explain the ongoing struggle between the forces of good and evil.[3] The very nature of this struggle, therefore, necessitates the creation of the twin figures of Messiah and Antichrist.[4] Critical scholars also believe that the sources for this Antichrist myth are to be found in those same Jewish apocalyptic writings from which the images of the Book of Revelation are drawn.[5]

While the New Testament writers are not ignorant of these sources, they are not the well from which the data is drawn to create an "Antichrist myth." More likely, these Jewish sources serve as a means to explain and clarify specific events associated with the dawn of the messianic age using familiar images. Indeed, the very nature of the Old Testament redemptive drama—from the account of the fall and the prophecy of a struggle between the Serpent and the coming Redeemer (Gen. 3:15) to the Maccabean wars and the profanation of the Jerusalem temple—has already alerted us to the fact that the birth of Jesus will fulfill ancient prophecy and bring the conflict between Christ and the Serpent to its decisive climax. Thus Antichrist is not mythological. His destiny is foretold in the Old Testament alongside that of the Messiah he will so energetically oppose (see Dan. 11:36–37). The coming of the Messiah onto the center stage of human history stirs a satanic reaction.

This connection between the New Testament fulfillment of Old Testament expectation can be seen in the renewed attempt by Satan to engage in a preemptive assassination of the promised seed, who will eventually bring about his demise. This tactic was already manifest when Cain killed Abel. In Matthew 2:13–18, we read of the so-called "slaughter of the innocents" by Herod, who is himself a type of Antichrist.[6] Just as Moses was delivered from the antichristic Pharaoh who tried to control the Israelite population through infanticide (at the time of his birth, Exod. 1:22; 2:1–10), so too, Jesus is spared from a similar satanic adversary, Herod, who tries to kill Israel's king by taking the lives of all young Hebrew males in Bethlehem.[7]

The temptation of Jesus by Satan also has ties to the struggle between the two seeds (see Matt. 4:1–10).[8] The passage is loaded with redemptive-historical significance. Leading up to the temptation, Matthew's Gospel shows us Jesus, the obedient Son, fulfilling the obedience required of Adam (Gen. 2:17) and Israel. Following the basic outline of the exodus, Jesus returns from Egypt (Matt. 2:13–23) and is baptized and declared to be the Son of God (Matt. 3:13–17) before embarking upon forty days of testing in the wilderness. This clearly reflects the basic history of Israel—the conflict with Pharaoh, the deliverance through the Red Sea, the establishment of the Sinaitic covenant on Mount Sinai, followed by forty years in the wilderness. We also should not overlook the fact that Jesus's answers to Satan's questions are taken from Deuteronomy 6–8, a passage that describes Israel's wandering through the wilderness.[9] Not only does Jesus prove himself to be the true obedient Son who will fulfill all righteousness, but Jesus establishes the means with which the people of God are to oppose Satan and his minions. Jesus does not summon the power of deity nor call upon the hosts of heaven to destroy Satan. Rather, Jesus opposes Satan with God's Word, the same weapon the saints must use in their struggle with Antichrist.

The Two-Age Model as an Interpretive Grid

Before proceeding to examine the three streams of Antichrist teaching in the New Testament, it is important to summarize the basic eschatological framework of the New Testament and its impact upon the doctrine of Antichrist. The New Testament writers universally speak of God's sovereign control of history as the outworking of two qualitatively distinct and successive eschatological ages known as "this age" and "the age to come."[10] Throughout the New Testament, "this age" is used in reference to the present course of human history, while "the age to come" is used of the eschatological age of redemption promised throughout the Old Testament, which is now realized with the coming of Jesus Christ and manifest for all to see in our Lord's triumph over death and the grave in his bodily resurrection and exaltation. After Jesus's victory on Easter, the fate of Satan and all his confederates (John's antichrists, Paul's Man of Sin, and the dragon, the beast, and the false prophet of the Book of Revelation) is sealed. Jesus has conquered death and the grave, proving that the curse is now reversed (1 Cor. 15:55) and ensuring that in the new creation there will be no place for Satan and those who serve him (2 Cor. 5:17; Rev. 21:5; 22–27).

The period of time between the first advent of Jesus Christ until his second advent—the time between the establishment of Christ's kingdom as described in the Gospels and the consummation of all things—is the same period of redemptive history described in Revelation 20 as a "thousand years." This means that the so-called "millennium" is a present reality and not a future hope. This also means that the New Testament writers do not anticipate an earthly golden-age millennium (either before or after our Lord's return) but expect the consummation of all things when Jesus comes back—the resurrection, the final judgment, and the creation of the new heaven and new earth. The "thousand years" spoken of in Revelation 20:1–10 is that same period of time in which citizens of "this age" await "the age to come"—though given the fact of the present reality of the kingdom of God (Matt. 12:28; Luke 10:1–20; 17:20–21; Rom. 14:17) and the work of the Holy Spirit (Eph. 1:13–14), "the age to come" is already a present reality for the believer in Jesus Christ.

The tension between the "already" and the "not yet" characterizes much of the New Testament eschatological hope as Christians await the final consummation of Christ's present kingdom on the great and glorious day of the Lord Jesus. This tension is also apparent in the fact that the New Testament writers speak of a "spirit of antichrist" already active (1 John 4:3) and a power of lawlessness, which is at work during the apostolic age but restrained by God until the time of the end (2 Thess. 2:7–8; Rev. 20:1–10).

Jesus and Paul speak of "this age" and "the age to come" as two successive and qualitatively distinct eschatological periods. In three places in the Synoptic Gospels, our Lord explicitly contrasts "this age" with "the age to come." In Matthew 12:32, Jesus speaks of the impossibility of forgiveness for blasphemy against the Holy Spirit, "either in this age or in the age to come." In Luke 18:29–30, Jesus speaks about the kingdom of God in response to the unbelief expressed by the rich young ruler. Jesus says, "I tell you the truth, . . . no one who has left home or wife or brothers or parents or children for the sake of the kingdom of God will fail to receive many times as much in this age and, in the age to come, eternal life." And finally, in Luke 20:34–36, Jesus declares, "The people of this age marry and are given in marriage. But those who are considered worthy of taking part in that age and in the resurrection from the dead will neither marry nor be given in marriage, and they can no longer die; for they are like the angels. They are God's children, since they are children of the resurrection."

From such texts it is clear that our Lord understands these two ages as successive and qualitatively distinct. "This age," says Jesus, is characterized by marriage and things temporal. "The age to come," on the other hand, is characterized by resurrection life and immortality; hence the impossibility of natural, earthly life continuing after the general resurrection that occurs at our Lord's return (John 6:39–40, 44, 54). The line of demarcation between these two ages is the return of Christ (Matt. 13:39), which presents a very serious problem for premillenarians who contend that people in natural bodies continue to populate the earth during Christ's millennial rule after the resurrection of the righteous. If "the age to come" is the age of resurrection in which there is no marriage or sexual relationships, just how is it that people somehow escape this universal event so as to repopulate the earth *after* Christ returns? This is an impossibility, which makes premillennialism highly untenable.

Paul sets out the same eschatological understanding of history in Ephesians 1:21, speaking of the present exaltation of Jesus Christ, who is "far above all rule and authority, power and dominion, and every title that can be given, not only in the present age but also in the one to come." Like Jesus, Paul sees these two ages as consecutive and distinct, although Paul adds to our understanding the important point that Christ's rule is already a present reality that began with his resurrection and exaltation.[11]

The impact of this two-age eschatological framework upon the question of millennialism in general and upon the doctrine of Antichrist in particular becomes very apparent when we examine how these terms are used throughout the New Testament. Whenever the term "this age" is used, it is always in reference to things temporal, things destined to perish. Consider the following things the biblical writers declared about "this age." The end of the age will be preceded by signs (Matt. 24:3), and Christ himself will be with us until this age ends (Matt. 28:20). There are material rewards in this age (Luke 18:30), and the people of this age marry and are given in marriage (Luke 20:34). According to Mark, the present age is an age of homes, fields, and families (Mark 10:30).

The Gospels also record our Lord as saying that there will be no forgiveness in the age to come for speaking blasphemy against the Holy Spirit (Matt. 12:32) and that it is a period of judgment when the weeds are thrown into the fire (Matt. 13:40). It is also an age of eternal life (Mark 10:30; Luke 18:30) and when, as we have seen, there is no longer marriage or giving in marriage. It is an age, says Paul, when life is "truly life" (1 Tim. 6:19).

Paul puts it in decidedly ethical terms. We are not to be conformed to the pattern of this age (Rom. 12:2), for this present age is evil (Gal. 1:4). The wisdom of this age is the godless speculation of the philosophers (1 Cor. 1:20) and is characterized by rulers who do not know the truth (1 Cor. 2:6–8). In fact, says Paul, Satan himself is the "god of this age" (2 Cor. 4:4) for the ways of this age are evil (Eph. 2:1–2). Paul exhorts those who are rich in this age not to put their hopes in their riches for the age to come (1 Tim. 6:17), for we are to live godly lives now as we await the age to come (Titus 2:12).

In every case, the qualities assigned by the biblical writers to "this age" are always temporal in nature and represent the fallen world and its sinful inhabitants awaiting the judgment to come at our Lord's return. This becomes clear when we see "this age" as the biblical writers intend—an age that stands in stark contrast to the eschatological "age to come."

Much more sinister than his predecessors, Antichrist is the supreme manifestation of the spirit of this present evil age.[12] Antichrist is a blasphemer beyond all others (Rev. 13:6). He proclaims himself to be God (2 Thess. 2:4), manifests the power of Satan (2 Thess. 2:9; Rev. 13:2), and will bring about the final end-times apostasy (2 Thess. 2:3). Empowered by Satan, Antichrist will wage war upon the saints (Rev. 13:7) and receive the worship of all the earth's inhabitants (Rev. 13:8). His mysterious number, 666, in a symbolic sense is the identifying mark of this present evil age (see Rev. 13:18), since the number 6 is the number of man and its triple repetition indicates that the Antichrist can never attain the fullness of Christ and the age to come. Antichrist is, therefore, destined to always fall short of the divine glory he craves.[13] These are all themes to be developed in more detail in subsequent chapters.

This means that "the age to come" is an age of eternal life and immortality. It is characterized by the realization of all of the blessings of the resurrection and consummation. It is not an age in which people await the consummation. When we consider those additional texts in which Paul speaks of the consummation of the kingdom of God, the evidence against premillennialism becomes even stronger. According to Paul, evildoers will not inherit this kingdom (1 Cor. 6:9–10). Flesh and blood cannot inherit the kingdom (1 Cor. 15:50). Those who live evil lives will not enter this kingdom (Gal. 5:21), nor will the immoral (Eph. 5:5). Thus, it is clear that "the age to come" refers to that period of time *after* the resurrection, the judgment, and the restoration of all things. Those who participate in "the age to come" are no longer characterized by the temporal but by the eternal—a point particularly problematic for all forms of premillennialism, which insist upon an earthly existence of some sort in a millennial age of halfway consummation after Christ's return. This two-age structure is also highly problematic for preterists, who see "this age" as the Jewish era and "the age to come" as that which follows God's judgment upon Israel in AD 70.[14] It is this misunderstanding of the relationship between these two ages that creates the impetus to so ardently defend the view that Antichrist has already come and has been defeated.

Prophetic Perspective and the Abomination of Desolation

Understanding the way in which several key prophecies regarding the Antichrist are framed in the New Testament is important to interpreting them correctly. It is my contention that several of the prophecies (especially in Daniel) regarding Antichrist and his predecessors involve *double fulfillment*, which simply refers to the fact that certain prophecies are fulfilled more than once. Such prophecies are usually connected to an immediate or imminent fulfillment in the lifetime of the prophet and again to a more distant fulfillment in the messianic age (at our Lord's first or second advent). This phenomenon is also known as "prophetic perspective." The prophet foretells what appears to be a single event in his immediate future, but as redemptive history unfolds, it becomes clear that there are multiple fulfillments of the original prophecy. This is true with the biblical data predicting the coming of an end-times foe of God's people—the Antichrist.

Before we discuss what Jesus meant when he predicted an act of sacrilege that would bring about the desolation of the Jerusalem temple—the so-called "abomination of desolation"[15]—we need to understand that a number of Old Testament prophecies, along with certain aspects of the prophecy Jesus uttered in the Olivet Discourse, have more than one fulfillment.

According to Herman Ridderbos, many biblical prophecies refer to "things that appear to be centuries apart in the fulfillment [and] are sometimes comprehended by Jesus' prophecy in the same temporal frame and within the same local framework." According to Ridderbos, such prophecy is "something different than a diary of future events. . . . The function of prophecy is consequently not that of a detailed projection of the future, but is the urgent insistence on the certainty of the things to come. This explains why, at the end of the vista, the perspective is lacking. The prophet sees all kinds of events that will come and he sees in all of them the coming of God. But he cannot fix a date for the events, he cannot distinguish all phases in God's coming. To him it is one great reality."[16]

This is an important point. The prophet is not concerned with *when* certain things will come to pass but with the fact that they *will* come to pass. Keeping this in mind as we look at the biblical data regarding Antichrist will explain how Daniel can predict more than one event in a single prophecy—for example, the prophecy of a great blasphemer in Daniel 11, which refers to both Antiochus IV (Dan. 11:21–35) and the Antichrist at the time of the end (Dan. 11:36–45).

A number of commentators believe that this telescoping of imminent and future fulfillment (prophetic perspective or double fulfillment) is found in several of the prophetic books of the Old Testament. It is also found in the Olivet Discourse (Matthew 24; Mark 13; Luke 21), in which our Lord sets forth his most comprehensive teaching regarding the course of future events. As the discourse unfolds, it becomes clear that Jesus is speaking of both imminent and future events. Some of these are fulfilled by the events of AD 70, while others remain to be fulfilled at the end of the age.[17] The events associated with the destruction of Jerusalem and the temple may also serve as a type (a foreshadowing) of a universal and final cataclysm (antitype) yet to come at the end of the age.

The imminent desolation of the holy place (the Jerusalem temple) by the armies of Titus in AD 70, predicted by our Lord in Matthew 24:15, fulfills Daniel's prophecy of such an event

(Dan. 9:27; 11:31; 12:11). But the actions of Titus's armies actually fulfill Daniel's prophecy a second time—Antiochus IV was the first to make the holy place desolate in 167 BC. Antiochus erected an altar to Zeus on the altar of Yahweh, and then some two hundred years later the armies of Titus started a fire in the temple before looting its sacred objects, profaning the temple and leaving it desolate a second time. This is what Daniel predicted and what Jesus restates. As Vos says, it is plain "that Jesus shaped the matter in his mind after the same fashion" as the desecration of the Jerusalem temple by Antiochus, "only he projects the horrible event from the past in which it had once taken place into a future beyond his own point of speaking."[18] But Jesus's mention of the "abomination of desolation" may also function as a prophetic picture of what will happen at the end of the age on a universal scale in Christ's church. If this is the case, Daniel's prophecy is not only fulfilled by Antiochus IV's desecration of the temple in 167 BC but again by Titus and his Roman legions in AD 70, and then possibly again on a universal scale by an end-times Antichrist.[19]

TRIPLE FULFILLMENT

Prophetic perspective is clearly found throughout the Olivet Discourse. Take, for example, our Lord's warning to his disciples in Matthew 24:4–13, where Jesus speaks of false christs, wars and rumors of wars, famines, and earthquakes before stating in verse 14 that the gospel must be preached to the whole world as a testimony. In verses 4–13, Jesus is speaking of events that will happen in the lifetime of the disciples; then he immediately jumps ahead to the time of the end in verse 14, seen in the reference to the universal preaching of the gospel to the ends of the earth, affirming the missionary calling of Christ's church (Matt. 28:16–20).

DO YOU THINK IT HAS?

The same thing can be seen when Jesus speaks of the imminent destruction of Jerusalem by the Roman army. When Jesus enters Jerusalem on Palm Sunday, he warns his disciples, "The days will come upon you when your enemies will build an embankment against you and encircle you and hem you in on every side. They will dash you to the ground, you and the children within your walls. They will not leave one stone on another, because you did not recognize the time of God's coming to you" (Luke 19:43–44). In Luke 21:20, Jesus is even more specific about what will happen to Jerusalem: "When you see Jerusalem being surrounded by armies, you will know that its desolation is near." This is clearly a prophetic prediction of an imminent event within the lifetime of the disciples, namely, the Jewish War so graphically detailed by Josephus. Says Jesus, "They will fall by the sword and will be taken as prisoners to all the nations. Jerusalem will be trampled on by the Gentiles until the times of the Gentiles are fulfilled" (Luke 21:24). That Jesus is predicting the imminent events of AD 70 and the Jewish diaspora is indisputable.

In Matthew's account Jesus is also speaking of an imminent fulfillment when he warns his disciples about a particular aspect of the desolation coming upon Israel's temple:

> So when you see standing in the holy place "the abomination that causes desolation," spoken of through the prophet Daniel—let the reader understand—then let those who are in Judea flee to the mountains. Let no one on the roof of his house go down to take anything out of the house. Let no one in the field go back to get his cloak. How dreadful it will be in those days for pregnant women and nursing mothers! Pray that your flight will not take place in winter or on the Sabbath. For then there will be great distress, unequaled from the beginning of the world until now—and never to be equaled again. If those days had not been cut short, no one would survive, but for the sake of the elect those days will be shortened.
>
> Matthew 24:15–22

Once again, the reference to the desecration of the temple ("the abomination that causes desolation") and a time of unequaled distress for the city of Jerusalem is a prediction of the events of AD 70.[20] The desolation and profanation of the temple, coupled with the siege of Jerusalem by skilled and combat-hardened Roman legions, is the worst cataclysm ever to come upon Jerusalem, and, according to Jesus, it will never be equaled again. The desolation of Israel and the dispersion of the Jews to the ends of the earth is a great tragedy.

Notice that later in that same discourse Jesus telescopes his attention to the time of the end, speaking of cosmic signs that accompany his return to earth at the end of the age (Matt. 24:29).[21] Only then does Jesus go on to tell his disciples, "At that time the sign of the Son of Man will appear in the sky, and all the nations of the earth will mourn. They will see the Son of Man coming on the clouds of the sky, with power and great glory. And he will send his angels with a loud trumpet call, and they will gather his elect from the four winds, from one end of the heavens to the other" (Matt. 24:30–31). Jesus speaks of an imminent event (the destruction of Jerusalem) and future events (the end of the age and his second advent) in what is a virtually seamless manner.

In light of this tension between things imminent and things future, Charles Cranfield has pointed out that "neither an exclusively historical nor an exclusively eschatological interpretation is satisfactory. . . . We must allow for a double reference, for a mingling of historical and eschatological."[22] Thus when Jesus speaks of an abominating sacrilege, he is likely not only predicting the events of AD 70, he may also be speaking of events that occur at the time of the end—especially if the apostle Paul is speaking of the same thing when the apostle refers to "the man doomed to destruction. He will oppose and will exalt himself over everything that is called God or is worshiped, so that he sets himself up in God's temple, proclaiming himself to be God" (2 Thess. 2:3–4). This connection, Vos believes, enables us to draw a line from Daniel to both Jesus and Paul and provides the continuity necessary to make sense of what would otherwise be three unrelated streams of data in the New Testament regarding the Antichrist.[23] This is also the view of Anthony Hoekema in his influential statement and defense of Reformed amillennialism, *The Bible and the Future*.[24] This seems to make the best sense of the passage and allows us to take seriously Jesus's utilization of prophetic perspective.

In Defense of Prophetic Perspective (Double Fulfillment)

In his helpful study entitled *The Language and Imagery of the Bible*, G. B. Caird points out that the phenomenon of prophetic perspective is found throughout the Old Testament prophets.

> The prophets looked into the future with bifocal vision. With their near sight they foresaw imminent historical events which would be brought about by familiar human causes; for example, disaster was near for Babylon because Yahweh was stirring up the Medes against them (Isa. 13:17). With their long sight they saw the day of the Lord; and it was in the nature of the prophetic experience that they were able to adjust their focus so as to impose the one image on the other and produce a synthetic picture. . . . To prove the truth of this assertion, there is fortunately a simple test ready at hand in the life story of Jeremiah. At the outset of his ministry (626 BC) Jeremiah predicted the destruction of Jerusalem by an enemy from the north (Jer. 1:14–15; 4:6; 6:1, 22; 10:22), and in a synthetic vision he saw this as God's judgment, depicting it as the return of chaos and even using the words *tohu wabohu* (waste and void), which occur elsewhere only in the account of creation in Genesis 1:2.[25]

Caird goes on to cite Joel 1:15 and 2:1, in which local judgment anticipates a universal judgment yet to come, and Joel 3:14 (which teaches a universal judgment) along with Joel 3:1, 21, in which the knowledge of such universal judgment would reverse the fortunes of Judah and Jerusalem (local).[26]

Given the fact that double fulfillment can be found in the prophets (Joel, Amos, Isaiah, and Jeremiah) as well as in the Olivet Discourse, this phenomenon is the means through which we should endeavor to understand the apparently conflicting data in both Testaments regarding an imminent Antichrist (or antichrists) and a future eschatological foe who appears at the time of the end. The events of AD 70 recapitulate the desecration of the temple by Antiochus IV while at the same time pointing us ahead to the end of the age.

A number of writers reject the idea of prophetic perspective and double fulfillment altogether.[27] The most common objection to double fulfillment of these prophecies is that this view supposedly enables the interpreter to have his cake and eat it too. Instead of making a decision as to whether an event, such as the destruction of the temple in AD 70, has a past or future fulfillment, the interpreter simply affirms both are true. While avoiding making such hard interpretive decisions may be tempting, the strength of this argument is greatly weakened if there are specific instances of double fulfillment found in Scripture, thereby providing some degree of external control upon the whims of the interpreter.

In his book *Perilous Times*,[28] Ken Gentry presents three arguments against double fulfillment as set forth above. Gentry's first argument is that the events depicted in John's vision in Revelation are soon to come to pass (Rev. 1:1, 3; 22:6, 10). The angel tells John that "the time is near" (Rev. 1:3). This fact, Gentry believes, means that the destruction of the Jerusalem temple in AD 70 along with the appearance of the beast/Antichrist (Nero) fulfills those things foretold by John, Paul, and Jesus. Given the preterist understanding of the course of redemptive history and the events of AD 70, nothing then remains of a future Antichrist yet to be fulfilled. Not only does this argument collapse if the Book of Revelation was written after AD 70 (see the appendix), but the fact that Revelation depicts the entire period of the time between our Lord's first and second advents weakens Gentry's contention considerably.[29]

Gentry's second argument is that "we really stretch credibility if we argue that all the many details of the beast (and why not all of Revelation?) are to be fulfilled in incredible detail again later."[30] Gentry misses the fact that we are not arguing that everything in Revelation is fulfilled twice—only those portions where there are hints in the text, such as Revelation (e.g., Rev. 17:9–14 while an eighth king is yet to come). This would have greater weight if we did not have sufficient biblical warrant to assert that double fulfillment is indeed found in the writings of Israel's prophets (especially Daniel) and in the words of our Lord in the Olivet Discourse. This point has been established above.

A third reason double fulfillment is not viable, according to
Gentry, is that "the beast clearly belongs to the first century
Roman era."[31] But the persecution of God's people brought
about by the beast more likely applies to the reign of Domitian (AD 95) than to Nero (before AD 70).[32] Furthermore, this
would be true if the Roman beast does not serve in the Book of
Revelation as a type of all anti-Christian empires and government that will subsequently arise throughout the inter-advental
period bent on persecuting the people of God. Nero is the type
of all the evil figures and self-deifiers who follow in his wake
who are bent on receiving that worship rightfully meant for
God and who use the sword to persecute the people of God.[33]
The historical events in Revelation are not at odds with the
eschatological if the relationship between the two is type and
shadow.

4

Many Antichrists Have Already Come

The Doctrine of Antichrist in the Epistles of John

The Meaning of the Term *Antichrist*

Many people are surprised to learn that the word *Antichrist* (*antichristos*) appears only in John's Epistles (1 John 2:18, 22; 4:3; 2 John 7) and is never even mentioned in the Book of Revelation.[1] It is even more of a surprise when people discover that John's teaching about the Antichrist bears very little resemblance to the Antichrist of either popular culture or the *Left Behind* novels. The term *Antichrist* simply refers to a false thing (anti) taking the place of a real thing with great antagonism present between the substitute and the real—Christ and an archfoe.[2]

John's Epistles were likely written in the latter part of the first century. John's purpose in writing is, in part, to inform his readers about the fact that "many antichrists" (note the plural) have already come (1 John 2:18). He's also letting his readers know just who these people are and what they are teaching. "Many deceivers, who do not acknowledge Jesus Christ as coming in the flesh, have gone out into the world. Any such person is the deceiver and the antichrist" (2 John 7). Therefore, the presence of these individuals in the first-century church is taken by the apostle to be an important indication that it is already the "last hour" (1 John 2:18). This is yet another way of speaking of the "last day" (John 6:40; see also John 5:25) or of the "last times."[3]

For first-century Christians, it was a fact of life that these antichrists were present who did not acknowledge that Jesus had come in the flesh. Clearly, in John's discussion of Antichrist, his focus fell upon a specific heresy on the part of certain individuals within the church who, sadly, had fallen away from the orthodox faith and were deceiving others. If many antichrists were already present when John wrote his Epistles before the end of the first century, then these antichrists cannot be relegated strictly to the time of the end as is the Antichrist of film and evangelical fiction. For John, antichrist is a present reality. The fact that many antichrists are present proves it is already the last hour.

John's warning about many antichrists opposing the faithful points us in the direction of the twin evils of heresy and apostasy. False teachers will inevitably arise and entice others to believe as they do. That this phenomenon arises within the church—as opposed to some form of external persecution by forces outside the church—is clear from the context. According to John, Christians are not to "love the world or anything in the world" (1 John 2:15). It is not that the world itself is evil. Rather, as John sees things, the world is a place temporarily controlled by the power of evil.[4] While God loves the world and sent his beloved Son to die to redeem the world (1 John 2:2), Christians must be very careful not to be enticed by those things that can draw them away from their master ("the cravings of sinful man, the lust of [the] eyes," 1 John 2:16). This is why John warns his readers so affectionately yet directly, "Dear children, this is the last hour; and as you have heard that the antichrist is coming, even now many antichrists have come. This is how we know it is the last hour" (1 John 2:18). In fact, John goes on to point out that these individuals did indeed love the world too much, since "they went out from us, but they did not really belong to us. For if they had belonged to us, they would have remained with us; but their going showed that none of them belonged to us" (1 John 2:19).

John's description of these individuals, whom he calls "antichrists," raises the question as to whether the term *Antichrist* is connected to the "false Christs" mentioned by Jesus in the Olivet Discourse (Matt. 24:24; Mark 13:22). A number of writers believe this connection to be fairly obvious.[5] The question remains as to how this series of antichrists is connected to that mysterious individual Paul speaks of—the Man of Sin—who sets himself up in the temple of God demanding to be worshiped (2 Thess. 2:1–12). If John's antichrists were a present reality before the close of the first century, how does his understanding of this matter relate to the widely held assumption among our contemporaries that the Antichrist awaits his revelation at the time of the end and not before? These are all important matters, which we will now address.

The Enemy Within—Many Antichrists Have Already Come

Throughout his first two Epistles, John makes three primary points about Antichrist. First, John tells us that antichrist is already present when he writes his first Epistle. Second, he says that there are many antichrists, not just one. Therefore antichrist is not a specific individual but a class of false teachers who deny that Jesus has come in the flesh. "Who is the liar? It is the man who denies that Jesus is the Christ. Such a man is the antichrist—he denies the Father and the Son" (1 John 2:22). Third, John tells us that antichrist may not even be an individual person or persons at all. Instead, antichrist may represent a system of heretical thought, specifically the denial that Jesus Christ has come in the flesh. As we read in 1 John 4:2–3, "This is how you can recognize the Spirit of God: Every spirit that acknowledges that Jesus Christ has come in the flesh is from God, but every spirit that does not acknowledge Jesus is not from God. This is the spirit of the antichrist, which you have heard is coming and even now is already in the world." There are not only "antichrists" (specific individuals who deny that Jesus has come in the flesh), but there is also a "spirit of antichrist," which seems to speak of a heresy then spreading throughout the church and not even necessarily to the individuals who teach such things. Some have advocated that John is correcting an earlier tradition in which antichrist was seen as a supernatural opponent. John's goal here, it is argued, is to "depersonalize" Antichrist, removing the need for undue speculation.[6]

B. B. Warfield's Challenge—A Composite Photograph?

One of the most important treatments of John's doctrine of antichrist from a Reformed perspective is B. B. Warfield's 1921 essay, "Antichrist," which provides a wealth of thought-provoking insights. Although I disagree with Warfield on several points, he effectively challenges a number of widely held assumptions. He writes:

> We read of Antichrist nowhere in the New Testament except in certain passages of the Epistles of John (1 John ii. 18, 22; iv. 3; 2 John 7). What is taught in these passages constitutes the whole New Testament doctrine of Antichrist. It is common, it is true, to connect with this doctrine what is said by our Lord of false christs and false prophets; by Paul of the Man of Sin; by the Apocalypse of the Beasts which come up out of the deep and the sea. The warrant for labelling the composite photograph thus obtained with the name of Antichrist is not very apparent. . . . The name of Antichrist occurs in connection with none of them, except that presented in the passages of the Epistles of John

already indicated; and both the name and the figure denoted by it, to all appearance, occur there first in extant literature.[7]

According to Warfield, John's doctrine of antichrist stands alone. Antichrist should not be confused or combined with Paul's Man of Sin nor the beast of Revelation. In other words, John is speaking of something altogether unique. Although Warfield has not convinced me that there is no direct connection between the antichrists of John's Epistles and these other New Testament figures, Warfield's challenge that this connection is simply assumed rather than proven is an issue that certainly merits consideration.

Since John's Epistles are the only place in Scripture where the term *Antichrist* is actually used, the connection between John's doctrine and that of Paul or even that found in John's Book of Revelation needs to be demonstrated rather than merely assumed. Although many scholars disagree with Warfield's contention that these individual antichrists are not part of what Warfield calls a "composite photograph" of a specific individual,[8] it is certainly possible that John's antichrists, Paul's Man of Sin, and the beast of Revelation have no connection whatsoever and that these are all distinct phenomena.

Warfield believes that John is dealing with some legend that has arisen in the church, since Warfield sees no "Anti-Messiah in the Old Testament."[9] While Warfield stands outside the scholarly consensus on this point, he is quite correct to point out that John introduces Antichrist terminology in a corrective fashion in order to clear up a serious misconception that already existed in the minds of his readers:

> We learn merely that there were people who declared "Antichrist is coming!" It appears to be implied that Antichrist was thought of as an individual, and his coming as, though certain, yet still future—as apparently, in fact, a sign of the impending end. We cannot go beyond that; perhaps not quite so far as that. And as to who it was who were asserting, "Antichrist is coming!" John leaves us completely in the dark. Possibly he is adducing a current Christian belief. . . . It appears far more probable, however, that John is adducing not an item of Christian teach-

ing, but only a current legend—Christian or other—in which he recognizes an element of truth and isolates it for the benefits of his readers.[10]

That John is correcting some popular superstition becomes clear, Warfield argues, when we look at exactly how John corrects the popular misconception:

> The phrase which, John tells us, his readers heard—"Antichrist is coming!" does not in its very language, to be sure, project his coming into the future. It is the certainty rather than the futurity of Antichrist's coming which it emphasizes; and it perhaps, as heard by his readers, put them in a quiver of expectation of his coming—creating some situation as that against which our Lord had warned his followers (Mark xiii. 21 f.). . . . John meets the situation thus produced by a very definite assertion, that, so far from being a matter of future expectation, the coming of Antichrist had already taken place. Antichrist is not a future, but a present phenomenon; not a thing to be looked forward to in nameless dread, but a thing to be courageously met in our every day living.[11]

Therefore, according to Warfield, antichrist is not some personal, future foe awaiting his revelation only at the end of time; he is already with us in some real sense.[12] This also means that John's antichrists are no doubt referring to the same or similar phenomena as the false christs predicted by Jesus (Matt. 24:24; Mark 13:22). In fact, says Warfield, it is our Christian duty to boldly face such opponents. This, Warfield argues, John has made certain, for the revelation of antichrist is one of the characteristics of the "last hour" in which we are already living:

> John makes this assertion with the utmost emphasis (iv. 3). This thing, he says, "is now in the world—already," that post-posited "already" carrying with it the utmost strength of assertion. There is no doubt about it at all; Antichrist is here among us, now, already. In doing this John does not so much separate Antichrist from "the last hour" with which he had been connected as correct the notion which perhaps had been entertained of the phrase "the last hour." "The last hour" no more than Antichrist is a matter of

the future; it too belongs to the present. The time we are living in—that is "the last hour" means just the Messianic period, the period after Messiah has come. We may call it, with reference to the true coming of our Lord, the inter-Advental period. Of course, there could be no Antichrist until this "last hour" had come. How then could there be an Antichrist before there was a Christ? The fact then, that Antichrist has come (*gegonasin*, ii. 18)—that the phenomenon is "now in the world—already" (iv. 3)—is proof enough that the time we are living in is "the last hour" (ii. 18). Thus, with the dismissal from reality of a distinctively future Antichrist, John dismisses from reality a distinctively future "last hour." The "last hour," as he knows it, began with the coming of Christ, and fills the whole spacious period which extends till He shall come again.[13]

This means that with the coming of Christ we have the coming of the last hour as well as the coming of many antichrists.

Not only is antichrist not merely some individual personification of evil assigned to the end of time, antichrist may not even be a specific individual at all. As John has been telling us, there are many antichrists! The fact that many such antichrists are already present demonstrates that the last hour has already come. Warfield says that John "not only, however, dismisses Antichrist from the future; he deprives him of his individuality. In the place of an Antichrist, he substitutes 'many Antichrists.' And he declares that, already when he wrote, still in the first Christian century, a multitude of these Antichrists had come into existence. . . . There can be no question then, that John volatizes the individual Antichrist into thin air and substitutes for him a multitude of 'Antichrists.' We may say, no doubt, that they embody the spirit of Antichrist."[14]

Not only is antichrist not an individual in John's Epistles, John makes it clear that in some way, the antichrist imagery represents the most egregious of doctrinal errors—the denial that Jesus is the Christ—and is clearly tied to a system of heretical thought. Warfield argues,

John not only erases the individual Antichrist from the scroll of prediction, but reduces him just to a heresy. "Who is the liar," he demands, "but he who denies that Jesus is the Christ? This is the Antichrist—he who denies the Father and the Son" (1 John ii. 22). "Every spirit," he declares, "which confesses that Jesus Christ come in the flesh is of God; and no spirit which does not confess Jesus, is of God: and this is that Antichrist of which you have heard that it is coming: and it is now in the world already" (iv. 3). "There are many seducers," he declares again, "who went out into the world, even those who do not confess Jesus as Christ coming in flesh." This is the Seducer and the Antichrist (2 John 7). In one word, "Antichrist" meant for John just denial of what we should call the doctrine, or let us rather say the fact of the Incarnation. By whatever process it had been brought about, "Christ" had come to denote for John the Divine Nature of our Lord, and so far to be synonymous with "Son of God." To deny that Jesus is the Christ was not to him therefore merely to deny that he is the Messiah, but to deny that he is the Son of God; and was equivalent therefore to "denying the Father and the Son"—that is to say, in our modern mode of speech, the doctrine—the fact—of the Trinity, which is the implicate of the Incarnation. To deny that Jesus is Christ come—or is the Christ coming—in flesh, was again just to refuse to recognize in Jesus Incarnate God. Whosoever, says John, takes up this attitude toward Jesus is Antichrist.[15]

It must be pointed out that whatever antichrist is—given the imagery used by John—antichrist clearly involves explicit doctrinal error and heresy regarding the person and work of Jesus Christ, specifically his incarnation and the necessary relationship that Jesus bears to the Father. Therefore, in the sense spoken of by John, Antichrist is any heretic, including the multitude of false teachers and the pernicious proto-gnostic heresy already present during the time of John's writing, denying the coming of the Son of God in the flesh.[16] To deny the incarnation of Christ is to be an antichrist, John says. Any false teacher who denies the incarnation of our Lord is effectively doing the work of antichrist and reflects the spirit of antichrist. In fact, the very presence of such individuals is a sign that it is "the last hour." Since antichrist was present in John's time, the only conclusion that can be drawn is that we have been in the "last days" ever since!

It should also be clear that John's multitude of antichrists can be directly related to the warnings that our Lord gives us about false christs—false teachers who would be characteristic, in part, of the "last days" (see Mark 13:21–23). This is also probably related to Jude's warning about the need to contend for the apostolic faith in the face of unbelief (Jude 3–4), and that of 2 Peter 2:1–22, where we are warned of false teachers who attempt to secretly introduce heresies. Indeed, Warfield's conclusion aptly sums up the central thesis of John's warning to his dear children. "So long as a Divine Christ is confessed in the midst of a gainsaying world, so long there will be, as in John's day, many Antichrists."[17]

A Connection between John's antichrists and an Antichrist?

There are a number of things we need to say in conclusion. First, according to John, many antichrists have already come (1 John 2:18, 22; 4:3; 2 John 7). Note the postpositive grammatical construction—now, have already come (1 John 4:3).[18] This means that such antichrists are not strictly a future foe limited to the time immediately before the end of the age. Antichrists are a past and present reality. It is also vital to note that these are individuals who arise from within the believing community and who then fall away, taking others with them. If there is a connection to be made between this series of antichrists and a final Antichrist, it is likely to be found here, since Paul's Man of Lawlessness appears at or during a time of great apostasy (a theme we will take up in chapter 6). These many antichrists (plural) are the manifestation of the spirit of antichrist (1 John 4:3). The fact that many antichrists have already come means that it is the last hour—i.e., the world has entered into the final phase of its history.

Second, antichrist is anyone who denies that Jesus has come in the flesh. The focus throughout the discussion in John's Epistles is clearly upon a very specific heresy. The context

clearly indicates that antichrist is a primarily internal threat
(apostasy). Christians are not to love the world (1 John 2:15).
Antichrists are people who went out from the church (1 John
2:19) because they love the world more than the truth. Believers,
on the other hand, have God's anointing, which is connected
to a knowledge of the truth (1 John 2:20–21). They will not
fall away and will take up their sacred duty of opposing these
antichrists with the divinely appointed weapon—the truth of
the gospel. If antichrists are proponents of error, they must be
opposed with the truth.

Third, John's antichrists are very likely connected to the false
christs mentioned by Jesus in the Olivet Discourse (Matt. 24:24;
Mark 13:22). The presence of false christs—false teachers and
prophets along with these many antichrists—should not surprise us. We are warned throughout the New Testament that
this will be the case from the time Jesus came until he comes
again (see 2 Tim. 3:1–9; 2 Peter 2:1–22).

Fourth, John provides the interpretive grid through which
we should understand the historicist view regarding the papacy
and any possible connection to the Antichrist and the beast.
The Roman Catholic Church is certainly orthodox in its teaching on the Trinity and Christology (unlike those of whom we
are warned in 1 John). Yet in Canon 9 of the Council of Trent's
decree concerning justification, the Catholic Church officially
denies the gospel (specifically justification *sola fide*). Even if
the pope is not Antichrist, Tridentine Catholicism clearly falls
under the apostle Paul's indictment in Galatians 1:6–9 regarding another gospel.[19] Furthermore, historicists have argued that
Rome imposes false worship on God's people (the adoration
of the saints and the use of images and unbiblical rituals) and
puts the papacy and the merits of the saints in place of the sole
mediation of Jesus Christ when it declares that the pope is the
Vicar of Christ on the earth.[20]

In the strictest sense, then, Warfield is correct, and we would
be wise to heed his caution. John's heretical antichrists are not
the same thing as the beast of Revelation, which is external
persecution of the church by the state—specifically through
the power exercised by the Roman Empire and its imperial

cult. Therefore, we must not simply equate John's antichrist imagery to the beast of Revelation to form what Warfield describes as a "composite photograph" without sound theological justification.

But the final manifestation of the beast and false prophet (when tied to Paul's Man of Sin) seems to indicate that John's series of antichrists (whether John here envisions this or not) will indeed give way to a final end-times persecutor of the people of God, in which the state uses its powers to impose the false teaching described by John on the people of God. In fact, both John (Rev. 20:1–10) and Paul (2 Thess. 2:1–12) speak of Satan's power as currently restrained, in some way, until the time of the end. And this may be why John here speaks of a series of antichrists and not an Antichrist. Indeed, John believes many antichrists have already come. And this is how we know it is the last hour.

5

THE DRAGON, THE BEAST, AND THE FALSE PROPHET

The Doctrine of Antichrist in the Book of Revelation

The Old Testament Background

Biblical history is replete with accounts of great empires and powerful tyrants who oppress the people of God. Understandably, secular historians locate the roots of the epic struggles between Israel and its neighbors in a combination of socioeconomic, political, and military factors. But the story of redemption indicates that this struggle is experienced by the people of God because of one reason—their allegiance to the Creator-Redeemer who has revealed himself in the pages of the Old and New Testaments. It is this allegiance to Yahweh that makes Israel an object of scorn in the eyes of all those who seek the glory that

[handwritten margin note: small portion of Israel]

rightly belongs to God alone. This allegiance also makes Israel a target of satanic wrath and ire, since it is from Israel that the seed of the woman will come.

The very nature of Yahweh's covenant promise—"I will be your God and you will be my people"—makes plain that those who serve Yahweh are serving the true and living God. And if Yahweh is the true and living God, then all the other so-called "gods" of the pagan nations are but mere idols, the figment of the sinful human imagination. Therefore, the struggle between men and nations depicted throughout the Old Testament is the historical outworking of a great cosmic struggle between two seeds (Messiah and Antichrist).[1]

The practical implications of Yahweh and Israel's mutual loyalty—formally expressed in the form of covenant—could not be greater. Those who serve Yahweh and obey his commandments are not free to worship any government or its leader, no matter what such loyalty to Yahweh might cost them. It was Israel's own Messiah and mediator of the covenant who cited a familiar proverb to his disciples: "No one can serve two masters. Either he will hate the one and love the other, or he will be devoted to the one and despise the other" (Matt. 6:24). Indeed, Yahweh demands full and total allegiance from his people.

The first table of the law that God graciously gave to his people at Mount Sinai (Exod. 20:1–11) indicates that Yahweh regards it a great evil for his people to worship and serve anyone but him. What is more, his people must respond to him as he has commanded in his Word. This is why throughout the story of redemption, Satan continually seeks to deceive God's people or beguile them to follow after the false gods of their pagan neighbors. To follow false gods is to deny the terms of the covenant in which Israel confesses loyalty to God. The stakes could not be higher. In Matthew 10:32–33, Jesus told his disciples that "whoever acknowledges me before men, I will also acknowledge him before my Father in heaven. But whoever disowns me before men, I will disown him before my Father in heaven." This makes apostasy and all forms of religious syncretism the twin evils that can potentially befall the people of God.

Whenever the people of God remain faithful to God's covenant promises, the powers that be will inevitably resent the fact that the loyalty of God's people is nontransferable. The biblical record describes tyrant after tyrant seeking to sever God's people from union with their covenant Lord—a union grounded in God's presence with his people through word and sacrament (ceremonies of covenant ratification). This is especially true in the Book of Revelation where the primary menace to God's people is not the Antichrist *per se* but a mysterious beast who is empowered by the dragon (Satan) and who arises from the sea in order to wage war upon the saints (see Rev. 13:1–7).

As Israel's prophets have foretold, the end-times enemy of Yahweh is that one who not only speaks blasphemy against the true and living God but who even dares to declare himself to be Yahweh's equal (see Dan. 11:36–37). Since this foe cannot in any sense harm God, instead he will wage war upon Christ's church. This conflict between those loyal to Yahweh and the allies of the Serpent (in this case the beast) lies at the heart of the apocalyptic images found in the Book of Revelation.

In John's apocalyptic vision, the future course of history is depicted from the time of Christ's death and resurrection until our Lord returns to raise the dead, judge the world, and make all things new while ushering in everlasting righteousness through the definitive establishment of his kingdom.[2] In fact, Revelation contains a series of visions, each of which views the entire period of redemptive history from Christ's first coming until his second advent. Much like different camera angles on the same event,[3] the series of visions found throughout Revelation also intensify toward the time of the end, pointing ahead to a great climax of the redemptive drama centered in the absolute victory of Jesus Christ over all of his enemies at the end of the age.[4]

Not only does John make extensive use of symbols and apocalyptic motifs, most of which are drawn from the Old Testament,[5] but his vision cannot be divorced from its historical context. The very same Roman government that the apostle Paul had called "God's servant" in AD 55 in Romans 13:1–7 was then engaged in the open persecution of Christ's church at the time John was given his vision while on the island of Patmos some forty years later.[6] The reason for this persecution is simple. When Christians confess that "Jesus is Lord," they are simultaneously affirming that Caesar is not.

Not only does John's vision reflect the transformation of the Roman Empire from God's servant (as Paul had said) into a vicious beast who wages war on the faithful, John also offers an explanation for such a dramatic transformation of the Roman Empire as evidenced by the rise of an anti-Christian imperial cult and emerging emperor worship. Such a dramatic turn of events can only be the work of the dragon (Satan). Those who are familiar with the Old Testament will immediately recognize Satan's fingerprints and detect the telltale trace of sulfur in the fact that the imperial cult demands full allegiance from its subjects and will persecute all who do not bow the knee to Caesar and confess him as Lord. Those who know the Old Testament know all about the great empires of Assyria, Egypt, Babylon, Persia, Greece, and the city of Sodom—Rome's prede- cessors—and the role they have played in opposition to God's redemptive purposes.[7] This succession of great empires who do the Serpent's bidding is the primary lens through which John views the Roman Empire in its new role as the oppres- sor of God's people.

From the better-known figures of history (such as Egypt's Pharaoh and Nebuchadnezzar of the Babylonian Empire) to less widely known historical figures (such as Nimrod, Antiochus IV Epiphanes, Herod the Great, or Titus), a number of cruel individuals have sought to oppose the purposes of God using the power of the state, including economic deprivation and the force of arms. But there was one despicable individual who manifested a hatred of all things good, perhaps more than all others, and who had taken his place on the stage of history in the years before John was given his vision on Patmos. Lucius Domitius Ahenobarbus, commonly known as Nero (AD 37–68), serves as the pattern (type) of all those across the ages who have been identified as Antichrist and who have followed in his maniacal wake.

The Role of Nero

The image of a despotic Nero lurks in the background throughout much of Revelation with good reason. Even though his reign lasted a mere fourteen years, not only did Nero further enshrine emperor worship begun under Gaius (Caligula) by strengthening the so-called "imperial cult," but Nero's personal depravity is almost beyond description. In many ways, Nero is evil personified.

According to the accounts of his various biographers, Tacitus, Suetonius, and Cassius Dio, Nero murdered his brother and rival to the throne at the prompting of his mother, with whom he may have had sexual intercourse. He later arranged for his mother's "accidental" death. He killed his pregnant wife (and child) in a fit of rage by kicking her in the stomach. He then found a young man who looked much like his wife, had him castrated, and then married him in a public ceremony.[8]

In fact, Nero mocked all societal convention. He raped a vestal virgin (a capital crime) and arranged for a young Christian woman to be tied nude to the horns of an enraged bull, mocking her Christian modesty and chastity.[9] He encouraged orgies in which commoners participated with members of imperial rank (something unthinkable in Roman society); he even married a male servant (taking the female role himself), and in a public spectacle, he acted as though he was giving birth. Throughout all of this despicable behavior, Nero sought to reverse the natural order of things, mocking not only Roman societal convention but the Creator himself.[10]

Nero lived for personal pleasure and self-indulgence. He participated in chariot races staged so that he would win. He proposed and built huge capital projects benefiting himself and his pursuit of pleasure. Nero was even accused of instigating the burning of Rome so as to make room for his next building project, the so-called "Golden House" (which Renan calls "the plaything of his delirious imagination").[11] But Nero blamed Christians for starting the fire, and subsequently many of them were put to death.[12]

What makes the reign of Nero so important in understanding the Book of Revelation is not his gross personal immorality (as bad as it was) but the fact that Nero presided over the first period of state-sponsored persecution of Christians by Roman authorities (the so-called Neronian persecution). Nero was personally responsible for turning Christians into human torches, for feeding them to wild animals in the Coliseum,[13] and for the deaths of apostles Peter and Paul,[14] all of which was followed by the destruction of the Jerusalem temple in AD 70, which occurred shortly after Nero's death.

These events not only changed the course of redemptive history but they also changed how Christians viewed the Roman Empire. The empire, which had tolerated Jews (and Christians as long as they remained somewhat associated with the synagogues—the situation when Paul wrote Romans 13:1–7), now regarded Christianity as an illegitimate religion and Christians as enemies of the state. Nero and the emperor cult are clearly in John's mind when the apostle speaks of the mark of the beast, which is a symbol of homage to the Roman leader and which is placed on the back of the hand or the forehead.[15] Those who refuse to receive this imperial mark are prevented from buying and selling. This dreaded mark is also tied to the mysterious number of the beast—666 (see Rev. 13:11–18). This is a theme we will take up momentarily.

Nero is also in John's mind when he speaks of a beast suffering a fatal wound, only to come back to life with more ferocity than ever (Rev. 13:3; 17:11). Although Nero committed suicide under somewhat mysterious circumstances—setting the stage for great mischief to follow[16]—was John actually predicting that Nero would come back to life either literally or figuratively (the so-called "Nero myth") in what would become the supreme manifestation of Antichrist? Nero, supposedly, had been seen alive in Parthia and other widely scattered portions of the empire, preparing an army in order to reclaim his throne.[17] Rumors spread everywhere that Nero wasn't really dead and that he was soon to return, reclaim his throne, and take revenge on all his enemies.[18] The Nero myth is enshrined in both Jewish and Christian extrabiblical writings (the *Sibylline Oracles* and the

Ascension of Isaiah).[19] In the fourth *Sibylline Oracle* we read: "A mighty king shall like a runaway slave./Flee over the Euphrates' stream unseen,/Unknown, who shall some time dare loathsome guilt of matricide, and many other things,/Having confidence in his most wicked hands./And many for the throne with blood Rome's soil while he flees over Parthian land./And out of Syria shall come Rome's foremost man [Nero]."[20]

The question as to whether any future Antichrist will be some sort of Nero *redivivus* has been one of the most hotly debated points in the church's reflection upon this doctrine.[21] In the eyes of many, Nero is the beast of Revelation.[22] Others see Nero as a type of all godless leaders who oppress God's people throughout the age.[23]

The Counterfeit Trinity of Revelation 13

Even a cursory reading of the thirteenth chapter of the Book of Revelation reveals three distinct foes of Jesus Christ: (1) the dragon, who stands on the shore of the sea, (2) the first beast from the sea, who receives the dragon's power, throne, and authority (vv. 1–2), and (3) yet another beast, which comes out of the earth (v. 11). The function of this second beast (called the "false prophet" in Rev. 16:13) is to entice people to worship the first beast. The identity of these three figures along with their overt blasphemy against the Most High God means that what is primarily in view is not so much John's interest in contemporary Roman history and politics (a particular emperor), but that his vision depicts another battle in the ongoing war between the two seeds, in this case, the godless character of Roman rule and its ongoing persecution of Christians.

What is recorded in Revelation 13 reflects the fact that a dramatic turning point in the history of redemption has already taken place with the coming of Jesus Christ. Through our Lord's death and resurrection, the dragon has already been decisively defeated by the Messiah (see Col. 2:15). Although our salvation has been secured through Christ's death upon the cross and through his resurrection from the dead, the dragon is enraged

by his defeat and wages war upon the saints (Rev. 13:7) because
he knows his time is short (Rev. 12:12).

The Book of Revelation, therefore, depicts an already defeated foe waging his last desperate efforts in a war he knows
he has already lost. In this final attempt to escape his inevitable
fate, the dragon now enlists the aid of two beasts to do his bidding, one from the sea (Rev. 13:1–10) and one from the land
(Rev. 13:11–18). While the final outcome is never in doubt, the
particular circumstances that bring us to the climactic end of
redemptive history have long fascinated God's people.

Critical to understanding John's vision in Revelation 13 is his
statement that the first beast has "ten horns and seven heads,
with ten crowns on his horns, and on each head a blasphemous name." This beast "resembled a leopard, but had feet
like those of a bear and a mouth like that of a lion. The dragon
gave the beast his power and his throne and great authority"
(vv. 1–2). This immediately harkens any reader who is familiar
with the Old Testament back to Daniel's vision of a great beast,
who is ultimately slain and who is conquered by the Son of
Man and his everlasting kingdom (Dan. 7:7, 11–14). Not only
does the beast of John's vision possess military power second
to none—"Who is like the beast? Who can make war against
him?" (Rev. 13:4)—but when "one of the heads of the beast
seemed to have had a fatal wound, . . . the fatal wound had
been healed. The whole world was astonished and followed
the beast" (Rev. 13:3).

This obvious parody of Christ's resurrection,[24] coupled with
the military prowess and deceptive ways of the beast, gives the
dragon exactly what he craves. "Men worshiped the dragon
because he had given authority to the beast." Not only did men
worship Satan because of the might of the beast, "they also
worshiped the beast" (Rev. 13:4). Clearly, then, what is in view
is a state (government) that is empowered by Satan and that
claims divine rights and prerogatives unto itself. Bauckham
is quite correct when he calls this a "deification of power" in
which military power (perhaps we could add economic power
as well) masks the inevitability of the beast's destruction by
Christ and his kingdom.[25]

The overtly anti-Christian nature of this beast's reign can be seen in what follows: "The beast was given a mouth to utter proud words and blasphemies and to exercise his authority for forty-two months" (Rev. 13:5)—the forty-two months are most likely a reference to the inter-advental age.[26] Taken from Daniel 7:25 ("a time, times, and half a time," see also Dan. 12:7), this same period of time appears in the preceding chapters of the Book of Revelation. In Revelation 11:2–3, the Gentiles are said to "trample the holy city" (the church—i.e., the dwelling place of God in the new covenant)[27] for forty-two months or 1,260 days. This is the same time period in which the two witnesses proclaim the gospel (Rev. 11:3). In Revelation 12:6, John refers to the time of the protection of the woman in the wilderness (the church) as spanning 1,260 days and then again later as "a time, times, and half a time" (Rev. 12:14). As Beale points out, these are all references to the same period of time, indicating that the manifestation of the beast likewise "spans the time from Christ's death and resurrection to the culmination of history."[28] This means that the beast's efforts to oppose the gospel extend from the time of the Neronian persecution into the present and will continue until the end of the age, when the beast is destroyed by Christ at his second advent (Rev. 20:10).

In Revelation 13, we read that the beast "opened his mouth to blaspheme God, and to slander his name and his dwelling place and those who live in heaven" (v. 6). This is a vision of a government that not only takes divine rights and prerogatives unto itself (e.g., worship), but this government and its leaders speak great blasphemies against Christ and his kingdom. This can be seen in the fact that the beast wears crowns with blasphemous names, thereby assuming the prerogatives of deity. This imagery is quite significant in helping us to understand the beast's identity. When coupled to the obvious reference to a counterfeit Trinity (the dragon, the first beast, and a second beast who is the false prophet), what is in view is a satanic parody of the Triune God as well as a satanic parody of our redemption (the death and burial, the resurrection, and the parousia of Christ), when the beast is killed and comes back to life to begin its reign of terror all over again.[29] John's point is that when empowered by the dragon, the state oversteps its bounds and deifies itself or its leader. As Caird puts it, "All political power is the gift of God; but when men deify the state, either directly by a religious cult or indirectly by demanding for it the total loyalty and obedience that is due to God alone, it ceases to be human and becomes bestial."[30] What is in view then is primarily an anti-Christian power, centered in the seat of government, using the resources of that government against Christ's church in an effort to thwart the preaching of the gospel.

The False Prophet: State-Mandated False Religion

In verses 11–18 of Revelation 13, John sees a second beast from the earth who is also known as the false prophet (cf. Rev. 16:13; 19:20; 20:10). The purpose of this beast is to procure worship of the first beast and ultimately of the dragon. John reports in verse 11 that "I saw another beast, coming out of the earth. He had two horns like a lamb, but he spoke like a dragon." This beast is also a parody of Christ, who is the Lamb of God (John 1:29), and who has already been identified as such, earlier in Revelation (5:6). He appears as a Christlike figure, but his words come from Satan, who is the father of lies and incapable of telling the truth (see John 8:44). In Revelation 13:12–18 we read the following:

> He exercised all the authority of the first beast on his behalf, and made the earth and its inhabitants worship the first beast, whose fatal wound had been healed. And he performed great and miraculous signs, even causing fire to come down from heaven to earth in full view of men. Because of the signs he was given power to do on behalf of the first beast, he deceived the inhabitants of the earth. He ordered them to set up an image in honor of the beast who was wounded by the sword and yet lived. He was given power to give breath to the image of the first beast, so that it could speak and cause all who refused to worship the image to be killed. He also forced everyone, small and great, rich and poor, free and slave, to receive a mark on his right hand or on his forehead, so that no one could buy or

sell unless he had the mark, which is the name of the beast or the number of his name. This calls for wisdom. If anyone has insight, let him calculate the number of the beast, for it is man's number. His number is 666.

While the beast from the sea is empowered by the dragon, the second beast is given the power to perform miraculous signs to deceive the world's inhabitants so that they worship the image of the beast from the sea. This means that the second beast from the earth compels those who serve him to take his blasphemous mark (which is the name of man and is tied to the first beast). As Sweet insightfully notes, the real threat raised by the dragon and his allies is not the sword (as frightening as that is) but its power to deceive and to draw people away from Christ and his church, which involves an exchange of light for darkness.[31] In other words, his military power, while great, is not as significant as his ability to deceive. This reflects the dragon's true nature as the father of lies.

John tells his readers that the key to resolving these mysterious words is wisdom—i.e., God-given insight. The beast's dreaded number—666—is the number of man. The imagery associated with the second beast clearly points in the direction of false religion, reinforced by the military and economic power of the first beast. John is not predicting some form of technology off in the distant future associated with the beast's tyranny at the end of the age—although the beast may indeed utilize whatever technology is available to further his purposes. When John was given his vision in the midnineties of the first century, Nero had brutalized God's people twenty years earlier, and then the persecution waned, but it only recently had intensified again under Domitian.[32] It looked like the beast had come back to life. According to Caird, "Emperor worship was never, before Domitian, forced by an arrogant imperialism upon a reluctant populace."[33]

The reference to worshiping the image of the beast (Rev. 13:15) is also not limited to the time of the end as taught by dispensationalists and other futurists. John has already told his readers of the situation in Pergamum, where Satan has

his throne and where a martyr named Antipas had been put
to death some time earlier for remaining a faithful witness
(Rev. 2:12–17). The reference to Satan's throne being present
in Pergamum is not only a reference to the many pagan religions found there—for which the town served as a kind of
headquarters—but also entails the fact that Pergamum was a
well-known center of emperor worship.[34]

If John is referring to the same kind of situation in Revelation
13:11–18 as was the case in Pergamum, then we should see the
reference to worshiping the image as a contemporary event.
More importantly, these words of John's vision resound with
echoes from the Old Testament account of Shadrach, Meshach,
and Abednego, who were commanded to worship the image
of a pagan king. The young men were told, "As soon as you
hear the sound of the horn, flute, zither, lyre, harp, pipes and
all kinds of music, you must fall down and worship the image
of gold that King Nebuchadnezzar has set up. Whoever does
not fall down and worship will immediately be thrown into a
blazing furnace" (Dan. 3:5–6). Like Nebuchadnezzar, Roman
emperors (such as Domitian) were demanding that Christians
bow their knees to Caesar and confess him as Lord, thereby
renouncing their allegiance to Jesus Christ.[35] The penalty for
not doing so was death. Antipas, apparently, had already suffered such a fate.

These important facts have led many to connect John's two
beasts to Roman imperial power (the beast from the sea) and
to the *commune Asiae*, the provincial town councils throughout
Asia Minor who ensured that local citizens paid proper homage to the Roman emperor (the second beast from the land).[36]
This is, likely, a proper identification.

It will come as no surprise that there are a number of interpretations of this vision held by Christians. The dragon, who
had waged war on the people of God (Rev. 12:17, in fulfillment
of Gen. 3:15), is easily identified as Satan. But the identity of
the two beasts who do the dragon's bidding has been the subject of much debate. Some of the church fathers saw in the
beast a personal Antichrist who would come at the time of the
end. This is also the view of dispensationalists such as John

Walvoord, who believes the time frame for the fulfillment of this prophecy is the seven-year tribulation period predicted in Daniel 9:27, and that what is in view is an end-times world leader and his supreme enabler (the false prophet).[37] Historic premillenarians, such as George Ladd, also see this vision as a description of an end-times Antichrist and his persecution of the church.[38] All of these views assume that the beast and the Antichrist are one and the same and downplay (or ignore) the reference in the opening chapter of Revelation to the imminence of the events when John was given his vision (Rev. 1:3) as well as the Neronian persecution and the historical circumstances we have just described. Whatever application we may draw from this vision about future events, the scene of the vision is clearly contemporary with the events associated with the Roman persecution of Christians and not isolated to the time of the end.

Others have seen these two beast figures as primarily symbolic of satanic power to persecute the church throughout the ages. Amillenarian William Hendricksen believes the first beast is symbolic of Satan's hands, while the second is symbolic of Satan's head. In other words, while presented in the geopolitical form taken by the end of the first century (i.e., the Roman Empire), the first beast refers to civil authority that is inspired by Satan to turn against the church, while the second beast is a reference to false religions and philosophies.[39] While Hendricksen is on the right track in terms of application for Christians beyond John's original audience (a serious weakness with preterism), Hendricksen does not give sufficient weight to the historical context—the Roman Empire as a true and historical type of those governments yet to come. Contemporary amillenarians such as G. K. Beale and Dennis Johnson[40] avoid Hendricksen's interpretive misstep by keeping the historical context firmly in mind.

While historicists see John's vision as a prophecy of the papacy,[41] preterist interpreters such as David Chilton see in the first beast of Revelation 13 a description of the Roman Empire under the leadership of Nero. But the second beast (Rev. 13:11–18), Chilton believes, arises within Israel in the days before the destruction of the Jerusalem temple and is the false prophet of whom Jesus warned in the Gospels (Matt. 24:5, 11).[42] Most preterists believe the mark of the beast and the number 666 are a direct reference to Nero,[43] while Chilton maintains that the number's theological significance (as the number of man in opposition to God) is every bit as important as its tie to Nero.[44] Not only does preterism collapse if it can be shown that the Book of Revelation was written after the events of AD 70, but the weight of the evidence we have just seen indicates that John is referring to a self-deifying state persecuting the people of God throughout Asia Minor (Nero-Domitian) and not to the apostate people of God (Israel).[45]

Along with a number of commentators, I believe that John is referring to the imperial power of Rome and the worship of its emperor in this vision but that the first-century Roman Empire does not fully exhaust the meaning of the vision.[46] In other words, the critical question to be dealt with is whether the Roman Empire's persecution of the church at the time of John's vision completely exhausts the scope of the prophecy. Do the events of AD 70 or even the events surrounding the Domitian persecution in AD 95 fulfill this prophecy? Or is it better to understand the Roman Empire's persecution of the church in the first century as a picture of what Christians will face from various anti-Christian governments until such persecution culminates in an Antichrist at the time of the end? The latter, I am satisfied, is what is in view in the vision of Revelation 13—especially in light of Revelation 17.

The Return of the Beast in Revelation 17

Before we move ahead to look at a possible connection between the king who suffers a mortal wound (Rev. 13:3) and the list of kings in Revelation 17:9–14, it is important to notice that John's vision of two beasts empowered by the dragon to persecute and deceive Christ's church is derived from two Old Testament passages: Job 40–41 and Daniel 7:1–7. Job 40–41 speaks of two beasts, one from the land (behemoth, Job 40:15–24) and one from the sea (leviathan, Job 41:1–34). It also alludes to a time at (or near) the dawn of creation when the dragon was defeated, although a future final battle is still anticipated (Job 40:19). In several Jewish sources, these two beasts are understood as satanic opponents of God and are symbolic of those powers of evil that will be destroyed on the last day.[47] John's vision clearly reflects the final outcome of the struggle between Christ and the Serpent in the messianic age—a struggle that Christ decisively wins despite the dragon's efforts to wage war upon the saints.

As we have seen in the previous section, the opening verses of Revelation 13 draw heavily upon Daniel 7:1–7. The beast from the sea has seven heads and ten horns (cf. Dan. 7:20, 24). It wears ten crowns on its ten horns, tying it directly to Daniel's fourth beast, where the ten horns are interpreted as ten kings (Dan. 7:24). The fact that the dragon wore the diadems in the previous chapter (Rev. 12:1) is quite significant, since it means that at some point the dragon attempts to exercise his rule through two surrogates—the two beasts from sea and land.[48] According to Daniel 7:19–22, this particular beast, along with the horn (king) that arises in its midst, is crushed by the Ancient of Days:

> Then I wanted to know the true meaning of the fourth beast, which was different from all the others and most terrifying, with its iron teeth and bronze claws—the beast that crushed and devoured its victims and trampled underfoot whatever was left. I also wanted to know about the ten horns on its head and about the other horn that came up, before which three of them fell—the horn that looked more imposing than the others and that had eyes and a mouth that spoke boastfully. As I watched, this horn was waging war against the saints and defeating them, until the Ancient of Days came and pronounced judgment in favor of the saints of the Most High, and the time came when they possessed the kingdom.

This passage likely indicates that the final destruction of this beast comes at the time of the end, which means that the beast will reappear immediately before the end of the age.[49] It is also significant that this beast is a blasphemer who wages war upon the saints, connecting him directly to the boastful figure in Daniel 7:8–11. In other words, John is seeing the same thing Daniel did—this time through the lens of Christ's death, resurrection, and parousia—the same redemptive work the beast attempts to mimic so as to deceive the world's inhabitants so that they worship him instead of Jesus.

Notice, too, that John's vision expands upon the vision in Daniel 7 because John's vision not only involves Daniel's fourth beast (the Roman Empire) but, since John's vision incorporates the imagery of all four of Daniel's beasts (Dan. 7:1–6), there is reason to believe that the beast John sees in Revelation 17 is ultimately greater than Rome, which is the beast's first historical manifestation after the time of Antiochus IV.[50] This, too, is evidence that identification of the beast with the Roman imperial cult is correct (Revelation 13), but the Roman imperial cult does not exhaust the full meaning of the prophecy, which may telescope ahead to the time of the end (double fulfillment). John describes the current suffering of much of the church in Asia Minor when he writes, but the struggle Christians are facing at the hands of pagan Rome points ahead to the time of the end when the beast appears yet again. It is this end-times beast who is most often identified as Antichrist.[51]

HE SEEMS TO WANT IT BOTH WAYS

There is additional evidence to support this interpretation found in Revelation 17:9–14. The numbers Daniel and John use in reference to the beast are also critical to understand the meaning of John's vision. Given the pattern of usage throughout the Book of Revelation, the seven heads (Rev. 17:9–10) and ten horns (Rev. 17:12) are probably not to be identified with a specific ruler either in John's time or even later on, since as Caird points out, "the [horns] belong wholly to the time of the future" (i.e., after AD 95) when the monster rises again from the Abyss.[52] Just as Jesus returns at the end of the age, so too, apparently, the beast has a future resurrection of sorts when he comes up from the Abyss yet again (Rev. 17:8). This is very likely related to Revelation 20:1–10 and the binding of Satan that begins the millennial age (the thousand years) but which ends when Satan is released from his prison in the Abyss (Rev.

20:7).[53] As Beale points out, "The beast's imitation of Christ will be shown to be a sham in the end. Whereas Christ's resurrection results in his being 'alive forever' (1:18), the beast's resurrection results in his 'destruction.'"[54]

The problems with the specific identification of the seven heads and ten horns are significant.[55] When you attempt to tie John's list of kings—either the seven kings of Revelation 17:10, who are followed by an eighth, or the ten kings of Revelation 17:12, who fight against the Lamb—to a historical individual, the critical question is, "With which Roman emperor do you start?" If you start with Julius Caesar, you end up with Nero as the sixth king, who rules only a short time. But Nero is supposedly the head of the beast who suffers a mortal wound and will return. Also, Nero is not the reigning emperor when John writes; Domitian most likely is.[56] If you start with Augustus, the first official emperor, then do you even include the three short-term rulers in the calculation, men such as Galba, Otho, and Vitellius, who were never officially deified by the Roman Senate? Such calculations are almost impossible to make from the information at hand, despite the confidence of some that this can be done definitively.[57]

But identifying a particular emperor as one of the seven heads or ten horns misses John's primary point. It is the symbolism of numbers involved that is the key to understanding the meaning of the vision, not identifying the particular individual who may or may not be ruling when John writes.[58] As Beasley-Murray points out, it is altogether misguided to even attempt to do so since John's focus falls not on the historical but on the eschatological.[59] John is not giving us a refresher course in Roman history. He's preparing Christians for the inevitable struggle against the forces of the beast.

What, then, do the numbers symbolize? Throughout the Book of Revelation, seven is the number of completeness, while the number ten likewise points to the beast's completeness of power and worldwide effect.[60] This means that John is probably not giving us a precise chronology of Roman emperors so much as he is describing the satanic character of the beast's attempts to overthrow the kingdom of God, which endures throughout the entire inter-advental period despite Satan's waging of war upon the people of God. The current manifestation of the beast when John wrote is seen in imperial Rome, regardless of whether the calculation begins with Julius or Augustus. The two beasts are waging war on the saints, persecuting God's people and preventing them from engaging in ordinary commerce because they do not worship the beast or his image (Rev. 13:17). The church in Smyrna was already experiencing such economic hardships, and many of its members were even facing arrest (see Rev. 2:8–11). The two beasts who come from sea and land are already a present foe when John records this vision.

But the point of this particular vision (Revelation 17) is that the same beast who was already persecuting the saints will appear yet again, this time in conjunction with the second advent (Rev. 19:19–21). As John states in Revelation 17:8, "The beast, which you saw, once was, now is not, and will come up out of the Abyss and go to his destruction. The inhabitants of the earth whose names have not been written in the book of life from the creation of the world will be astonished when they see the beast, because he once was, now is not, and yet will come." The last of the three verbs John uses here (yet will come) is the word *parestai*, which is derived from the noun *parousia*, used throughout the New Testament to denote the second advent of Christ.[61] The beast will rise again from the Abyss and deceive many at the time of the end (cf. Rev. 20:7–10).

Not only does the beast astonish the whole world through this parody of Christ's death and resurrection, but the vision of Revelation 17 depicts the beast as having a rider—a mysterious female prostitute, identified as "MYSTERY, BABYLON THE GREAT, THE MOTHER OF PROSTITUTES, AND OF THE ABOMINATIONS OF THE EARTH," who is "drunk with the blood of the saints" (Rev. 17:3–6). John ties this woman directly to the city of Rome (the city with seven hills, 17:9), then he lists a series of kings (seven) who will be followed by an eighth king, before giving us yet another list of ten different kings allied with the beast, who will eventually turn upon the prostitute, Babylon the Great, killing her (Rev. 17:9–17). John later calls this woman, "the great city that rules over the kings of the earth" (Rev. 17:18). Not only do the kings of the earth wage war upon the Lamb; the self-destroying power of evil is also seen in the fact that the kings of the earth also turn against the harlot.

Preterists often identify this woman as apostate Jerusalem,[62] while historicists see this as a reference to the Roman Catholic Church.[63] Dispensationalists most often believe this is a prophecy of an alliance between an apostate church with revived Roman political power during the seven-year tribulation period,[64] although prophecy pundit Dave Hunt also sees this as a reference to the Roman Catholic Church.[65] None of these identifications, however, fit the data given us in the vision.

The identification of Babylon as a seductive harlot informs us that her power lies in her ability to seduce. In fact, the kings of the earth have committed fornication with her (Rev. 18:2–3). This cannot be said of Israel. The picture is not so much one of immorality but acceptance "of the religious and idolatrous demands of the ungodly earthly order."[66] Her influence is upon the inhabitants of the world, who have consumed her intoxicating wine. There are many echoes here from the Old Testament. Israel had engaged in spiritual adultery against Yahweh (see Isa. 1:21; Jer. 2:2–37; Ezek. 16:36–63; Hos. 2:5), just as this woman does. This imagery explains the uncanny ability of the woman to seduce the people of the world. There is also an echo from the prophecy of Jeremiah (chapter 51) that foretells of the destruction of Babylon (especially v. 13) so that the temple might be rebuilt, now fulfilled yet again.[67] That the great city is tied to the commerce of the world is clear from Revelation 18 (vv. 3, 9–19). As long as Babylon provides the kings and their merchants with wealth, they will drink from her cup, only to be seduced by her in a *quid pro quo* of sinful benefit. This is what the city of Tyre had done, committing fornication with kings through economic trade tied to idolatry (see Isa. 23:17).

By now the symbolism should be clear. Rome is "the Babylon of her age,"[68] and in her inevitable destruction she serves as a perpetual symbol of how the City of Man can never attain either the glory or the dominion of the heavenly city, which even now is coming down from heaven (Rev. 21:2). Thus Babylon is the city of Rome, while at the same time it is symbolic of "the prevailing economic-religious system in alliance with the state and its related authorities existing throughout the ages."[69] For the apostle John, the idolatrous evil that the city of Rome represented through the combination of economic might and emperor worship will appear again and again throughout the inter-advental period. The nations will gladly ally themselves with this symbolic Babylon (the City of Man). They are willingly seduced in exchange for economic gain. One day, they will turn on the whore and destroy her, only to mourn her death, because even though the merchants hate the whore for what she has done to them, they need her to continue their economic gain (Rev. 18:11).

Is the Beast the Antichrist? Yes and No

Understanding this symbolism, says John, "calls for a mind with wisdom. The seven heads are seven hills on which the woman sits. They are also seven kings. Five have fallen, one is, the other has not yet come; but when he does come, he must remain for a little while. The beast who once was, and now is not, is an eighth king. He belongs to the seven and is going to his destruction" (Rev. 17:9–11). The key to understanding the vision is not in calculating the current ruler of Rome (whether that be Nero or Domitian). The key figure in the vision is the eighth king, or emperor, who is still future when John is given his vision (Rev. 17:11). Some have tied this to Nero, as one who supposedly comes back to life (Rev. 13:3) and is supposedly the Antichrist—the archenemy of Christ and his church (Nero *redivivus*).[70] But as Dennis Johnson points out, the meaning of this series of kings, six of whom have already come and gone, is simply that "the church must persevere not only under the pressure of present levels of suffering (the seventh king), but also under the coming, crushing conspiracy of its enemies at the end (the beast to arise as an eighth king)."[71] John directs us to a seventh and eighth king yet to come, not to a ruler already present when he was given this vision.

As we have seen, however, it is probably better not to speak of Nero (as a particular emperor of Rome) come back to life in either a literal or figurative sense. Rather, we should speak of the beast (not its emperor) come back to life, complete with all of its self-deification and hatred for God's people, in the form of an end-times anti-Christian government, which is the final manifestation of the beast's ability to deceive and amaze the people of the earth. This eighth king is yet to rise.

The identification of the beast as Antichrist has generated a great deal of confusion. John, whom I take to be the author of those three New Testament Epistles bearing his name as well as the recipient of the angel's vision and therefore the author of Revelation, never uses the term *Antichrist* of the beast. If the beast is the Roman Empire and its imperial cult and the first in a series of godless governments that will arise and persecute God's people throughout the inter-advental period, then the beast cannot be Antichrist in the sense that John uses the term in his Epistles—which specifically refers to heresy (internal), not persecution by the state (Rome).

The reason people identify the beast as Antichrist has to do with the connection between the possibility of a Nero *redivivus* and an eighth king, who is yet to come. In other words, the eighth king is the end-times archfoe of God's people and may properly be labeled the "Antichrist" if by that designation we mean that this particular personage is the final manifestation of the beast (the eighth king) and if we take John to mean that the series of antichrists mentioned in his Epistles does indeed culminate in a final Antichrist. Without such qualification, we risk using the term in a confusing and even, perhaps, unbiblical way.

666 and the Mark of the Beast

If you are a futurist and believe that the beast of Revelation 13 is not connected to the Roman Empire of the first century and remains yet to be revealed at the end of the age (i.e., during the seven-year tribulation period, as dispensationalists teach),

then you will not look at the mark of the beast through the lens
of the New Testament and the historical situation when John
was given his vision. Instead you will understand this mysterious mark as something still hidden in the future. And given
the breakneck pace of the advances being made in all forms
of technology, it is only natural that futurists would see John's
reference to the mark of the beast as somehow connected to the
technological advantage by which the beast and false prophet
will enslave the inhabitants of the world and deceive them into
worshiping the Antichrist.

As futurists see it, when John speaks of the mark of the
beast, he's essentially predicting that some future form of technology will be utilized by Antichrist to dominate and control
the world's population. According to Peter and Paul LaLonde,
"The Bible says that the mark of the beast and its accompanying technology will be installed by the antichrist—not as an
end in itself, but as a means of managing the new world order
that is even now being created."[72] Tim LaHaye has capitalized
on this apprehension regarding Big Brother with yet another
best-selling novel in the *Left Behind* series, *The Mark: The Beast
Rules the World*.[73]

The futurist approach to Revelation is misguided because it
pushes off into the distant future what was already a serious
threat to Christians in the first century (emperor worship) by
ignoring the historical context for the visions of Revelation 13
and 17 we have just labored to establish. Instead, John's comments about the mark of the beast should be seen against the
backdrop of the imperial cult and the worship of the Roman
emperor. The emperor's blasphemous image was everywhere
in John's world (Asia Minor), from coins to statues identifying various emperors as deities in most major cities.[74] John's
reference to the mark being placed upon the back of the hand
or the forehead makes perfect sense in light of the widespread
first-century practice of branding or tattooing slaves—a mark
of shame and subjugation.[75]

The theological significance of this practice of marking slaves
is simply that those who have this mark of the imperial cult
are property of the beast—followers and servants who do his

will. In other words, this mark (*charagma*) identifies those who worship and serve the beast. That such a *charagma* specifically refers to the imperial stamp on official documents indicates that whatever John means by this mark is directly tied to the state's usurpation of that authority and honor which belong to God alone.[76] John has already exhorted the persecuted Christians in Smyrna, "Do not be afraid of what you are about to suffer. I tell you, the devil will put some of you in prison to test you, and you will suffer persecution for ten days. Be faithful, even to the point of death, and I will give you the crown of life" (Rev. 2:10). Surely, this exhortation extends beyond the people of Smyrna to Christians in every age.

As for the number of the beast (666), some historical background would be helpful here as well. The Greco-Roman world did not use Arabic numbers as do we, so instead, letters were assigned numeric value. Using the sum totals of the numerical equivalent of letters to identify words or persons is known as gematria.[77] The most obvious candidate derived from the sum total of the numbers 6-6-6 is Nero Caesar, since the Greek form of Nero's name when transliterated into Hebrew may indeed total 666. This is not an unreasonable conclusion and is widely accepted.[78]

The attempt to calculate the identity of the beast with this degree of specificity, however, is disputed on a number of grounds. Such calculations do not involve the exact use of Hebrew letters, and Caesar is not the only title for Nero. None of the church fathers, apparently, were aware of any connection between 666 and Nero.[79] In fact, it was not until 1831 that the specific identification of these numbers with Nero using gematria was first suggested by four German scholars.[80] And then finally, as John says, this requires wisdom, not knowledge, to calculate. In other words, spiritual insight is required, not cleverness or skill in math.

The attempt to calculate the number of the beast using gematria can also be problematic because this kind of methodology can be manipulated to refer to almost anyone, in what has come to be known in certain circles as the "pin the tail on the Antichrist" game. For example, Ronald Wilson Reagan was once identified as the beast because his three names each have six letters.[81] So have a host of others (a matter we took up in chapter 1). Another problem with gematria is that from our vantage point two thousand years after the fact, it is relatively easy to turn a particular name into a number, but it is far more difficult to work from the number back to a specific name,[82] which is what the text seems to imply—"This calls for wisdom. If anyone has insight, let him calculate the number of the beast, for it is man's number. His number is 666" (Rev. 13:18).

While these objections are not sufficient to overturn what appears to be an obvious connection of some sort between the number 666 and Nero, these points do urge us to be a bit cautious about identifying Nero as that one to whom John was referring and then simply leaving the matter there.

In fact, the preoccupation with identifying just who it is, exactly, to whom this number refers creates an unfortunate tendency to downplay (or even ignore) the theological significance of this number. What the number 666 represents is at least as significant as the beast's human identity.[83] When John tells us that this is "man's number," he may even mean that this number does not refer to a specific individual, such as Nero, but to a series of individuals who behave as Nero did. As Beale points out, "The omission of the article in 13:18 indicates the general idea of humanity, not some special individual who can be discerned only through an esoteric method of calculation. Therefore, in both verses ἀνθρώπου [man] is a descriptive or qualitative genitive, so that the phrase here should be rendered 'a human number' (so RSV) or 'a number of humanity.' It is a number common to fallen humanity."[84]

In light of the beast's attempt to parody the redemptive work of Christ so as to receive the worship of the nations, the idea that this number is to be understood as the number of fallen humanity makes a great deal of sense. If seven is the number of perfection, the number six comes close, but never reaches the goal. As Beale points out, "The beast is the supreme representative of unregenerate humanity, separated from God and unable to achieve divine likeness, but always trying. Humanity was created on the sixth day, but without the seventh day of rest Adam and Eve would have been imperfect and incomplete. The triple six emphasizes that the beast and his followers fall short of God's creative purposes for humanity."[85]

If Beale is correct, and I think he is, this does not mean that John does not have Nero in mind at all. In fact, some have argued that Nero is indeed the individual who first bears the number 666, but the number has symbolic meaning as well. According to Beale, "Some believe both that John had Nero in mind and also that the number had a symbolic meaning, which is quite possible. . . . Bauckham has argued that John used the Nero legend not to focus on an individual but to construct a history of a succession of emperors paralleling the death, resurrection and final return of Christ; accordingly, Nero, and the imperial power, are symbols for any state power that overreaches its proper limits by trying to grasp what properly belongs only to Christ and God."[86] This, it seems to me, fits well within the scenario we have set forth above.

What, then, is the mark of the beast? It may indeed be directly tied to Nero as indicative of his personal wickedness and hatred for God's people, but Nero does not exhaust what is implied by taking the number—worshiping the state or its leader in order to avoid persecution for confessing that Christ is Lord. The beast is manifest to some degree throughout the inter-advental period but is restrained until the time of the end through the preaching of the gospel or the providence of God (see 2 Thess. 2:1–12; Rev. 20:1–10).

The meaning of the number is at least as significant as identifying to whom it applies. The number of man, 666, is "perfectly imperfect" in contrast to the number of perfection—seven. The thrice repeated number "6" implies endless work without rest. The creational pattern was for humans to work for six days and then rest on the seventh as did the Creator. But in this case, those who take the mark of the beast work endlessly and never do enter the hoped-for Sabbath rest.

When placed in the larger context of the New Testament, Christians are said to be "sealed" unto Christ in their baptism (Rom. 4:11; see also Rom. 6:1–11). The mark of the beast may be the theological equivalent of the rejection of baptism (in the case of apostasy) or the rejection of Christ's lordship through the confession that Caesar (or any other political figure) is Lord. This comports with the New Testament's repeated warnings about apostasy being connected to the final manifestation of the beast (see 2 Thess. 2:1–12; Rev. 20:7–10).

Even as the image of godless Nero lurks in the background, this phenomenon reoccurs throughout the course of the present age whenever someone confesses that "Caesar is Lord." I'll never forget the gasp that went through the room when a video on Nazi Germany was shown in an adult education class at our church. German schoolchildren in an old newsreel sang with glee, "Hitler is our Savior. Hitler is our Lord." That is as clear an image of what is means to "take the mark" as anything I can imagine.

Surely Nero is the forerunner or type of all those wicked and godless leaders who come after him and who take that which belongs to God unto themselves and then mock the natural order of things. Such leaders reject all conventional norms of morality and use power for personal gain and pleasure. This explains why Christians have frequently spoken of a Nero *redivivus* in connection with the beast. It is not that Nero comes back to life but that what Nero represented will be a fact of life until the end of the age. For it is not until the seventh trumpet sounds that "the kingdom of the world has become the kingdom of our Lord and of his Christ, and he will reign for ever and ever" (Rev. 11:15).

Although the various manifestations of the beast and the false prophet throughout the inter-advental age may utilize technological advances to further the cause of the beast and false prophet in their persecution of God's people, the mark of the beast cannot be tied specifically to new advances in technology apart from a proper theological context. John is not speaking of an event isolated to the time of the end as dispensationalists teach. He is warning the faithful across the ages of the cost of following Christ. There are indeed times when the confession "Jesus is Lord" will enrage some tyrannical leader.

Attempts by historicists to tie the ceremonies of the Roman Catholic Church to the mark of the beast have merit insofar as the Roman Church has, at times, prevented those who denied its authority from buying and selling. The Roman Catholic Church's relationship to a number of governments (monarchies)—especially those of the late Middle Ages (the Holy Roman Empire and its remnants)—may well serve as a model of sorts for an end-times marriage between heresy and the state, as in those grotesque instances in which the church takes up the sword and the state imposes false religion. Reformed Protestants were keenly aware of the relentless persecution of the faithful in the Netherlands at the hand of Spanish armies in the name of the pope and the Roman Catholic Church during the so-called Council of Troubles in the 1570s.[87] This is one of the main reasons why many Reformed Christians have believed the papacy to be the seat of Antichrist and the subject of John's visions.[88]

Of course, such persecution of Christians could also occur in a thoroughly secular nation (such as the former Soviet Union) or in a nation with no real Christian history (China). It might even occur in a nation that previously had been largely Protestant (Nazi Germany) or a nation dominated by pluralistic civil religion (the United States). It could happen anywhere the leaders have in the past or may in the future manifest beast-like characteristics by taking unto themselves what rightfully belongs to God and waging war upon the saints, only to be crushed by the Lamb.

6

THE MAN OF LAWLESSNESS

The Doctrine of Antichrist in 2 Thessalonians 2:1–12

The Situation in the Thessalonian Church

In Acts 17:1–9, we read of the apostle Paul's tumultuous time in the city of Thessalonica during the days when a Christian church was first established in that city. As was his custom, Paul goes into the local synagogue and reasons with the Jews from the Old Testament, trying to convince them that Jesus is the Christ (v. 3). When a number of Jews are persuaded by Paul's message, the trouble begins. It is not long before rioting breaks out (v. 5), and Paul and Silas are forced to flee to neighboring Berea. Eventually, they make their way to Corinth (Acts 18:1–17). The two Thessalonian letters were likely written in AD 50–51, shortly after Paul settled in Corinth, to help the struggling but faithful church he had left behind in Thessalonica.[1]

The first Thessalonian letter was a response to a report from Timothy (1 Thess. 3:6), while Paul's second letter supplements the first. It is in his second letter that Paul speaks of an ominous figure he calls the "Man of Lawlessness," who is also known as the "Man of Sin." This figure is understood to be Paul's sole reference to the Antichrist.

As for Paul's discussion of this evil individual, some historical background is necessary. According to the Jewish historian Josephus, in AD 40 the Roman emperor Gaius (more popularly known as Caligula) attempted to set up his statue in the Jerusalem temple. According to Josephus, Gaius took "himself to be a god." Therefore, this maniacal act is connected to emperor worship and the imperial cult, but it never came to pass due to the timely intervention of King Agrippa.[2] Nevertheless, Gaius's attempt to set up such a desecrating image would have been seen by our Lord's disciples, many of whom were still in Jerusalem at the time, as a potential fulfillment of our Lord's warning about the abomination of desolation "standing where it does not belong" (Mark 13:14). Certainly, this act of sacrilege would have been in the recent memories of both Jews and Christians when Paul came to Thessalonica and proclaimed the gospel, especially when the apostle warns the Thessalonians in his second letter, "Don't let anyone deceive you in any way, for (that day will not come) until the rebellion occurs and the man of lawlessness is revealed, the man doomed to destruction. He will oppose and will exalt himself over everything that is called God or is worshiped, so that he sets himself up in God's temple, proclaiming himself to be God (2 Thess. 2:3–4)."[3]

When Paul speaks of a Man of Lawlessness setting himself up in the temple, no doubt some of his readers thought of Caligula's image. Many certainly recalled Antiochus Epiphanes and his act of desecration of the Jerusalem temple in 167 BC, since Paul's discussion is clearly framed against the backdrop of Daniel's prophecy (11:30–45) of an end-times enemy—an Antichrist, if you will—who will attack the people of God both from within ("smooth words"—Dan. 11:32) and without ("destroy" and "annihilate"—Dan. 11:44).[4]

The first critical question faced by Paul's interpreters has to do with the identification of the Man of Lawlessness. Paul's Thessalonian readers clearly knew what he meant, since he reminds them, "Don't you remember that when I was with you I used to tell you these things?" (2 Thess. 2:5). While Paul's readers had the benefit of Paul's personal instruction regarding these matters when he had been present with them some months earlier, the matter is much more difficult for us. We don't know for sure what Paul told the Thessalonians when he was with him, but we can make a pretty good guess based upon the contents of Paul's two letters.

Contemporary Interpretations of 2 Thessalonians 2:1–12

	Identity of Man of Sin	Identity of the Restrainer	Paul's Reference to the Temple of God (2:4)
Preterism (prophecy is already fulfilled)	Nero or succession of Roman emperors	The Jewish commonwealth or the Roman Empire	Paul is referring to the Jerusalem temple, still standing before AD 70
Historicism (prophecy refers to the papacy)	The current pope or the papacy as an office	The preaching of the gospel	Paul is speaking of the church
Dispensationalism (the prophecy is yet future)	Future Antichrist	The Holy Spirit	A rebuilt temple in Jerusalem
Reformed Amillennialism (the prophecy is future)	Future Antichrist	The angel of Revelation, the providence of God, or the preaching of the gospel	Paul is speaking of the church

In his first letter, Paul had spoken of his work being hindered by Satan (1 Thess. 2:17–18), and in this very chapter (2 Thess. 2:1–3), Paul speaks of false reports that the day of the Lord had already come, which were circulating throughout the church, deceiving many. Given such hindrance and deception on the part of Satan, Paul very likely told the Thessalonians that the secret power of lawlessness was already at work. But the apostle also encouraged them that God was restraining such evil until the proper time, which was the time of final judgment. Therefore, the Thessalonians should not be taken in by such obvious falsehoods as they were hearing.

Contemporary Interpretations

There are a number of attempts made by Christian interpreters to identify the Man of Lawlessness. Those who hold to a preterist interpretation of New Testament eschatology believe that Paul is making a reference to Nero[5] or to the succession of Roman emperors,[6] which ties this passage to the events of AD 70. Still other preterists identify this act of sacrilege as the Jewish high priest continuing to offer sacrifices in the temple after Christ had died on the cross to do away with such sacrifices.[7] If preterists are correct, Paul's prophecy has already been fulfilled.

So-called historicists are of one mind about Paul's meaning. The Man of Lawlessness is either the current pope (at the time they were writing), or the papacy as an office.[8] According to Iain Murray, at that time it was the "unanimous belief that the Papal system is both the 'man of sin' and the Babylonian whore of which Scripture forewarns (2 Thessalonians 2; Revelation 19). In the conviction of sixteenth century Protestants, Rome was the great Anti-Christ, and so firmly did this belief become established that it was not until the nineteenth century that it was seriously questioned by evangelicals."[9]

The dispensationalists on the other hand, believe the Man of Sin to be an eschatological (end-times) figure who performs his despicable act in a rebuilt temple in Jerusalem at some point after making a seven-year peace treaty with Israel (see Dan. 9:24–27). Since the Jerusalem temple is not currently standing, it must be rebuilt. This explains why dispensationalists are so eagerly awaiting the rebuilding of the Jerusalem temple, since that will, supposedly, serve as a critical sign that the coming of the Lord is drawing near.[10]

There are also futurists (nondispensationalists) who see the Man of Sin as an eschatological (end-times) figure, who is in some sense a Nero *redivivus*. This includes some of the church fathers and historical premillenarians such as George Ladd, who does not see in this prophecy a specific fulfillment. Ladd believes that Paul is describing a pattern of events (of which the Roman Empire is the archetype) in which various states and governments will repeatedly become the persecutor of God's people. The state will take divine rights and prerogatives unto itself, manifest in the act of worship of the state or its leader.[11] There are still others (including a number of Reformed amillenarians) who believe Paul's words will remain mysterious by and large until this man is revealed at the time of the end, when believers will understand that to which Paul is referring because they have been forewarned by this prophecy.[12]

A second set of questions centers around the identity of the mysterious "restrainer" who holds back the power of lawlessness, which was already at work when Paul wrote this letter. Preterists believe the restrainer to be the second Jewish commonwealth[13] or the Roman Empire itself.[14] But the latter view begs the immediate question as to how the persecutor can also be the restrainer. The passage certainly seems to imply that the restrainer is good, since the language implies, at the very least, a struggle between good and evil.[15]

According to historicists, the restrainer is the preaching of the gospel that has kept the Roman Catholic Church from overcoming those who have rejected the errors of Rome.[16] The dispensationalists believe the restrainer to be the Holy Spirit, who is subsequently removed when the seven-year tribulation begins.[17] According to a number of Reformed amillenarians, the restrainer is somehow tied to the angel of Revelation 20:1–10.[18] Still other Reformed amillenarians hold that the restrainer is the general providence or power of God that holds back the power of lawlessness until the end.[19]

An Interpretation of 2 Thessalonians 2:1–12

This passage is critical in formulating a doctrine of Antichrist. Paul's reference to a Man of Sin (literally a Man of "Lawless-

ness"—*anomias*) is quite possibly the exegetical connection between two otherwise distinct tendencies found in Scripture. On
the one hand, we have a series of antichrists (heresy) arising
from within the church (spoken of in John's Epistles). On the
other hand, we have the rise of a persecuting beast in the Book of
Revelation who wages war on God's people through the means
of the power of the state—something external to the church.
Paul might offer the means to tie these two things together.

The context for Paul's discussion of the Man of Sin is that
the apostle is attempting to respond to two groups within the
Thessalonian church who were struggling with the notion of
the Lord's second advent. One group was worried about the fate
of those who died before the Lord's return (1 Thess. 4:13–17).
Would those who died before the parousia miss out on the benefits of the resurrection? Then there were others in the church
who were idle (1 Thess. 5:14; 2 Thess. 3:6–10). A number of
people, apparently, had concluded that if the Lord was returning
soon, they would not engage in any activity whatsoever—work,
evangelism, and so on.

In his first letter Paul tells us that the Lord has not yet come
back but that he can return at any moment (1 Thess. 4:17–5:11).
When he does, the dead in Christ will rise first. This would allay
any fears people had about their loved ones who died before
the return of Christ somehow missing out on the benefits of
the bodily resurrection. Paul also reminds the congregation
that the coming of the Lord should motivate them to work and
not be idle (5:14).

In 2 Thessalonians 2, however, Paul responds to those who
were teaching that the "day of the Lord" had already come (v. 2);
he emphatically points out that Christ's coming will be preceded
by two very specific signs that had not yet been fulfilled when
this Epistle was written in AD 50–51. These two signs are an
apostasy and the appearance of this Man of Sin (vv. 3–4). Thus,
it is clear that the Lord had not yet returned when Paul wrote
his second Epistle to the Thessalonians in AD 50–51, as some
were erroneously teaching.

Some critical scholars have used this apparent discrepancy
in Paul's teaching to argue that 2 Thessalonians was written

by a pseudonymous author.[20] But the tension between the unexpected and sudden nature of our Lord's return, which is paradoxically preceded by two very specific signs, is virtually identical to what we see in the Olivet Discourse when Jesus speaks of his coming as near (Matt. 24:42–44) and yet preceded by definite signs, such as the preaching of the gospel to the ends of the earth (Matt. 24:14). The point is that since no one knows when the Lord will return, and yet certain events must precede the coming of the Lord, including the revelation of the Man of Lawlessness, Christians must always be ready and must not be preoccupied with setting dates.[21] In this, Paul echoes the teaching of Jesus (see Matt. 24:36).

In 2 Thessalonians 2:1–2, Paul identifies the specific problem he will now address. "Concerning the coming of our Lord Jesus Christ and our being gathered to him, we ask you, brothers, not to become easily unsettled or alarmed by some prophecy, report or letter supposed to have come from us, saying that the day of the Lord has already come." Some in the Thessalonian church were teaching that the day of the Lord had already come—thus Christians are not to expect either the parousia or resurrection in the future, as these things had, supposedly, already occurred.[22] This error may spring from a misunderstanding of the imminent nature of the second advent, stemming from an over-realized eschatology, which sees everything as already fulfilled now that Christ has come. In 1 Thessalonians 5:5–8, Paul writes, "You are all sons of the light and sons of the day. We do not belong to the night or to the darkness. So then, let us not be like others, who are asleep, but let us be alert and self-controlled. For those who sleep, sleep at night, and those who get drunk, get drunk at night. But since we belong to the day, let us be self-controlled, putting on faith and love as a breastplate, and the hope of salvation as a helmet."

Some may have taken the reference to the kingdom as presently inaugurated ("we belong [presently] to the day") to mean that the kingdom has already been consummated.[23] Paul will now correct this misunderstanding, since this is not what he had taught them earlier. The Thessalonians are about to get a lesson in understanding the already and the not yet!

Over-realized eschatology was also a problem in Corinth, where certain false teachers were denying the resurrection of the body (1 Cor. 15:12–24). Later in his ministry Paul speaks of two men in the Ephesian church who were teaching that the Lord had already returned, and he pointedly rebukes them by name. "Avoid godless chatter, because those who indulge in it will become more and more ungodly. Their teaching will spread like gangrene. Among them are Hymenaeus and Philetus, who have wandered away from the truth. They say that the resurrection has already taken place, and they destroy the faith of some" (2 Tim. 2:16–18).

The erroneous views that the Lord has already returned or that the resurrection occurs at death (so there is no resurrection of the body) were not unheard of, even in the apostolic church. The first Christians lived with a distinct and pronounced eschatological tension—the Lord has died, the Lord has risen, the Lord has ascended (the already), but the Lord will come again at any moment (the not yet). This tension is clearly taught by both Jesus and Paul to prevent both date-setting and idleness.[24] According to Paul, two very specific signs must precede our Lord's return—an apostasy and the revelation of the Man of Lawlessness.

Paul's response to the erroneous notion that the day of the Lord had already come is to remind the Thessalonians not to be alarmed or unsettled by the rumors they were hearing. Paul makes it clear that such reports have not come from him—he had taught them otherwise when he had been with them—and this letter is the way in which this false teaching will be corrected. Paul uses his apostolic authority to correct this particular error.

In 2 Thessalonians 2:3–4, Paul indicates that the reason people are not to be startled is that two signs must be fulfilled before the Lord returns. "Don't let anyone deceive you in any way, for that day will not come until the rebellion occurs and the man of lawlessness is revealed, the man doomed to destruction. He will oppose and will exalt himself over everything that is called God or is worshiped, so that he sets himself up in God's temple, proclaiming himself to be God." Paul is crystal clear. Two things must occur before the Lord returns. First, there must be a rebellion (apostasy). Second, there must be a revelation of the Man of Lawlessness. The question for us is, "Are these events still in the future, or were they fulfilled by the events of AD 70?"

The Apostasy

As for the rebellion (*apostasia*), the word Paul uses here is used throughout the Septuagint (LXX) and elsewhere in the New Testament to speak of a religious crisis of some sort facing God's people—a falling away from the faith in some sense. As Beale points out, "Such a meaning is apparent because of the immediate context of false teaching (vv. 1–2 and vv. 9–12) and the clear allusions to Daniel's prediction of an end-time opponent who will bring about a large-scale compromise of faith among God's people."[25] This seems to connect Paul's comments to both John's and our Lord's warnings about false teachers and people who claim to be believers but who fall away and take a number of followers with them (see Matt. 24:10–12, 23–24; 1 John 2:18–19).

Some dispensationalists have erroneously argued that *apostasia* can mean something like "departure," so that Paul is speaking here of the rapture, which occurs immediately before the Antichrist is revealed. But the word never bears that meaning, as dispensationalists like Wuest and others have claimed.[26] The word means a rebellion against God, specifically an apostasy (a falling away from the truth) on the part of God's people. Thus professing Christians, not Jews, must be the ones who fall away.[27] While there were some apostates in the apostolic church just as there are in ours, God restrains false teachers and antichrists from gaining the upper hand until the appointed time.

Because the final apostasy has not yet taken place, the Thessalonians can be assured that the Lord has not yet returned, nor has the day of the Lord already occurred.[28] The timing of the apostasy is in some way connected to the second condition (the revelation of the Man of Lawlessness) as concomitant events.[29] You cannot have one without the other. Either the falling away occurs first so that the Man of Sin can appear, or else the apostasy is a consequence of the Man of Sin's appearance.[30] It may very well be that the Man of Lawlessness orchestrates such an apostasy through his blasphemous actions and his satanic powers of deception (2 Thess. 2:9–12). Whether the apostasy is a cause or an effect of the appearance of the Man of Sin, the two things are clearly connected.

The Revelation of the Man of Lawlessness

The other thing that must happen before the Lord returns is the revelation of the Man of Lawlessness. In contrast to preterist and historicist interpretation of this revelation as something that has already occurred, there are a number of reasons why Paul is most likely referring to "a future apostasy throughout the worldwide church and antichrist's influence in the church, which is the inaugurated end-time temple of God."[31] In other words, Paul is not speaking of the temple in Jerusalem (either the historic temple destroyed by the Romans in AD 70 or a rebuilt temple yet to come). Paul is instead using the temple as a metaphor for the church, since the church is now indwelt by the Spirit of God in this present age.

It is important to notice that Paul says the lawless one will be revealed (*apocalypsis*)—language that seems to make him a counterfeit redeemer with a counterfeit unveiling. The same verb is used by Paul of Jesus in the previous chapter (2 Thess. 1:7) and is used again in this chapter in reference to the coming of the Man of Sin in verses 6 and 8. The revelation of the Man of Lawlessness mocks the revelation of Jesus Christ.[32] The Man of Sin is a counterfeit and a usurper. This fits with the counterfeit Trinity in the Book of Revelation (the dragon, the beast, and the false prophet), which mimics our Lord's death, resurrection, and second advent in the beast who was, who is, and who will come again only to be judged and destroyed by Christ himself.

In Paul's discussion of this individual, there is a loud echo from Daniel 11:31, 36 and 12:10–11.[33] The prophet Daniel foresees a time in the future when the daily sacrifice will cease and God's temple will be desecrated. In Daniel 11:30–45, the prophet speaks of the final enemy of God both deceiving the people of God and then causing them to forsake the covenant (apostasy). Very likely, this means that Daniel foretells three different events—one associated with the coming of Antiochus Epiphanes and the profanation of the Jerusalem temple during the Maccabean wars in 167 BC, another tied to the dawn of the messianic age and the destruction of the Jerusalem temple in AD 70, and then finally to an end-times profanation of the holy place by the archfoe of Israel's Messiah.

Daniel's prophecy (especially 11:32, 36) is clearly in Paul's mind when he speaks of an apostasy and the Man of Lawlessness. But Daniel assigns this particular figure to the time of the end.[34] This would certainly seem to indicate that Paul is not speaking of the events of AD 70 but of the end of the age when the blasphemer faces his maker on the day of judgment. This is why, as Leon Morris so aptly puts it, "all attempts to equate the Man of Lawlessness with historical personages break down on the fact that Paul was writing of someone who would appear only at the end of the age; the Man of Lawlessness is an eschatological [future] figure."[35]

Since this Man of Lawlessness "sets himself up in God's temple" (2 Thess. 2:4), an act that implies the exercise of great authority,[36] and then proclaims himself to be God, many take this to mean that Paul is speaking of the Jerusalem temple. As we have seen, preterists tie this to events associated with the Jewish rejection of the gospel and the desecration of the Jewish temple in AD 70, while many futurists see this as a prophecy of a rebuilt temple in Jerusalem at the time of the end. Historicists are surely on the right track here when they argue that the reference to the temple is a reference to the church.[37] This identification explains why historicists identified the Man of Sin with the papacy. Although I adopt the historicist understanding of Paul's use of the word *temple* as a metaphor for the church,

I do not believe that this prophecy is fulfilled by the papacy but rather by a particular individual yet future.

As Beale points out, the word temple (*naon*) is found nine other times in the New Testament outside of 2 Thessalonians, where it is almost always used of Christ or the church.[38] In the five other times Paul uses the word, it does not refer to a literal temple in Israel, past or future (1 Cor. 3:16–17; 6:19; 2 Cor. 6:16; Eph. 2:21; 2 Thess. 2:4). In both Matthew and John the word is used of the temple that will be destroyed before Christ raises it up, or of the true temple, which is his body (Matt. 26:61; John 2:21). Paul refers to believers as constituting the temple of God because they are in union with Christ, through faith (1 Cor. 3:16–17; 2 Cor. 6:16; Eph. 2:19–21).[39]

Furthermore, in 1 Thessalonians 4:3–8, Paul depicts Christians in a manner that parallels the passage in 1 Corinthians 6:18–19, although the word *temple* is not specifically used. Paul is making the point that the people of God constitute the dwelling place of God's Spirit. In Revelation 11:1–7, the saints are pictured as a sanctuary,[40] and in Revelation 13:6, the beast attacks the people of God, described as the "tabernacle" (NASB). Taken together, this is strong evidence in favor of the view that Paul is not referring to the Jerusalem temple but to the church.[41]

There are a number of other important redemptive-historical shifts that have taken place after the death and resurrection of Christ that underlie Paul's overall theology, especially his eschatology.[42] All of these points support the interpretation that the temple spoken of here by Paul is the church, not the temple in Jerusalem. We can enumerate them briefly. First, after Christ's death and resurrection, true Israel is Christ and his people (see Gal. 6:16). Second, Christ's people are now his temple, indwelt by his Spirit. This can be seen on the day of Pentecost—the outpouring of the Spirit in Acts 2:14–41 is the reality foreshadowed by the Spirit filling the tabernacle in Exodus 40:34–38. Third, both national Israel as the covenant community and the temple as the place of sacrifice have come to an end (Luke 21:6; Heb. 7:11–10:22).[43] When Christ died upon the cross, the veil in the Jerusalem temple was torn from top to bottom. The temple is now *ichabod*—its glory has departed. No believers are present there. Neither is God's Spirit.

It is important to keep in mind that the temple represents the church because, in order to fall away, the people who fall must be part of the believing covenant community into which the Man of Lawlessness will make his entrance and so deceive and blaspheme. In defending the preterist interpretation of this text, Gentry asserts that those who fall away are Jews who rebel (*apostasia*) against Roman political authority, which sadly led to Rome's military intervention and subsequent devastation of Israel in AD 70. Gentry sees in this apostasy a religious element as well—Israel's rejection of the Messiah.[44] But this does not fit with Paul's metaphorical use of temple imagery. How can an apostate people (the Jews) fall from the orthodox faith when they are already apostate? Such apostasy implies professing believers falling away from Christ's church, not Jews who have already rejected their Messiah.

Therefore, the scene depicted by Paul is one in which the Man of Lawlessness (who mimics Christ) deceives people within the believing community (the church) through satanically empowered signs and wonders (2 Thess. 2:9–12). Nowhere does Paul say the Man of Sin does this in the old covenant community (Israel) with its temple. That Jesus spoke of such apostasy as one of the signs of the impending judgment upon Israel is certain (Matt. 24:10–12). But such signs were not only warnings to the apostles, since the apostles are representatives of the church, they are spoken to them and to us as well. This, then, is not only a warning to the Thessalonians, it is a warning to all Christians about what must happen before the Lord returns—there must be an apostasy and the revelation of the Man of Sin.[45]

When Paul warns the Thessalonians of someone to come who "will oppose and will exalt himself over everything that is called God or is worshiped, so that he sets himself up in God's temple, proclaiming himself to be God" (2 Thess. 2:4), he is referring to an end-times individual who will commit this heinous act in Christ's church, not in the Jerusalem temple past or future. And this despicable act is, in some way, connected to a final apostasy that immediately precedes the final judgment (2 Thess. 1:8–10; 2:8).

While the acts of Antiochus Epiphanes in 167 BC and Titus in AD 70 fulfill the various prophecies of Daniel 11 in part, Paul telescopes those provisional fulfillments of Daniel's prophecy—what Ridderbos calls "a proleptic-prophetic" character of such prophecies[46]—to what will happen in Christ's church immediately before the end of the age. A great apostasy will occur in Christ's church in connection with the revelation of the Man of Lawlessness, who will exalt himself over God and demand to be worshiped. This may indeed indicate that the series of antichrists described by John in his Epistles will give way to an Antichrist once God's restraint is lifted.[47] This occurs at the time of the end, not in connection with the destruction of the Jerusalem temple.

The Mysterious Restrainer

In 2 Thessalonians 2:5, Paul reminds the Thessalonians of two related matters. The first is that he has already warned them about such false teaching. The second has to do with the fact that he has already set forth in general terms what the future would hold. "Don't you remember that when I was with you I used to tell you these things?" Then Paul goes on to speak in much more specific terms regarding the fact that both the power of lawlessness as well as the Man of Lawlessness are presently being restrained. "And now you know what is holding him back, so that he may be revealed at the proper time. For the secret power of lawlessness is already at work; but the one who now holds it back will continue to do so till he is taken out of the way" (2 Thess. 2:6–7). These latter two verses raise the very difficult question of just who, or what, is presently preventing the Man of Lawlessness from appearing on the scene. The Thessalonians knew what Paul meant, but we must make an educated guess. Speculation abounds as to what, exactly, Paul means when he speaks of both an act of restraint ("what is holding him back") as well as someone or something ("the one who now holds it back") that is presently restraining the power of lawlessness.

Since Paul has made the point that the day of the Lord is not at hand since the apostasy has not yet occurred and the Man of Lawlessness has not been revealed, Paul must now address the question as to why this has not yet happened. Paul's interpreters are greatly divided about the identity of the restrainer, who holds at bay the secret power of lawlessness, which Paul says is already at work at the time of the writing of his Epistle. Beale identifies at least seven different interpretations of this passage, some of which we've already mentioned.[48] The problem for interpreters is that Paul switches from speaking of a restrainer in the neuter (*to katechon*—"restraint"), to the masculine (*ho katechone*—"the restrainer"). The interpretive problems here are tremendous, especially since they are qualified by the fact that something (when Paul writes) is currently doing the work of restraint.[49]

As we have seen, some preterists believe that this restrainer is the second Jewish Commonwealth (e.g., B. B. Warfield) or the Roman Empire itself (e.g., F. F. Bruce, Kenneth Gentry). Historicists believe this refers to the preaching of the gospel (John Calvin, for one), while some dispensationalists believe that this is a reference to the Holy Spirit (e.g., J. Dwight Pentecost). Reformed amillenarians, on the other hand, tend to connect this to a supernatural power perhaps manifest in the angel of Revelation 20 (e.g., Jay Adams, Cornelius Venema) or to the providential power of God in exercising the restraint until the time of the end (e.g., Herman Ridderbos). In fact, Ridderbos sees the restrainer as a "supernatural power or ruler ordained by God (in Revelation 20, 'A strong angel') who checks the final revelation of the power of Satan, until the time set for the Man of Sin has come."[50] Geerhardus Vos believes that "Paul likewise understood by the *katekon* [restraint] and the *katekone* [restrainer] something supernatural and far superior to the might of Rome. . . . The fact remains that it is impossible for us to form concrete conceptions of how the restraint of the mystery takes place."[51]

Vos is very likely on the right track about this power being supernatural, especially in light of Beale's contention that the angel's restraint of Satan (Revelation 20) is likely tied to the preaching of the gospel. Not only was Paul's preaching already having an impact upon the forces of darkness—which explains why Satan was trying to hinder him—but this also fits with our Lord's words that the gospel must first be preached to all nations before his return (Mark 13:10). Indeed, our Lord himself had promised that the gates of hell will not prevail against his church (Matt. 16:18).[52] Something, perhaps the preaching of the gospel, is already restraining the power of lawlessness, keeping it from prevailing. If Paul's restrainer/restraint is in any way connected to the angel of Revelation 20, then the case becomes all the stronger that Paul is indeed speaking of the preaching of the gospel as presently holding back the power of evil. As Beale notes,

> This is further in line with Revelation 20:1–9, where during the church age an angel restrains (literally "binds") Satan's power to decimate the church. Then, at the end of the age, the restraining power is removed, so that Satan unleashes against the church his antichrist who will deceive and cause apostasy on a worldwide scale. When he is on the verge of destroying the covenant community, he himself will be destroyed at Christ's final coming. . . . Consistent with this perspective is the Apocalypse's repeated allusion to evil figures being "given power" by God to carry out wicked actions (Rev. 6:4; 7:2; 9:13–15; 13:5, 7, 14–15).[53]

It seems to me that this argument makes the best sense of Paul's point that even though the powers of evil were already at work, they are also presently being restrained until God's appointed time. As Leon Morris wisely reminds us, all the speculation about Paul's language here ends up obscuring the obvious point (whatever the restrainer is or is not). "Some power was in operation, and . . . the Man of Lawlessness could not possibly put in his appearance until this power was removed. The Thessalonians knew this. Therefore they should have known that speculations about the presence of the day of the Lord were necessarily false. Necessary preconditions had yet to be fulfilled."[54] The mystery of lawlessness was already being restrained so that the Man of Lawlessness could not appear.

According to Paul, at some point in the future[55] the restraint will be removed, and then as we read in 2 Thessalonians 2:8, "The lawless one will be revealed, whom the Lord Jesus will overthrow with the breath of his mouth and destroy by the splendor of his coming." While the principle of lawlessness is already at work in AD 50 and is currently being restrained when Paul writes this letter, at some point in the future the restraint will be lifted. Only then will the Man of Lawlessness be revealed, and that for a very specific divine purpose: the final judgment.

The verb "to reveal" (*apocalypsis*) is clearly tied to the second coming of Christ to judge the world, raise the dead, and make all things new, and this passage is no exception. As Beale puts it, "the end-time enemy will be revealed so that his followers are further deceived and judged along with him."[56] This means that the lifting of the restraint has for its goal the final judgment upon all the forces of evil, not merely the revelation of the Man of Sin that comes about as a consequence so that God's purposes will be fulfilled. This, too, is very strong evidence that the events of AD 70 do not fulfill this prophecy. The scope of eschatological judgment mentioned here is the visible revelation of something previously invisible, namely, the glory and splendor of Christ himself.[57] The passage has an air of finality about it. It is not likely that Paul is speaking of something that is localized to judgment only upon unbelieving Israel or limited to the destruction of Nero. This point becomes stronger when we notice that Paul is quoting from Isaiah 11:4, a text in which Yahweh, the mighty warrior, is said to judge the whole earth. "With righteousness he will judge the needy, with justice he will give decisions for the poor of the earth. He will strike the earth with the rod of his mouth; with the breath of his lips he will slay the wicked." The Man of Lawlessness will be destroyed by the glory of the Lord's appearing, something Paul did not think to be either secret or localized to Jerusalem (see 1 Thess. 4:16 and the mention of the shout, the trumpet, and the loud command in connection with the bodily resurrection from the dead at our Lord's second advent). Jesus is that mighty warrior of whom Isaiah had spoken, and when his glory is revealed it will be to judge the earth.

With the restraint lifted, Satan's power is made fully manifest through this individual, about whom Paul says, "The coming of the lawless one will be in accordance with the work of Satan displayed in all kinds of counterfeit miracles, signs and wonders, and in every sort of evil that deceives those who are perishing. They perish because they refused to love the truth and so be saved" (2 Thess. 2:9–10). Thus, the lawless one is an individual empowered by Satan and whose miracles mimic those of Christ himself. This is the means by which he brings about the final rebellion and certifies his claims of divinity in the church. He is the deceiver and usurper *par excellence*. The Man of Sin may indeed be the final Antichrist to which the series of antichrists mentioned by John have pointed us. No longer restrained, he deceives almost without measure.

That this event is tied to our Lord's second advent is made clear in 2 Thessalonians 2:11–12. Paul writes, "For this reason God sends them a powerful delusion so that they will believe the lie and so that all will be condemned who have not believed the truth but have delighted in wickedness." God's judgment comes upon all those who have embraced his eschatological enemy through the form of powerful delusion, so that all who are taken in by this man are therefore objects of final judgment. Divine condemnation is the ultimate fate of those who are already perishing (2 Thess. 2:10; cf. Rev. 20:1–10).

Preterists, such as Gentry, are surely far from the mark when they assert that Paul is referring to God's coming in judgment upon Israel and possibly to the great fire of Rome (AD 64) during the reign of Nero.[58] Dispensationalists are equally wide of the mark when they assert that the Man of Sin's blasphemy takes place in a rebuilt temple in Jerusalem three and a half years after signing a peace treaty with Israel. No, Paul's Man of Sin presides over an end-times apostasy in Christ's church. He is the culmination of that series of antichrists already plaguing the apostolic church, and he is presently being restrained by the preaching of the gospel, until such time as God lifts his supernatural restraint and the Man of Lawlessness is finally revealed. And when that day comes, the second coming of the Lord will not be far behind.

7

KNOW YOUR ENEMY

The Antichrist in Church History

The Church Fathers

The purpose of this chapter is not to provide an exhaustive history of the doctrine of Antichrist. Bernard McGinn has already produced a substantial history of this doctrine—especially patristic and medieval developments—in his book *Antichrist*.[1] There is no need to duplicate his efforts. Instead, the purpose of this chapter is to offer a brief survey of certain aspects of the church's reflection upon this doctrine, specifically as they relate to some of the themes discussed earlier in this study. There is much to learn from our fathers in the faith as they wrestled with this doctrine and sought to make sense of the biblical data.

The earliest Christian documents that mention Antichrist contain very little theological reflection, apart from a brief mention of him in connection with a particular biblical passage. The *Epistle of Barnabas*, written soon after the close of the apostolic age, identifies the fourth beast of Daniel 7 as the Roman Empire, while specifically referring to the beast as Antichrist.[2] A similar reference surfaces in the writings of Polycarp, bishop of Smyrna, who was born about AD 70 and likely martyred about AD 156. In 7.1 of his *Epistle to the Philippians* (written about AD 135), Polycarp quotes from 1 John 4:2–3 and 2 John 2:7 and contends that antichrist is the spirit of heresy.[3] This is similar to the emphasis found in John's Epistles, to the effect that the threat from antichrist arises from within and is not connected to state-sponsored persecution like the beast of Revelation 13.[4] In his *Dialog with Trypho*, Justin Martyr (who was put to death in Rome about AD 165) speaks of the appearance of the "man of apostasy" who speaks "strange things against the Most High" and ventures to "do unlawful deeds on the earth against us Christians." Justin is clearly alluding to 2 Thessalonians 2:3 but does not specifically speak of this individual as Antichrist.[5]

One of the most important early discussions of Antichrist is found in the work of Irenaeus, who was born in Asia Minor, where he met Polycarp when still a young man.[6] Irenaeus later became bishop of Lyon in Gaul. In his work *Against Heresies* (about AD 180),[7] Irenaeus set forth the opinion that Antichrist will be a Jew, a notion that had come from Papias (another writer from Asia Minor whose work remains largely fragmentary).[8] Appealing to the best manuscripts and eyewitnesses (probably a reference to Polycarp), Irenaeus believes Antichrist recapitulates the apostasy that occurred in the beginning with Adam and Eve. This apostasy could be seen in the present (the gnostics of his own age), and a similar apostasy will appear again at the time of the end.[9] Just as Christ, who is the Word made flesh, recapitulates all that is good, so too Antichrist must come in the flesh to recapitulate all that is evil.[10]

In addition, Irenaeus believed that the Roman Empire eventually would be divided among ten kings,[11] and at the end of time an Antichrist will arise and lead a final apostasy (in fulfillment of Dan. 7:8; 8:23; Matt. 24:15; 2 Thess. 2:3). The Antichrist's rule will complete the six thousand years of world history (Sabbatical pattern), followed by a millennial age, when Christ reigns upon the earth.[12] While Irenaeus cautions his reader against undue speculation in this regard, he identifies 666 with Lateinos, the ancient king of the Latins, or with Teitan—a royal name for a tyrant. He believed that Antichrist will be an apostate Jew, sitting in the temple in Jerusalem, demanding to be worshiped as God.[13] In fact, Irenaeus connects Paul's prophecy of a Man of Sin (2 Thess. 2:1–12) to the prophecies in Daniel 8:12 and 9:27, the fulfillment of which is assigned to the time of the end.[14]

The first Christian writing specifically dealing with Antichrist was written by Hippolytus, himself a student of Irenaeus. Hippolytus served as an elder in the church in Rome for nearly thirty-five years and died a martyr in AD 235.[15] In his treatise *On Antichrist* (AD 200),[16] which is part of a larger work on Daniel and the earliest surviving Christian commentary on any book of the Bible, Hippolytus builds upon the earlier work of Irenaeus, although there are a number of distinctive elements.[17] Like his mentor, Hippolytus believed that Antichrist will be a Jew and a counterfeit of the true Christ. Antichrist will be born in Babylon and will come from the tribe of Dan—he is spoken of in Genesis 49:9 and Deuteronomy 33:22 as a lion's cub and therefore cunning and deceptive.[18] As a false redeemer, Antichrist will persuade the Jews that he is the Messiah. The forerunners of Antichrist are also identified as several Old Testament figures: the Assyrian king (Isa. 10:12–19), the Babylonian king (Isa. 14:4–21), and the prince of Tyre (Ezek. 28:2–10). As Hippolytus puts it, "For a deceiver seeks to liken himself in all things to the Son of God. Christ is a lion, so Antichrist is also a lion; Christ is a king, so Antichrist is also a king. The Savior was manifested as a lamb; so he too will in like manner, appear as a lamb, though within he is a wolf."[19]

Hippolytus also states that Antichrist will rebuild the temple in Jerusalem[20] and will deceive Christians, who are symbolized by the two witnesses who preach against him before being killed. Three and a half years of tribulation will follow before

Christ returns to destroy him. The two beasts of Revelation 13 are yet future and will rule in the manner of Caesar Augustus, "by whom the empire of Rome was established."[21]

Hippolytus also sets forth a rather bizarre chronology of the end. Christ will not come at the end of the six thousand years of world history—the schema of history set forth by Irenaeus—but instead, Christ will return in the middle of the final thousand years marking some five hundred years between Christ's return in humility and his return in glory.[22] According to McGinn, Hippolytus is the "earliest witness to what later became known as the 'refreshment of the saints,' a brief period between the Antichrist's defeat and Christ's return when the surviving faithful were supposed to live in peace while awaiting the manifestation of the kingdom of God."[23] While many have seen in this a kind of proto-premillenarianism (chiliasm), recent studies, such as that by Charles Hill, have shed new light on this assumption, pointing out that Hippolytus believed that the first resurrection takes place when the soul of a martyr joins Christ in heaven, not when Christ returns to raise the dead—a position inconsistent with premillennialism.[24]

The belief that Antichrist will be a Jew who will preside over a rebuilt temple in Jerusalem and then proclaim himself as Israel's Messiah is, according to Bousset, "the universal belief" of the church. A few men (Lactantius, Commodian, and Martin of Tours) identified this false Messiah who will deceive the Jews and commandeer their temple as a Nero *redivivus*.[25] The former view was taken up by the French monk Adso and widely popularized in the tenth century.[26] Adso's views were adopted and modified by the two great scholastic theologians, Albertus Magnus and Thomas Aquinas, thereby giving them great credence and influence.[27]

Origen and Augustine

A most influential figure in the early church and a contemporary of Hippolytus, Origen (AD 185–254) is another important contributor to the development of a doctrine of Antichrist, especially in his so-called "spiritualizing" method of interpreting biblical texts. In his *On First Principles*, which many consider to be the first attempt to write a systematic theology, Origen takes issue with those who attempt to understand those biblical texts that speak of the reign of the saints upon the earth in a literal way.[28] Those who understand the biblical passages that speak of eating and drinking in the kingdom, of an earthly city of Jerusalem, and so on in a literal way "are of the opinion that the fulfillment of the promises of the future are to be looked for in bodily pleasure and luxury . . . [and are] not following the opinion of the Apostle Paul regarding the resurrection of a spiritual body."[29] For Origen, it seems, there is always a deeper meaning to a text.

Not surprisingly, this spiritualizing method carries over into Origen's understanding of antichrist. According to Origen, there are two great extremes—virtue and its opposite. Perfection of virtue dwells in the person of Jesus, while that one who rejects virtue "embodies the notion of him that is named Antichrist." Virtue is found in the Son of God, while "the other, who is diametrically opposite, [is] termed the son of the wicked demon and of Satan, and of the devil."[30] Antichrist is not a person but a spiritual principle. He is not a man to be feared but a falsehood to be opposed.

In his *Commentary on John*, Origen restates this idea that antichrist is merely a spiritual principle. Alluding to 2 Thessalonians 2:8, where Paul speaks of Jesus destroying the lawless one with the breath of his mouth, Origen understands this to be a reference to the wisdom of God in Christ destroying the lie by means of the truth. "For that which is destroyed by the breath of the mouth of Christ, Christ being the Word and Truth and Wisdom, but the lie?"[31] When discussing the Olivet Discourse in his *Commentary on Matthew*, Origen identifies the abomination of desolation as a false word that stands in the place of Scripture, so that antichrist is anything that pretends to be true but is not.[32] Obviously, Origen's spiritualizing of the text mutates the Antichrist from a personal eschatological foe into a principle of evil.

The most important Christian theologian in the first thousand years of church history is St. Augustine (AD 354–430). Augustine addressed the subject of Antichrist in several places and yet in doing so managed to avoid much of the kind of speculative discussion found in Hippolytus and Irenaeus. In the opinion of Bernard McGinn, Augustine "was cool to legendary accretions to the story of Antichrist, [but] the bishop was still a major channel for the transmission of sober traditions concerning the Final Enemy to the Latin West."[33] In other words, when it came to Antichrist speculation, Augustine's focus was upon the exegesis of particular texts. This concern not to go beyond the biblical text enabled him to emphasize the significance of present and imminent threats to the church, rather than locating this threat exclusively to the time of the end as many earlier writers had done.[34]

In the *City of God* Augustine clearly affirms that Jesus Christ will destroy Antichrist at the time of the second advent before going on to affirm the impossibility of knowing when, exactly, this will occur. He adds that human conjecture cannot add anything to Scripture.[35] According to Augustine, Paul's discussion of the Man of Sin is a reference to Antichrist and the time of final judgment, but he's not sure what Paul means when he mentions the temple (the Jerusalem temple or the church). He goes on to describe a number of views, including the Nero *redivivus* theory, which he dismisses. Augustine says what is clear from the biblical text is that Antichrist will not appear until Satan is loosed from the Abyss (Rev. 20:1–10), for this is what gives Antichrist his power to deceive. This, says Augustine, is exactly what Daniel predicted, for the kingdom of Antichrist will assail the church before Christ returns to rescue his people. The ten kings and kingdoms mentioned by Daniel may or may not refer to Rome, but more likely they symbolize the entirety of the inter-advental age.[36] Augustine also finds it reasonable to believe that the Roman Empire must fall so that Antichrist might be revealed.[37]

In his sermons (homilies) on 1 John, delivered in AD 415, Augustine speaks directly to the nature and character of Antichrist. Antichrist is "contrary to Christ." This means that antichrists are "all heretics, all schismatics [who] went out from us, that is, they go from the Church." Since this is the case, Augustine says, "each person ought to question his own conscience, whether he be an antichrist." Antichrists are liars and deny that Jesus is the Christ. Thus the test as to whether one is an antichrist is not their confession "Christ is Lord," since even a liar can utter these words. The test is someone's deeds. "A more lying antichrist is he who with his mouth professes that Jesus is the Christ, and with his deeds denies Him. A liar in this, that he speaks one thing, and does another."[38]

McGinn draws the conclusion from this that Augustine believes that "the real Antichrist is anyone of us," and he takes this as an indication of Augustine's rejection of apocalyptic eschatology.[39] But Augustine is very clear in *City of God* that the mystery of lawlessness of which Paul speaks in 2 Thessalonians, which is currently restrained by God, is somehow tied to John's assertion that many antichrists have already come because it is the last hour. The series of antichrists of whom John speaks will indeed culminate in a final Antichrist. "As therefore went out from the Church many heretics, whom John calls 'many antichrists,' at that time prior to the end, and which John calls 'the last time,' so in the end they shall go out who do not belong to Christ, but to that last Antichrist, and then he shall be revealed."[40] While Augustine cautions against undue speculation about the end times, his view that Antichrist is both a present/imminent threat as well as finally revealed at the end of the age reflects the tension found in Scripture. This is not, as McGinn states, Augustine's belief that Antichrist is merely a reflection of the personal evil within each of us. While we all may be found liars whose deeds do not match our profession, the final Antichrist clearly falls in a different category, since he is empowered by Satan and is to be revealed at the end of the age.

The Medieval Church

After both Irenaeus and Hippolytus seemed to predict the end of the Roman Empire, after Hippolytus planted the seed that the critical eschatological date was about AD 500, and after Rome was sacked (AD 410 and again in 455) and then dissolved into a number of separate kingdoms, there could be only one conclusion: the end must be at hand. The fact that Rome was weakened politically, economically, and militarily, coupled with the realization that the barbarians to the north were a serious threat to the old Greco-Roman way of life, created a climate in the West where apocalyptic speculation was rife.[41] The restrainer had been taken out of the way—the Man of Sin was soon to appear. It was not a question of *if* but *when.*

Since it was possible that Antichrist could be revealed at any moment, many became preoccupied with the Antichrist's personal appearance and attempted to develop a "suspect sketch" from the biblical data. Some thought Antichrist would have flaming hair, while others thought he would have bloody or radiant eyes. He is depicted as missing teeth, with fingers shaped like sickles and with huge feet. Some writers believed he would be a miracle-worker and possess some distinguishing mark revealing his true identity.[42] Some even feared that the Antichrist was already alive, awaiting his revelation.[43]

One of the most stabilizing figures of the early Middle Ages was Gregory the Great, bishop of Rome from AD 590 to 604, at a time when Rome was being repeatedly and systematically pillaged by the Lombards. Gregory used the Antichrist motif as a means of furthering the moral reform of the church. While acknowledging that Antichrist is an eschatological foe, Gregory was primarily concerned with the threat to the church from heretics and hypocrites within.[44] What makes Antichrist such a feared foe in Gregory's estimation is that when he appears he will possess the power of the world while simultaneously manifesting a high degree of holiness. Given the tumultuous times, Gregory told the citizens of Rome that the end of the world was at hand since the signs of the end—wars and rumors of wars—were readily apparent for all to see, "like pages of our books."[45]

In AD 950 the monk Adso composed his letter to Gerberga, sister of Otto I, German ruler of the Western Empire, in which he set forth a summary of the biblical and traditional teaching regarding the Antichrist.[46] Not only does Adso provide a summation of patristic teaching (drawing upon Jerome's commentary on Daniel and Bede's work on Revelation, among others),[47] he composes his narrative description of Antichrist as a kind of negation of the very popular "lives of the saints." If the saints were known for their great personal holiness and piety, Antichrist will be known for his impiety. McGinn believes that Adso's narrative, which turns the "lives of the saints" motif on its head, "marks a major turning moment in the history of the Antichrist legend"[48] because this narrative concentrates upon the manifestation of Antichrist as a particular individual yet to appear and not as a moralistic tale.[49] When it comes to the Antichrist in Adso's estimation, Irenaeus and Hippolytus triumph over Origen and to a lesser extent St. Augustine.

According to Adso, the Antichrist "will perform deeds contrary to Christ" and yet will simultaneously deceive the masses by appearing Christlike. Adso takes the traditional view that the Antichrist will be a Jew from the tribe of Dan; he will be born in Babylon but end up in Jerusalem and take his place in a rebuilt, restored temple. Antichrist will perform false signs and wonders, and he will convert many kings and princes soon after he appears. His followers will take his mark on their foreheads, and he will rule for three and a half years.[50] Adso's work effectively institutionalizes the notion that Antichrist will be a false Messiah who possesses miracle power and a deceptive piety that enables him to masquerade as a false christ. Because Antichrist is so successful in his efforts to mimic Christ, he is utterly diabolical.

Antichrist was often depicted in medieval art, especially in images taken from the Apocalypse,[51] and was also a popular subject in medieval plays. One of the most popular of these plays, *Antichristus*, was one of the earliest dramas written in Germany (about AD 1160). The plays follow the general plot laid out by Adso, though with local adaptation. Similar plays appeared in Italy in the fourteenth century (*Lauda Drammatica Dell'Antichristo O Dell Giudzio Finale*), in France about 1240 (*Le Regne de l'Antechrist*), with the most famous being *The Coming of Antichrist* in 1328.[52] These plays not only popularized the idea

among the masses that Antichrist was a future foe who would
arise at the time of the end, but the visualization of Antichrist
kept speculation about him at the heart of church life and firmly
established in the popular imagination.[53] In fact, there was so
much Antichrist speculation throughout the Middle Ages that
by the end of the fourteenth century, Matthew of Janov could
comment that the Antichrist was so well known that when he appeared even small children could recognize him.[54] Both Luther
and Calvin make reference to the widespread speculation about
Antichrist in the church on the eve of the Reformation, and
both lament the fact that the Roman Catholic Church should
have been far more interested in the purity of the gospel than
in promoting end-times prognostication.[55]

Thus Antichrist speculation is neither recent nor an exclusively American evangelical fascination. The main categories
that characterize Antichrist speculation in contemporary America were already established in the medieval church. Antichrist
will be a Jew. He will perform false signs and wonders. He will
preside over the Jerusalem temple, receive worship, and appear
to be the Messiah himself. He will be the master of deceit, but
he will be opposed by the two witnesses of Revelation 11:3–12.
What are missing are dispensational characteristics—a seven-
year tribulation, a peace treaty with Israel, and the rapture of
believers before the Antichrist is revealed. Augustine's view is
clearly on the wane.

One final aspect of medieval speculation about Antichrist,
particularly important for our study, is that toward the end of
the period two distinct tendencies developed that opened the
door to the possibility the papacy itself could become the seat of
Antichrist. The first tendency has to do with the so-called Great
Reform movement in which the church sought to purify itself
from interfering politicians and corrupt clerics who practiced
simony and engaged in unchaste behavior. The second development was the influence of Joachim of Fiore (AD 1135–1202)
upon the apocalyptic theology of the church.[56]

When the Great Reform got underway, one of its most prominent figures, Hildebrand, who reigned as Pope Gregory VII
from AD 1073 to 1085, began to denounce as an Antichrist and

arch-heretic the so-called antipope, Wibert, the archbishop of Ravenna, who was established as "pope" by the German Emperor Henry IV at the Diet of Worms in 1076. Gregory VII also excommunicated Henry for having called a council that excommunicated Gregory and named Wibert as his successor. A certain Cardinal Beno, who was a supporter of the antipope, responded in an official decree that it was Hildebrand who was an Antichrist. Thus began a pattern of calling one's opponent "Antichrist" as well as resorting to drastic ecclesiastical sanctions when dealing with one's "Antichrist" opponents.[57]

In an important aside, when Pope Urban II conceived of the first crusade about the same time in 1095, some accounts of his call for mobilization to liberate Jerusalem from the Muslims indicate that he appealed to the necessity of Christians retaking Jerusalem so that Antichrist will arise and, in turn, begin the process of bringing about the events that are a prelude to the end. Given the widespread Antichrist speculation at the time, the idea that Christians could act in such a way as to hasten the coming of the Antichrist (and, therefore, the return of Christ) was only natural.[58]

In any case, as various reforming movements jockeyed for control and influence in the church, those seeking reform could label the defenders of the status quo as those doing the work of Antichrist in keeping the church impure, while such defenders could just as easily label Reformers antichrists because they disrupted the peace and harmony of the church.[59] To call someone an antichrist had not only ecclesiastical cache but political value as well. As McGinn points out, "If a pope accused an emperor of being an Antichrist or one of his minions, as both Gregory IX and Innocent IV accused Frederick II, this was not an attack on the Christian empire as such, but a denial that a particular occupant was really the emperor because of his manifest wickedness."[60]

One of the most influential figures from this period in the development of apocalyptic thought and the doctrine of Antichrist is Joachim of Fiore, an itinerant monk who produced a number of significant works, most notably an important exposition of the Apocalypse, which broke with the established teaching on

Antichrist and the end times.[61] Although he lived a monastic lifestyle, it is a mistake to think of Joachim as someone of little influence. As a counselor to popes and politicians, Joachim was very influential and rubbed shoulders with the likes of Richard the Lionhearted, Empress Constance, Pope Innocent III, and a young Frederick II.[62]

Lamenting the spiritual lethargy of his day, Joachim believed the church had fallen away from Christ's favor because of its lack of purity and its increasing worldliness. In Joachim's estimation, the solution was not to go back to the past (reform) but to seek for a new era in redemptive history, the era of the Spirit, which would bring about the desired reform of the church and the long-awaited Sabbath age. This work of the Spirit would bring about a new interest in monasticism, which Joachim saw as essential to the well-being of the church. This age would begin about AD 1200, or in the not-too-distant future.[63]

Breaking with Augustine on a number of points having to do with matters of eschatology, Joachim believed that a period of great blessing (a millennial age of sorts) would come after the defeat of the first Antichrist.[64] As Joachim saw things, since the Triune God is author of both Scripture and history, history would unfold along the lines of a trinitarian pattern. As part of this pattern, many antichrists will come before the manifestation of an Antichrist, who mimics Christ's threefold office of prophet, priest, and king. What remained was the third and final age—that of the Spirit.[65]

Joachim contends that the seven persecutions of the Jews in the Old Testament are parallels to seven times of persecution foretold in the New Testament. This can be seen in the seven-headed dragon of Revelation 12, which signifies seven tyrants who persecute the church. These include Herod and the Jews, Nero and Roman imperialism, Constantius and the efforts of heretics to persecute the church, Muhammad, "Mesemoth" and the sons of Babylon, Saladin and the Islamic armies who had just recaptured Jerusalem, and then a seventh king, who will be the first Antichrist. This seventh king, Joachim believed, would be the most evil of all of the kings just listed, a kind of *maximus antichristus*, who Joachim assumed was already alive and soon to be revealed.[66]

Since a third epoch in redemptive history (the age of the Holy Spirit) is yet to come, there will be the revelation of yet another final Antichrist at the end of this period, many years distant. Thus, Joachim posits the coming of two Antichrists—one imminent (the seventh king) and another at the end of the age of the Spirit, which Joachim believes is associated with the revolt led by Gog and Magog (cf. Ezek. 38–39; Rev. 20:7–10). Just as Jesus has two advents, so will Antichrist.[67]

In breaking with patristic tradition, Joachim does believe that Paul's reference to the Man of Sin taking his place in the temple of God in 2 Thessalonians 2:1–12 is a reference to the church and not to a rebuilt temple in Jerusalem. The fact that Antichrist might possibly appear in the church as a false priest implies that he might even be a false pope who is a member of a heretical sect and who deceives not only the faithful but the Jews as well. In opposition to this false pope will come a truly holy pope who will renew the faithful through his fearless preaching of the gospel.[68] Nevertheless, as McGinn points out, Joachim's willingness to even consider the possibility of an apostate pope represents a very important step "on the road to the full-blown conception of a papal Antichrist."[69]

Therefore, with the continuing emphasis upon reforming the church from those within it who do not have its best interests at heart (antichrists), and with the influence of the apocalypticism of Joachim indicating that the seventh king, Antichrist, might arise within the church, a significant shift has been made. Before the rise of Christendom and the conversion of Constantine, Antichrist was associated with the Roman Empire and the imperial cult. After the rise and subsequent corruption of Christendom, Antichrist may actually be the titular head of Christ's body on earth, the church, since Antichrist is, above all else, a false christ. This is a huge shift in perspective, especially when coupled to a rediscovery of the writings of Adso, which circulated widely during the same period. Add to this a number of significant and negative historical circumstances—the lack of success of the Crusades to permanently liberate Jerusalem, the rise to power of Frederick II (who was excommunicated for not supporting the Crusades and threatening papal lands, and who was labeled "the beast from the sea" by Pope Gregory IX), the continued efforts to reform the church, the divided church as seen in the rise of the so-called Avignon Papacy (1348–77) and the great schism within the church—all of which led to a situation in which forerunners of the Reformation began to speak openly of the papacy as Antichrist.[70]

Rejecting outright the Adsonian notion that the Antichrist is a particular individual, in 1377 John Wycliffe began to speak of the papacy as an antichrist institution in its very essence, a point taken up by the Lollards in 1388. The Hussite movement of Eastern Europe was thoroughly galvanized when Jan Hus was burned for heresy on July 6, 1415, by what was perceived by his followers as the Antichrist church (Rome). Thus when the Reformation got underway, there was ample precedent to see in the papacy (as an office) and in its current occupant (the pope) the very visage of Antichrist.

Luther and Calvin

As Christopher Hill points out, "With Luther and the adoption of Lutheranism as a state religion in many countries, the doctrine that the Pope is Antichrist, hitherto associated with the disputable lower-class heretics, acquired a new respectability."[71] While in many ways Luther stands in direct continuity with Augustine on matters of eschatology, as well as with the late medieval notion that the Antichrist might arise within the church, Luther does break with medieval tradition by vehemently arguing that the papacy is the true and final Antichrist. For Luther, the rise of the Antichrist in the person of the pope meant that the end of the age was at hand.[72]

Early in his career, Luther struggled with his newfound conviction that the papacy may indeed be the seat of Antichrist.[73] But as he wrestled with this thought and became clear in his own mind of its truth, Luther had no problem identifying the papacy as the Antichrist. He repeatedly and vociferously argued that the destruction of the papacy (which Luther thought to be imminent) was the sign that the end was at hand.[74] Luther believed the papacy had become the focal point of anti-Christian power during the rule of Pope Gregory I (590–604), making the Roman Catholic Church the great harlot depicted by John in Revelation 17–18.[75] The papacy was, along with Islam, the supreme obstacle to the success of the gospel.[76] In Luther's estimation, both pope and Turk must be opposed by all Christians.

Martin Luther is a man who means what he says and says what he means. Since Luther had so much to say about the papacy, several representative quotes will suffice. According to Luther, "We are convinced that the papacy is the seat of the true and real Antichrist."[77] In another place Luther writes, "One is not obliged to expect any other Antichrist [than the papacy]. To have a worse regime on earth, one that kills more souls than does that of the pope, is impossible; of its extortion of bodily goods I shall say nothing. Therefore we must by all means cry and pray to God against this archrascal among God's enemies until Christ comes to redeem us from him. The pope is really the guilty one. Let every Christian say 'Amen.'"[78]

Elsewhere Luther stated,

> Why is it that the pope is so full of heresies and has introduced one after the other into the world until people at Rome, especially at the pope's court, are downright Epicureans and mockers of the Christian faith? The reason is that they fell away from the faith of Christ and relied on works, that is, on their own righteousness. Which of all the other articles was then of any further use to the pope? What good does it do him that his lips highly praise the true God, the Father, Son and Holy Ghost, and that he presents the impressive guise of a Christian life? Despite all this he is and remains the greatest enemy of Christ. He is and remains the true Antichrist.[79]

Luther believed that Paul's reference to the Man of Sin sitting in the temple (2 Thess. 2:1–12) is a reference to Antichrist, which is the papacy.[80] Luther declared that the "pope is the masked and incarnate devil because he is the Antichrist," and that Christians have been "warned about this deadly pestilence by Daniel, Christ, Paul, Peter and others."[81] Thus the opposition of the papacy to the newly recovered gospel meant that the pope is that blaspheming "little horn" seen by Daniel in his vision. While Luther believes that the *Schwärmer* (enthusiasts) are antichrists (in the sense John uses the plural "antichrists" in his Epistles), the supreme manifestation of Antichrist is the papacy.[82] For Luther, the unrestrained nature of Rome's opposition to the gospel meant that the end is at hand. "You should know that the pope is the real, true and final Antichrist, of whom the entire Scripture speaks, whom the Lord is beginning to consume with the spirit of his mouth and will very soon destroy and slay with the brightness of His coming for which we are waiting (2 Thess. 2:8)."[83] In fact, says Luther, the pope "is the real, head Antichrist, whom, God willing, our Lord Christ will shortly thrust into the abyss of hell by his advent. Amen."[84]

Luther's view soon became the official view of the Lutheran Church. In the "Apology" of the Augsburg Confession, it is affirmed, "If our opponents defend the notion that these human rites merit justification, grace and the forgiveness of sins, they are simply establishing the kingdom of Antichrist. The kingdom of Antichrist is a new kind of worship of God, devised by human authority in opposition to Christ. . . . So the papacy will also be a part of the kingdom of Antichrist if it maintains that human rites justify."[85]

Like Luther, John Calvin had no doubts as to the fact that the pope was the Antichrist. But unlike Luther, Calvin is much more measured in his comments.[86] In his commentary on 2 Thessalonians 2:4, Calvin dismisses the notion that Antichrist will be a Nero *redivivus*, calling the idea "an old wife's fable." Furthermore, Calvin is not impressed with those who see in this passage a reference to the Roman Empire—an idea Calvin says is "too stupid to need lengthy refutation."[87]

For Calvin, the identity of Antichrist is not to be found by looking to the past nor to the future but by looking to the present threat facing Christ's church—the papacy. According to Calvin, "Anyone who has learned from Scripture what are the things that belong to God, and who on the other hand considers well what the Pope usurps for himself, will not have much difficulty in recognizing Antichrist, even though he were a ten year old boy." Since the pope claims divine rights and privileges that belong to God alone, he clearly manifests that pride the biblical writers associated with Antichrist.[88] Quoting from Hilary of Poitiers, Calvin reminded King Francis I in the preface to his famed *Institutes of the Christian Religion* that "it is wrong that a love of walls has seized you; wrong that you venerate the church of God in roofs and buildings; wrong that beneath these you introduce the name of peace. Is there any doubt that Antichrist will have his seat in them?"[89]

When discussing the identity of the Antichrist and Paul's reference to that Man of Sin who sits "in the temple of God," Calvin writes,

> This one word fully refutes the error or rather the stupidity of those who hold the Pope to be the vicar of Christ on the ground that he has a settled residence in the Church, however he may conduct himself. Paul sets Antichrist in the very sanctuary of God. He is not an enemy from the outside but from the household of faith, and opposes Christ under the very name of Christ. The question, however, is asked how the Church may be referred to as the den of so many superstitions, when it was to be the pillar of the truth (1 Tim. 3:15). My answer is that it is so referred to not because it retains all the qualities of the Church, but because it has still some of them left. I admit, therefore, that it is the temple of God in which the Pope holds sway, but the temple has been profaned by sacrileges beyond number.[90]

Unlike Luther, Calvin was inclined to avoid eschatological speculation about when the end might come, choosing instead to emphasize the fact that the gospel must be proclaimed to the ends of the earth before the end of the age. In his comments on 2 Thessalonians 2:6, Calvin addresses the question of that which restrains the mystery of lawlessness. "Paul declared that the light of the Gospel must first be spread throughout every part of the world before God would give Satan his rein in this way." Says Calvin, "I think that I hear Paul speaking of the universal call of the Gentiles. The grace of God was to be offered to all, and Christ was about to enlighten the whole world by his gospel."[91] When the gospel is preached to the ends of the earth, only then shall come the end. Calvin avoids any temptation to speculate when that might occur.

According to Calvin, the term *Antichrist* "does not designate a single individual, but a single kingdom which extends throughout many generations."[92] Connecting this to the prophecy in Daniel 9:27, Daniel foretold that "Antichrist would sit in the Temple of God. With us, it is the Roman pontiff we make the leader and standard-bearer of that wicked and abominable kingdom."[93] Thus Antichrist is a not a particular individual but a kingdom that opposes the true church and the gospel. And the head of that kingdom is the pope.

Calvin is also concerned to harmonize Paul's teaching with that of John. In his commentary on John's first Epistle, when John speaks of the presence of many antichrists in the early church, Calvin takes him to refer to "certain sects [that have] already arisen which were fore-runners of a future scattering."[94] Here, Calvin emphatically states, "All marks by which the Spirit of God has pointed out antichrist appear clearly in the Pope."[95] The many antichrists faced by the apostolic church are to be understood as forerunners of the papacy.

While Calvin is sure that it is the word of God that slays Antichrist, he is not certain "whether [Paul] is speaking of the final appearing of Christ, when he will be revealed from heaven as judge." While Paul may not mean this is accomplished in a single moment, "we must therefore understand . . . that Antichrist would be completely and utterly destroyed when the last day of the restoration of all things will come." In the meantime, Christ will scatter the enemies of the church through the preaching of the gospel.[96] As Berkouwer points out, "Calvin was not worried greatly that the name of Christ or of the church would be wiped out. He was concerned that the antichrist 'misuses a semblance of Christ and lurks under the name of the church as under a mask.'"[97]

The Reformed Tradition and the Papal Antichrist

As even a brief survey will demonstrate, the belief that the pope was Antichrist was the universal conviction of Reformed Protestants.[98] Not only did Luther's protégé Philip Melanchthon hold this view, so did Calvin's successor, Theodore Beza. Strasbourg Reformer Martin Bucer also set forth this view in his famous work, *De Regno Christi*, as did the pastor-theologian of Zurich, Heinrich Bullinger.[99] Heidelberg theologian Francis Junius's commentary on Revelation—whose notes on Revelation were included in some editions of the Geneva Bible—named the pope as Antichrist, as did the author of the Heidelberg Catechism, Zacharius Ursinus, in his own theological textbook, *Summe of Christian Religion*.[100]

English Protestants including Tyndale, Cranmer, Ridley, Latimer, and Hooper also embraced this view. When Mary Tudor began her reign, it was said that "Antichrist has come again." John Knox believed the papacy was Antichrist, as did King James, who produced his own gloss on Revelation in 1588 in which he too argued that the pope was Antichrist. The Puritans were of one voice on this as well. Oliver Cromwell's mentor and friend, Thomas Beard, published a book entitled, *Antichrist and the Pope of Rome* in 1625, while John Jewell's commentary on Thessalonians identified the pope as the Man of Sin. Other well-known Puritans including Thomas Goodwin, Richard Sibbes, and John Owen affirmed the same position.[101] This belief was institutionalized in the Westminster Confession of Faith: "There is no other head of the church but the Lord Jesus Christ: nor can the Pope of Rome in any sense be head thereof; but is that antichrist, that Man of Sin, and son of perdition, that exalteth himself in the church against Christ, and all that is called God."[102]

If the Reformers and their theological descendants were of one mind about the identity of the Antichrist, they were likewise of one mind when it came to the general approach that one should take to interpret the Book of Revelation. The so-called "historicist" interpretation of Revelation "was so widely held that for a long time it was called the Protestant view."[103] While historicist commentators differed widely about the details of the various prophecies John reveals in the Apocalypse, they were all in agreement about the identity of two of the principal figures in Revelation, the beast and the Babylonian harlot—these are both prophetic references to the Roman Catholic Church and the papacy.[104] Thus in John's Apocalypse the great movements of history are predicted, whether that be the emergence of Gentile empires who attack the Holy Roman Empire, the ascent of the papacy, or even the rise of Islam and the Muslim threat to the West.

Reading Paul's Thessalonian letter through the same interpretive grid, historicist interpreters believe that Paul's Man of Sin setting himself up in the temple of God is a reference to the papacy. The harlot Babylon is identified with the Roman Catholic Church, and her spiritual adultery is committed with the kings of the earth—France, Spain, and Italy, all of whom opposed the Reformation faith with the power of the sword. In the mind of the historicist, the Book of Revelation foretells the great struggles facing the church, giving rise to repeated attempts by Protestants to tie contemporary events to the biblical text. In other words, the Bible did indeed foretell of their present struggles and circumstances. This approach to the Book of Revelation also meant that by carefully dating biblical history and prophecy, one could actually calculate the date of the Antichrist's appearing, an endeavor that was soon taken up with great zeal.[105]

Antichrist Speculation among the Puritans

Scotsman John Napier (1550–1617), who invented logarithms as a means of calculating the number of the beast, also calculated in his book, *Plain Discoverie of the Whole Revelation of St. John* (1594), that a time of trouble for the papacy would begin in 1639 and would be followed by the day of judgment in 1688 or 1700. Napier's views received great attention and were disseminated widely.[106] Another influential figure in this new frenzy to calculate the date of the fall of Antichrist and time of the end was Thomas Brightman (1562–1607). Brightman wrote two books defending the thesis that the papacy was the seat of Antichrist. In 1615 he published his famous work, *The Revelation of St. John*, in which he argued that the fall of the Roman Antichrist and the Turk were imminent. He believed that Rome would fall about 1650 and that the Antichrist would be overthrown as early as 1686.[107] Brightman's works were also widely read and quite influential among the Puritans, including Goodwin, Owen, and Thomas Shepherd.[108]

As the decade of the 1640s began and civil war was becoming inevitable in England, Antichrist speculation was rampant. The times were tumultuous, and great changes were taking place in the international balance of power. The defeat of the Spanish Armada (1588), the apostasy of Henry IV of France (1593), the Thirty Years War (1618–48), and then the English Civil War (1642–46) were all interpreted through the lens of apocalyptic fervor. According to Robert Godfrey, it was a widely held consensus among the Puritans that the world would end about 1650–56. This date was determined by using a benchmark date of AD 390 (the date of the supposed consolidation of the papacy), and then adding 1,260 years, the number mentioned in both Daniel and Revelation. Brightman dated the fall of Rome and the conversion of the Jews at around 1650. Biblical scholar Joseph Mede (1586–1638) looked for these events to occur between 1650 and 1715.[109]

Buoyed by the rise of congregationalism (in response to "divine right" Presbyterians and to what was thought to be the "little popes" in the form of the bishops of the Church of England), Thomas Goodwin began to contend that the decline of the papacy (Antichrist) and the Turks as well as the conversion of the Jews would occur no later than 1650–66.[110] Obviously, this was a time of great political and theological upheaval with eschatological expectations to match.

But as political events overtook theological speculation, another key factor in the increasingly rampant Antichrist speculation was the ascendancy of William Laud as Archbishop of Canterbury in 1633. While many accepted the "official position" of the Church of England that the pope was the Antichrist, some

Puritans believed that "too much of Antichrist remained in the English church," while others felt the Church of England was already too far gone and had become apostate. Then, there was an Arminian party in the church that did not accept the view that the pope was Antichrist.[111] Since Laud was a member of that group,[112] some Puritans thought Laud himself might be Antichrist. Thus Antichrist was no longer safely overseas; he might be in their very midst "setting up his throne in England."[113] Others thought King Charles I (1600–1649) might himself be the Antichrist, since Charles was an avowed Arminian, was married to a Roman Catholic (Henrietta Maria, daughter of the king of France), and was widely rumored to be secretly engaged in discussions with Rome.[114]

Things were turning for the better, however, and it looked like the prophecies of the end just might be coming to pass. The English Civil War, bloody as it was, resulted in the defeat of Charles I by the Scots. The Solemn League and Covenant was signed the same year as the meeting of the Westminster Assembly (1643). The trial and execution of King Charles I in 1649 greatly fueled speculation about the defeat of Antichrist, since many of the Puritans and their forebears had predicted that the fall of Antichrist would occur about this time. Such tumultuous events brought about a whole new wave of millennial expectation and eager anticipation of the second advent, effectively fanning the eschatological flames that had been burning in England for some time.[115] But with the restoration of the Stuart monarchy in 1660, such speculation quietly died down as the papacy regained strength. A millennial age had not dawned, and Christ had not returned. What began with a bang ended with a whimper.

Even as millennial fever and Antichrist expectation died down in England, it was being exported to the New England colony in America by a number of Puritan divines, including John Cotton (1584–1652), a Cambridge graduate who took up ministerial duties in Boston. An avowed congregationalist, Cotton held tenaciously to the view that the pope was Antichrist—although he believed that the Antichrist had infected the Church of England as well—and firmly believed that there was little hope of converting the American Indians in any great number until Antichrist had fallen and the end-times glory of the church was manifest.[116] John Cotton's legacy lived on in two of the brightest lights of Colonial America, Cotton Mather and Jonathan Edwards.

Jonathan Edwards—Antichrist and 1866

Much of New England Puritanism was premillennial in its eschatological orientation. But the American variety of pre-millennialism of the period was quite optimistic—unlike the dispensationalism of our contemporaries—anticipating that the establishment of a thriving colony in the New World would hasten the demise of the antichrist Catholic powers (Spain and France). Furthermore, world events seemed to indicate that the revelation of Antichrist was soon at hand. This satanic apocalypse of the Man of Sin would be immediately followed, of course, by his destruction and the second advent of Jesus Christ. All of these great world events, interpreted in light of the imminency of the end of the world, typical of Puritanism, would inevitably usher in the golden age of God's kingdom on earth.[117] Thus, despite divergent views about the precise nature and character of a millennial age, most New England Puritans were sure it was soon to dawn.

Cotton Mather (1663–1728) was the intellectual heir of the New England variety of Puritan millennial expectation. While there was in Puritan New England a substantial development of differing millennial views (both "pre" and "post"), both varieties of millenarianism were necessarily tied to the rise of Antichrist, since this eschatological foe of God's people must be destroyed before the great blessings of the kingdom could be realized upon the earth. Mather watched world events closely from his Boston home and "above all . . . was convinced that Antichrist's destruction was imminent and that the millennium was right around the corner."[118] This was the accepted orthodoxy of Puritan New England.

Unlike many of his premillennial forebears, Jonathan Edwards (1703–58) moved in a very distinct postmillennial direction, leaving behind a strong postmillennial legacy at the College of New Jersey (Princeton), as well as upon American theology in general. Influenced by the millennial views of Daniel Whitby,[119] Edwards is considered by one historian to hold the "distinction of being America's first major postmillennial thinker."[120] While Edwards's millennial views are widely known and oft discussed, he is not as well known for his Antichrist expectations.

Edwards also believed that Antichrist's destruction was imminent and that the end of the age was near. Despite his Puritan sobriety, Edwards believed that he was living at a critical turning point in redemptive history in which Christ's kingdom was soon to reach its final eschatological glory. As an important component of his emerging postmillennialism, Edwards believed the fall of the papacy, the conversion of the Jews, the defeat of Islam, and a last days glory for the church were all soon at hand.[121] Like most Reformed Christians, Edwards's grievance against the papacy was twofold. The papacy protected the Roman Catholic Church from further doctrinal reformation, and insofar as the rest of Christendom sought reform, the papacy persecuted it.[122] Thus the final Antichrist must appear and meet his doom so that the church might enter its millennial glory now that reformation could go forth unopposed.

In his *A History of the Work of Redemption*, which began as a series of sermons first preached in 1739 and envisioned to set an entire body of divinity in redemptive-historical form, Edwards sets out his rather distinctive view of the future course of redemptive history. Edwards divides redemptive history into three periods—from the fall to the incarnation, from Christ's incarnation to the resurrection, and then that period from Christ's resurrection until the end of the world. In his discussion of the third redemptive period, Edwards devotes considerable attention to the doctrine of Antichrist, especially chapters 3, 4, and 7.

Edwards argues that the millennial age will not arrive until "Antichrist is fallen, and Satan's visible kingdom on earth is destroyed." However, immediately before this millennial age

dawns, which may be imminent, "we have all reason to conclude from the Scriptures, that just before this work of God
begins, it will be a *very dark time* with respect to the interests
of religion in the world." This dark period, which Edwards may
even have viewed as his own age, will witness the great work
of God gradually though powerfully wrought by the Spirit of
God, "poured out for the wonderful revival and promulgation
of religion. . . . This pouring out of the Spirit of God, when it
is begun, shall soon bring multitudes to forsake that vice and
wickedness that generally prevails."[123] Antichrist will soon come
and go.

Following the traditional Protestant line of argument closely,
Edwards believed that the papacy was Antichrist. But Edwards
framed the traditional doctrine in distinctive ways. He believed
that the rise of Antichrist was a gradual event that commenced
in AD 606 with the rise of a universal papacy.

> The rise of Antichrist was gradual. . . . In primitive times, he was
> a minister of a congregation; then a standing moderator of a
> presbytery; then a diocesan bishop; then a metropolitan, which
> is equivalent to an archbishop; then a patriarch. Afterwards he
> claimed the power of a universal bishop over the whole Christian
> church; wherein he was opposed for a while, but afterwards was
> confirmed in it by the civil power of the emperor in the year six
> hundred and six. After that he claimed the power of a temporal
> prince, and so was wont to carry two swords, to signify that both
> the temporal and spiritual sword was his. He claimed more and
> more authority, till at length, as Christ's vice-gerent on earth,
> he claimed the same power that Christ would have done if he
> was present on earth reigning on his throne: or the same power
> belongs to God, and was used to be called God on the earth; to
> be submitted to by all the princes of Christendom.[124]

Yet despite cautioning his reader about setting dates, Edwards calculated that Antichrist would fall in 1866, coupled
with the conversion of the Jews and a latter-day glory for the
church.[125] Edwards states, "I am far from pretending to determine the time when the reign of Antichrist began, which is a
point that has been so much controverted among divines and

expositors," although he goes on to identify 606 as the likely time. He continues, "It has been certain that the twelve hundred and sixty days, or years, which are so often in Scripture mentioned as the time of continuance of Christ's reign, did not commence before the year of Christ four hundred and seventy-nine; because if they did, they would have ended, and Antichrist would have fallen before now."[126] If one begins at AD 606 (the rise of the papacy) and then adds 1,260 years, one arrives at a date of 1866. This is precisely what Edwards did, although he was doing nothing but what other Puritan writers before him had done.

After revival broke out in the 1740s (the so-called "Great Awakening"), Edwards came to believe that the end was nearer than he first thought. In a section of his essay *An Humble Attempt* (1748) dealing with the imminent fall of Antichrist, Edwards states that the fifth bowl of judgment of Revelation 16 is the Reformation and the sixth bowl is the defeat of the French and Spanish armadas (slowing the flow of gold in the Antichrist coffers of Catholic countries France and Spain). Edwards writes that it is his view that the slaying of the two witnesses is in the past and that "God's Spirit will begin in a little time, which, in the progress of it, will overthrow the kingdom of Antichrist."[127] Thus, the seventh bowl of judgment could be poured out at any moment, although this time Edwards backed off from setting a date.

Moderating Trends

Just as the Antichrist expectation among the English Puritans began to wane after the Restoration under Charles II, so too did Antichrist speculation wane in America after the Revolution. While many of the Sons of Liberty saw the fingerprints of the beast in English attitudes toward American independence and taxation, men who were preoccupied with building a nation were not as worried about the end of the age nor about the threat of a foreign Antichrist when they were protected by the great ocean.[128] There were a number of millenarian sects in America and some speculation about whether

Catholic France's new emperor Napoleon might be the beast, enough so that Ernest Sandeen could write that "America in the early nineteenth century was drunk on the millennium."[129] Nevertheless, two factors brought about a subtle yet significant change in Antichrist speculation, especially among the Reformed. These two factors were Enlightenment skepticism and the identification of an institution (the papacy) as Antichrist, not a particular pope. Both in their own way led to a marked downplaying among Protestants of a focus on a specific individual as Antichrist.[130]

Those influenced by Enlightenment skepticism tended to see Antichrist as mythological, just as they were beginning to do with the narrative materials in the Gospels. Antichrist must be a figment of the human mind facing uncertainty. He is a product of human fear. Those who see the Antichrist in the papacy as an institution rather than a particular pope will likewise no longer seek to identify an individual as the Antichrist.

One important instance of such moderation is found in Charles Hodge (1797–1878), famed Princeton Theological Seminary professor and the author of a widely read and influential theology text, *Systematic Theology* (1872–73). Hodge, who was postmillennial, argued in his treatment on the signs of the end (volume 3 of *Systematic Theology*) that three specific signs are to precede the coming of Christ. The first is the universal preaching of the gospel, the second is the national conversion of the Jews, and third is the coming of Antichrist. Hodge believed the Reformers were largely correct in their belief that the papacy is Antichrist, and states that Antichrist is an institution, not a person, and that what is in view is primarily an ecclesiastical power. Therefore the papacy is not the only Antichrist because John says there were many. Since the word *Antichrist* is a generic term, Paul may be describing one manifestation and Daniel another. But what they have in common is a boastful figure exalting himself above God. Hodge believes that the prophecies of Antichrist had partial fulfillments in Antiochus Epiphanes, Nero, and the papacy, and "may still have a fulfillment in some great anti-Christian power which is yet to appear."[131] Antichrist may be tied to the papacy, but more remains to be fulfilled.

After discussing the historic Protestant position that the pope is the Man of Sin and that the Babylonian harlot is the Roman Catholic Church, Hodge offers the following modification of the historic Protestant position:

> The great truth set forth in these prophecies is, that there was future in the time, not only of Daniel, but also of the Apostles, a great apostasy in the Church; that this apostasy would be Antichristian (or Antichrist), ally itself with the world and become a great persecuting power; and that the two elements, the ecclesiastical and the worldly, which enter into this great Antichristian development, will, sometimes the one and sometimes the other, become the more prominent; sometimes acting in harmony, and sometimes opposed one to the other; and, therefore, sometimes spoken of as one, and sometimes as two distinct powers. Both, as united or as separate, are to be overtaken with a final destruction when the Lord comes. So much is certain, that any and every power, be it one or more, which answers to the description given in Daniel vii and xi and in 2 Thessalonians ii is Antichrist in the Scriptural sense of the term.[132]

For Hodge, then, Antichrist is an institution (the papacy) or a world power but not a particular individual. Antichrist is tied to apostasy in the church, so there is no need for a rebuilt temple in Jerusalem. There may indeed be some sort of religious dimension tied to political power, but the key features are blasphemy toward God, apostasy from the true faith, and the persecution of the saints. This Antichrist institution—in whatever form it takes, religious or secular—will be destroyed by Christ at his return. Since the Antichrist is an institution, Hodge is not interested in any particular candidate. Nor is he interested in speculating about when this might occur. This view, or variations thereof, becomes the mainstream Reformed/ Presbyterian doctrine of Antichrist.

Another example of a moderation of the traditional Protestant view is found in Louis Berkhof, who largely agrees with Hodge's basic assessment, although he is reticent to identify the papacy directly with Antichrist. While Berkhof prefers to speak of "elements of Antichrist in the papacy," unlike Hodge, Berkhof believes that Antichrist will be an "eschatological person, who will be the incarnation of all wickedness and therefore represents a spirit which is always more or less present in the world, and who has several types or precursors in history." This anti-Christian principle was already at work in the apostolic age and will reach its highest power at the end of the age. Daniel pictures its political manifestation, Paul its ecclesiastical manifestation, and John may picture both. According to Berkhof, Scripture clearly teaches that a particular individual is in view because he both imitates the incarnation of Christ and is personally cast into the lake of fire at the time of the end.[133]

The Roman Catholic Response

The very thought that the leader of the Roman Catholic Church is Antichrist is understandably repugnant to the Catholic faithful. Although some, such as Joachim of Fiore, had argued that a particular pope might be a deceiver of the faithful, the Protestant challenge that the papacy as an institution is Antichrist required a response. In the Reformation era, Luther's foe, Johann Eck (1486–1543), replied to Luther's comments about the papacy by returning the favor. Eck contended that Martin Luther was either the Antichrist or at the very least his forerunner.[134] A noted Dominican preacher of the period, Vincent Ferrer, had predicted shortly before Luther's birth that the precursor to Antichrist was already alive and even enumerated some of the characteristics of this person in his preaching. This not only raised Antichrist expectation on the eve of the Reformation, but once the Reformation got underway, it gave Roman apologists a convenient way to argue that Luther's efforts to recover the gospel were part of this revelation of Antichrist. This same theme can be seen in the book *Concerning the Antichrist* (1632), in which Dominican friar Tommaso Campanella identified Luther, Calvin, Wycliffe, and Muhammad as men who prepared the world for Antichrist. These were all precursor antichrists, preparing the way for *l'Antichristo Massimo*.[135]

At the time of the counter-Reformation and the promulgation of the decrees and canons of Trent (1545–63), Jesuit theologians began to make the case that the papacy could not be Antichrist because the Antichrist was still yet to be revealed—in effect, restating the views of many of the church fathers and Adso. In fact, the leading Jesuit theologian from this period, Robert Bellarmine, wrote extensively on the subject in his *Disputations*, written directly in response to the Reformation. Bellarmine argued that the Antichrist was still future because there were six signs connected to his coming, none of which were fulfilled in Bellarmine's day. While the Reformers were preparing the way for the future Antichrist, Bellarmine believed that Antichrist was a particular individual whose appearance would mark the end of world history. Therefore, the papacy cannot be Antichrist.[136] The other noted Jesuit theologian from this period, Francis Suarez (1548–1617), took the same basic approach as Bellarmine, likewise arguing that Protestants were wrong in their identification of the papacy as Antichrist, since Antichrist will appear at the time of the end.[137]

Various Reformers (and reforming movements) are often identified by Catholic writers as forerunners of Antichrist along the lines set forth by Vincent Miceli.[138] These figures and issues can be enumerated as follows:

2nd century —Gnostics, Docetists, Marcionites, Montanists

3rd century —Manicheans

4th century —Eutychians, Donatists, Macedonians, Arians

5th century —Monophysites, Nestorians, Pelagians

6th century —Semi-Pelagians

7th century —Monothelites

8th century —Iconoclasts

9th century —Iconoclasts

10th century —Simony and abuses

11th century —Berengerians (attacked transubstantiation)

12th century —Albigenses (dualists, followers of Mani, perfectionistic), Waldensians (simple evangelical sect)
13th century —Albigenses
14th century —Wycliffe
15th century —the "great schism," two antipopes at same time
16th century —Luther, Calvin, Zwingli, Henry VIII
17th century —Jansenists (Augustinians), rationalists
18th century —Jansenists, Quietists
19th century —Modernists, Old Catholics
20th century —Neo-Modernists, Teilhardists

The official Catholic position regarding the Antichrist is set forth in the *Catechism of the Catholic Church* (1994):

675. Before Christ's second coming the Church must pass through a final trial that will shake the faith of many believers. The persecution that accompanies her pilgrimage on earth will unveil the "mystery of iniquity" in the form of a religious deception offering men an apparent solution to their problems at the price of apostasy from the truth. The supreme religious deception is that of the Antichrist, a pseudo-messianism by which man glorifies himself in place of God and of his Messiah come in the flesh.

676. The Antichrist's deception already begins to take shape in the world every time the claim is made to realize within history that messianic hope which can only be realized beyond history through the eschatological judgment. The Church has rejected even modified forms of this falsification of the kingdom to come under the name of millenarianism, especially the "intrinsically perverse" political form of a secular messianism.[139]

SOUNDS LIKE DOUBLE-SPEAK

This view depersonalizes Antichrist (the church fathers thought he would be a Jew) and states that the deception of Antichrist is tied to self-deification and some form of apostasy before the time of the end (Christ's second coming).

8

THE ANTICHRIST

Figure of the Past or Future Foe?

Summing Up the Evidence So Far

We have come to the point in our study when it is time to summarize both the biblical data regarding Antichrist and the conclusions reached in earlier chapters. Based upon the ground we have already covered, it is my contention that Christ's church will face two significant threats associated with Antichrist. The first of these threats is a series of antichrists who arise within the church and are tied to a particular heresy—the denial that Jesus Christ is God in human flesh. This threat has been with us since the days of the apostles and will be present until the time of the end. The second threat is the repeated manifestation of the beast throughout the course of history, taking the form of state-sponsored persecution of Christ's church, which will finally culminate in an end-times Antichrist. It is likely that these two distinct threats combine into a single threat at the time of the end. To use Warfield's phrase, they do indeed form a "composite photograph."

Antichrist will be the supreme persecutor of Christ's church and will exercise his reign of terror through state-sponsored heresy, taking a form similar to the emperor worship John describes in Revelation. John depicts this as a counterfeit Trinity of sorts—an unholy collaboration between the dragon (Satan), the beast (the state), and the false prophet (the state's leader). Since this figure is a false christ who mimics our Lord's redemptive work, he will manifest his own death, resurrection, and second advent. In opposition to the City of God (the New Jerusalem) even now coming down out of heaven, the beast will seduce the harlot-city Babylon and proclaim it the "City of Man." The beast's number, 666, indicates that he can never enter God's rest nor rise to deity. All of this takes place against the backdrop of the Old Testament. The City of Man's first builder was Cain, followed in turn by Lamech, Nimrod, and a host of others. In Revelation 18, the city of man which first rose on the plains of Shinar has come full-flower in the form of Babylon the Great, only to meet its demise at the hands of those who built it.

The Christian confession that "Jesus is Lord" is the supreme offense to the beast, who craves the worship of his subjects. Whenever Christians refuse to pay this individual and his government the homage they demand, believers will pay the price. There will be economic consequences, and the faithful, at times, will be prevented from conducting ordinary commerce (buying and selling). Some will pay with their lives because the beast will ruthlessly kill those who will not worship him or his image.

Paul calls this evil end-times figure the "man of lawlessness" (or the man of sin) in 2 Thessalonians 2:1–12. Paul tells us that this individual arises within the church (the temple of God), proclaims himself to be God's equal, demands to be worshiped, and is empowered by Satan to perform deceptive signs and wonders. The Man of Sin is likely connected to the end-times beast John sees, who arises from the Abyss at the time of the end to do the bidding of the dragon (cf. Rev. 17:11; 20:7–10). Like Paul's Man of Lawlessness, the beast also craves the worship of the world's inhabitants and is empowered by his master to perform signs and wonders designed to deceive those who worship him. The language used of him, *Man* of Sin, coupled with the fact that he is cast into the lake of fire, seems to support the idea that what is in view is a particular individual who is said to rise from the Abyss when empowered by the dragon at the time of the end.

The beast's power is economic and military, but it is ultimately given him by the dragon. He will be a persecutor on the order of Pharaoh, Nebuchadnezzar, and Domitian and will commit acts of blasphemy that make the desecrations of Antiochus IV, Titus, and Nero pale by comparison. Therefore, these figures from redemptive history should serve to prepare us to face the future. For God not only destroyed them all, he delivered his people from their clutches, just as he will destroy the Antichrist and deliver his church when conditions become most desperate.

This final manifestation of Antichrist, then, is state-enforced heresy—the worship of the state and its leader—and is connected to a time of great apostasy (2 Thess. 2:3; Rev. 20:7–10). Antichrist's final destruction is brought about by the second advent of Jesus Christ (2 Thess. 2:8; Rev. 17:14; 19:19–21; 20:7–10). As Tregelles puts it, "Just as the Lord triumphed over Satan in His resurrection, so will He manifest His power in destroying the dominion of Satan, even though it may seem at the very time to be especially triumphing in opposition to God."[1] Just when the hour is darkest, Christ will appear in all his glory to judge the world, raise the dead, and make all things new.

Antichrist or antichrists?

The term *antichrist* is used in two senses throughout this discussion. The narrow or biblical usage of the term refers to those individuals spoken of in John's Epistles who are the manifestation of the spirit of antichrist within the church and who deny that Jesus is God come in the flesh (1 John 2:18, 22; 4:3; 2 John 7). Many such antichrists have already come and gone. Until the return of Christ, many more will come. In this sense, then, antichrist is both a past and present foe. As Warfield reminds us, John warns us about him not to satisfy our curiosity about dates and times, but to prepare us to do combat with him.[2] We combat the spirit of antichrist with the truth of the gospel, not with the force of arms.

According to John's Epistles, many antichrists were already present in the apostolic church—the fact that they are is the primary sign that it is "the last hour" (1 John 2:18). Through-out his Epistles, John describes antichrist in terms of heresy or apostasy, which means that this is an internal threat that arises within the church. These antichrists are likely related to our Lord's warnings about false christs (Matt. 24:4–5, 23–24; Mark 13:5–6, 21–22; Luke 21:8), Paul's warnings about false teachers (e.g., 1 Tim. 4:1; 2 Tim. 3:1–9), and Peter's warning about false prophets (2 Peter 2:1). In this narrow sense, then, antichrist is anyone who denies that Jesus Christ is God in the flesh. The spirit of antichrist is already present (1 John 4:3) and is probably tied to the secret power of lawlessness, which is presently being restrained (2 Thess. 2:7). While the end-times Antichrist has not yet come (or has not yet been revealed), many antichrists have already made their appearance.

The theological use of the term *Antichrist*, on the other hand, refers to the composite picture of that eschatological individual who opposes God and persecutes God's people at the time of the end and who is destroyed by our Lord at his second advent. John speaks of Antichrist's personal destruction in the lake of fire (Rev. 19:20). He is mentioned in Paul's second letter to the Thessalonians, where he is called "the man of lawlessness" (2:3), another indication that a particular individual (not an impersonal system of thought or an institution) is in view. He is described by John in Revelation 11:7; 17:8; and 20:7 as the beast who arises from the Abyss at the time of the end. In an obvious parody of the redemptive work of Christ, this beast of Revelation 11, 17, and 20 is the final manifestation (parousia) of the two beasts who were persecuting the church at the time

John was given his vision (Revelation 13). When we use the term *Antichrist* in its broad or theological sense, we are referring to this eschatological personage who appears at the time of the end.

The Man of Lawlessness: A Rebuilt Temple or the Church? Is He the Pope?

According to Paul (2 Thess. 2:1–12), the day of the Lord had not already come (as some feared) because two things had not yet occurred—a great apostasy and the revelation of the Man of Lawlessness. Even though Paul wrote 2 Thessalonians before AD 70 (AD 50–51), he is probably not referring to the events of AD 70 but to the time of the end (v. 8). The spirit of lawlessness (*anomia*) was already present when Paul wrote his letter, but it was presently being restrained (v. 7). This restraint probably refers to the preaching of the gospel and is Paul's description of what John refers to in Revelation 20:1–10 as Satan being "bound."

When the apostasy does occur, the revelation of the Man of Lawlessness is at hand (2 Thess. 2:3–8). These are concomitant events. The revelation of the one (the Man of Lawlessness) is connected to the other (the apostasy). Paul also connects the revelation of the Man of Lawlessness to the day of judgment at the second advent (vv. 8–10). This evil man is revealed so that he (and those who follow him) will be judged, bringing history to its final culmination.

When Paul refers to the Man of Sin sitting in the temple, he's referring to the church on earth when the apostasy occurs and when the Man of Lawlessness is revealed—not to the Jerusalem temple in either AD 70 (contra preterism) nor to a rebuilt temple in Jerusalem at the time of the end (contra futurists—including the church fathers, dispensationalists, and historic premillenarians).

Paul's reference to the Man of Lawlessness does not refer to the papacy, since Paul is not referring to a series of individuals who may come and go (an institution) but to a particular individual who is destroyed by Christ at his second advent.[3] That being said, Berkhof is correct when he speaks of "elements of Antichrist in the papacy."[4] The papacy has, at times, manifested characteristics like those described by Paul. The union of pope and prince in the sixteenth century intent upon destroying the Reformed churches may serve as a type of what the end-times revelation of the Man of Lawlessness and his blasphemous behavior will be like.

How Is Antichrist Related to the Beast of Revelation 13?

When John speaks of the two beasts in Revelation 13 (the beast from the sea and the beast from the earth), he is speaking of the Roman Empire and its imperial cult. The beast from the sea (vv. 1–10) refers to the imperial cult in Rome. The key figure in this is Nero, under whose reign the persecution of Christians began. Nero represents all forms of wickedness and ungodliness. Nero had Peter and Paul put to death in Rome. Nero blamed Christians for the great fire, which began a period of ruthless persecution of Christians in Rome. He was censured by the Roman Senate, took his own life, but was widely rumored to have survived or to have come back from the dead. The Nero *redivivus* myth underlies John's discussion of the beast and his mimicking of Christ's work of redemption—his death, resurrection, and parousia.

The beast from the earth (vv. 11–18) refers to the imperial cult and its priests in Asia Minor at the time John was given the series of visions we know as the Book of Revelation (about AD 95). The key figure in this imperial cult is Domitian (the beast come back to life) and the renewed persecution of Christians throughout the area, especially Pergamum (where Antipas had been martyred some time earlier, Rev. 2:13) and Smyrna (where Christians were facing severe economic repression and were unable to buy and sell, Rev. 2:8–11). The imperial cult (including the Commune of Asia) was much more active in Asia Minor than in Rome. Domitian was very active in persecuting Christians throughout Asia Minor, especially in those years immediately before John received his vision.

The identification of a city with seven hills (Rome) and a series of rulers (Caesars) then in power when John received his revelation means that the beast was a foe presently persecuting the apostolic church when John was given his vision. While preterists are correct to emphasize the significance of John's statement that "the time is near" (Rev. 1:3) and to recognize that John is writing to Christians already suffering from Roman persecution, ultimately the preterist interpretation cannot be sustained. Not only does the evidence point to John being given this revelation after AD 70 (see the appendix), but preterist interpretations of the beast, his image, and his number are not exhaustively fulfilled by Nero and the events of AD 70 with the destruction of Jerusalem and its temple (Rev. 17:9–14) since both Nero and the events associated with the destruction of the temple may point ahead to another fulfillment at the end of the age. This is especially the case if some of these prophecies have double fulfillments (e.g., the Olivet Discourse—Matt. 24:10–25) and if the beast of Revelation 17 is an eschatological figure (an eighth king) who will appear at the time of the end.

Futurist interpretations of the connection between the Antichrist and the beast of Revelation 13 are highly problematic as well. The biblical data clearly speaks of antichrists and the beast as present realities during the apostolic age. These images cannot be pushed ahead to the time of the end, thereby virtually ignoring the historical context of John's vision. Therefore, the dispensational variety of futurism (the idea that Antichrist is revealed at or about the time of the rapture and the dawn of the seven-year tribulation period in connection with a peace treaty with Israel) collapses under its own weight.

As we have seen, in 2 Thessalonians 2 Paul is not referring to the Jerusalem temple in any sense. He's referring to the church. If true, the futurist interpretation of this data means that Christians of the first century were wrong to assume that John was writing about events contemporaneous to them. John is *really* writing to people living at the time of the end, not to Christians in the first century. This, of course, is not the case.

What Is the Mark of the Beast?

The mark of the beast (the number of humanity—"perfectly imperfect") is tied to the state's usurpation of divine prerogatives and attributes. Those who take the mark of the beast do so in the context of the worship of the state and its leaders in such a way as to either deny their faith in Jesus Christ (apostasy) or confess that "Caesar is Lord." The number 666 may indeed be a reference to Nero, but Nero does not exhaust what is thereby signified, especially if Revelation was written after AD 70. This mark and number are a reoccurring phenomena tied to the continual reappearing of the beast seeking the worship and adoration that belongs only to the true and living God.

Gematria, or the practice or substituting letters for numbers, may indeed point in the direction of Nero. But even if Nero is referred to, we should be aware of the theological significance of the number. It is more important to understand what the number means than to identify the individual to whom it is referring. Six falls one short of seven (the number of completeness). The beast mimics Christ but always falls short. Six represents fallen humanity, always laboring, but never entering the Sabbath rest. The triple sixes indicate the beast who, along with the dragon (Satan) and the second beast (or false prophet), mimics the Holy Trinity and is condemned to fall short of completeness. The beast can never rise above humanity to deity.

At the time John used this image, slaves were branded or tattooed by their owners. Thus anyone who "takes the mark" is branded as a slave of the beast and consciously renounces Christ to their eternal peril. Our dispensational friends miss the point when they are preoccupied with investigating which forms of technology can be used to create body markings or a cashless society. They come closer to the truth when they warn us about government usurping its God-given role and seeking the adoration and worship owed to God by his people. This is a real and pressing threat to all Christians. The worship of the state or its leaders in all of its forms is a false religion. It is the very essence of the beast.

Therefore, any state that usurps divine authority and honor and insists upon the worship of the state or its leaders can be said to be engaged in this practice. This can be seen, for example, in the swastika and Nazi salute to Hitler—relatively recent manifestations of the mark. The usurpation of divine authority by the state is seen in the efforts of the second beast (Rev. 13:11–18), who is the false prophet (Rev. 16:13), to deceive the earth's inhabitants into worshiping the beast (the state) and his image (its leader).

Is an Antichrist Yet to Come?

Many antichrists will come and go, but the series of anti-christs faced by the church from the beginning will at some point give way to an Antichrist—the final heretic, arch-blas-phemer, and persecutor of God's people. According to Paul (2 Thessalonians) and John (Revelation 20), the spirit of law-lessness and Satan are already at work, but they are presently restrained through the preaching of the gospel. Both Paul and John expect that restraint to be lifted immediately before Christ returns. Therefore, various beasts (governments) and their lead-ers and henchmen will come and go until one final manifes-tation of satanic rage and deception breaks out immediately before the Lord returns.

The fact that such anti-Christian empires or nations and their satanically inspired leaders come and go means that many attempts by Christians in the past to identify the beast and the Antichrist may have merit, although the date-setting that was often attached to this does not. In an age when the Roman Catholic Church was able to exert political power and papal sanction against Protestants through allied nations and their armies, Protestants were absolutely justified in identify-ing the Roman Catholic Church and those nations allied with it (Spain, Italy, and France) as the beast and the papacy as the seat of Antichrist. Yet the preaching of the gospel restrained Catholic nations from destroying those churches that embraced the doctrine of justification, *sola fide*. Furthermore, historical circumstances have changed greatly in the centuries that have followed. The unholy alliance between pope and prince has been replaced by socialist democracies that are virtually secularized and threaten no one.

Based upon John's discussion of the beast and the harlot Babylon, the final manifestation of the beast and its leader will not be so much a Nero *redivivus* but a beast *redivivus*. If we want to know what the Antichrist and his kingdom will be like, we look to the Roman Empire and the imperial cult already present in the pages of the New Testament, taking the lives of God's people and preventing them from buying and selling. This is what the final beast will seek to do—wage war upon the saints because they refuse to worship him or his blasphemous image. But the beast will be destroyed by the Lamb who has already overcome him! If John is clear about anything, it is that the Lamb wins in the end, not the dragon. When Satan and his surrogates wage war on the saints and kill them (Rev. 13:7), John tells us that the saints come to life and will reign with Christ for a thousand years (Rev. 20:4).

Hope, Not Fear

One lesson we must learn is that we need to be very cautious about setting dates and identifying particular persons as the Antichrist. The biblical writers speak of things associated with the time of the end as a mystery (Rom. 11:25; 1 Cor. 15:51) or as something that requires wisdom in order to understand (Rev. 13:18; 17:9). We have been cautioned that this phenomena is connected to the great apostasy and is currently prevented from appearing by some form of divine restraint (2 Thessalonians with Revelation 20). Only God knows when these things will come to pass. Since God gives his people wisdom without measure (James 1:5), when the time comes, we will know what these prophecies mean. But not before.

We also need to learn to avoid predictions from the examples in our own tradition and the sincere but futile efforts by the Puritans and Jonathan Edwards to tie biblical prophecy to current events, to set dates, and to identify the Antichrist by name. As McGinn correctly points out, "No age in Christian history has lacked its own ingenious proofs of the imminence of the time of the end."[5] Yet this is the nature of an ongoing threat, especially when that threat is expected to come to a dramatic and climactic end. While our forefathers may have been largely correct in their identification of the beast (the signs were certainly present in some measure), it was simply not God's time for the restraint to be lifted and the beast to attain its final fury.

Will there be an Antichrist? Yes, there will. But we need to take note of Anthony Hoekema's caution in this regard: "We conclude that the sign of the antichrist, like the other signs of the times, is present throughout the history of the church. We may even say that every age will provide its own particular form of antichristian activity. But we look for an intensification of this sign in the appearance of the antichrist whom Christ himself will destroy at his Second Coming."[6]

Thus we must be very cautious, yet ever vigilant. Our focus should be upon the means by which God restrains the principle of lawlessness—the gospel—and we must not spend our energies upon useless speculation. Our hope as Christians lies not in our powers of prognostication but in the ultimate and final victory of the Lamb. As Geerhardus Vos reminds us,

> [The prophecy of Antichrist] belongs among the many prophecies, whose best and final exegete will be the eschatological fulfillment, and in regard to which it behooves the saints to exercise a peculiar kind of eschatological patience.
>
> The idea of Antichrist in general and that of the apostasy in particular ought to warn us, although this may not have been the proximate purpose of Paul, not to take for granted an uninterrupted progress of the cause of Christ through all ages on toward the end. . . . The making all things right and new in the world depend not on gradual amelioration but on the final interposition of God.[7]

We long not for an earthly utopia in which the City of Man becomes the City of God. The harlot Babylon cannot be fumigated and remodeled. We do not long for an earthy millennium in which a fallen world is whitewashed for a time, with sinful human nature still present beneath the serene veneer. No, we long for the same thing Abraham did—a heavenly country and a heavenly city (Heb. 11:16). For as God promised Abraham, even now he is preparing this very thing for his people. This will become a glorious reality when Jesus Christ returns, not before.

The New Testament never holds out the hope that Babylon (the City of Man) will become the New Jerusalem (the City of God). Vos is correct. The New Testament teaches that when the seventh trumpet sounds at the time our blessed Lord returns, then "the kingdom of the world has become the kingdom of our Lord and of his Christ, and he will reign for ever and ever" (Rev. 11:15). The dragon, the beast, the false prophet, and all who serve them will be cast into the lake of fire, no longer a threat to the peace and safety of the kingdom of God. As John says, "I saw the Holy City, the new Jerusalem, coming down out of heaven from God, prepared as a bride beautifully dressed for her husband. And I heard a loud voice from the throne saying, 'Now the dwelling of God is with men, and he will live with them. They will be his people, and God himself will be with them and be their God'" (Rev. 21:2–3). The great covenant promise has been finally realized—God will dwell in our midst—and no longer will there be any curse, no tears, no sadness, and no sorrow. Nor will there be any trace of the harlot Babylon.

Instead of fearing and dreading the Antichrist and worrying about the latest events in the Middle East or whether the number 666 appears on a household product ID, we should be longing for the second coming of Jesus Christ. For Satan and his cronies have already been defeated by the blood and righteousness of Jesus, although for a time they will run amuck because they know their time is short. Regarding the fate of our enemy, Martin Luther perhaps said it best: "One little word shall fell him." Amen. Even so, come quickly, Lord Jesus!

APPENDIX

THE DATE OF THE WRITING
OF THE BOOK OF REVELATION

A theological position is only as strong as its weakest point. The preterist interpretation of the doctrine of the Antichrist and the beast is based upon the fact that John was supposedly given his apocalyptic vision before the fall of Jerusalem in AD 70. This allows preterists to identify the beast of the Book of Revelation with Nero, thereby limiting antichrist to the series of heretics mentioned in John's Epistles who will plague the church until the Lord's return. According to preterists, the events of Revelation 13–18 lie in the past and were fulfilled in the first century. This means there will be no future manifestation of a Nero-like beast or an Antichrist who will persecute the church immediately before our Lord's return at the end of the age.

If it can be shown that the Book of Revelation was written after AD 70, the preterist interpretation of the beast as entirely a figure of the past is not tenable. While the case for the view of Antichrist and the beast presented in this book is surely strengthened by a post–AD 70 dating of Revelation (through the elimination of a competing view), the overall case for my position is not dependent upon the date when the Book of Revelation was written. It should be noted that not all of those who advocate a pre–AD 70 date for the writing of Revelation would fall into the preterist camp. Ken Gentry, the author of *Before Jerusalem Fell*, a significant book arguing for a pre–AD 70 date, holds the preterist position.[1] But a number of other noted advocates of an early date would not, such as John A. T. Robinson, J. M. Ford, and the three famed New Testament scholars who dominated biblical scholarship in the English-speaking world from 1860 to 1900, J. B. Lightfoot, B. F. Westcott, and F. J. A. Hort.[2] In my estimation, many of the prophecies regarding the Antichrist involve double fulfillment, which means that neither an exclusively preterist nor a futurist interpretation will make the best sense of the biblical data.

While many New Testament scholars and commentators readily acknowledge that there is no way to determine with certainty when the Book of Revelation was written and are, therefore, willing to acknowledge that a pre–AD 70 date for its composition is possible,[3] the consensus of current and historical New Testament scholarship is that John's vision was recorded long after AD 70, likely in the midnineties of the first century.[4] To this end, many commentators approvingly cite the sage words of J. P. M. Sweet: "To sum up, the earlier date may be right, but the internal evidence is not sufficient to outweigh the firm tradition [for the later date] stemming from Irenaeus."[5]

While counting the number of scholars who hold one view over another to see where the majority come down is not an argument in favor of a given position, this can tell us where the consensus of opinion falls and therefore indicate which side assumes the burden of proof. In this case, critical scholarship is largely in agreement with the vast majority of evangelical scholars who hold that Revelation was written about twenty-five years after Jerusalem fell to the Romans, probably during the time of the Roman emperor Domitian (81–96) about AD 95.[6] While there is no "smoking gun" proving beyond all doubt the post–AD 70 date for the writing of Revelation, a strong case can be made for the later date based upon the internal evidence within the Book of Revelation itself, a case which is only strengthened by our ever-growing knowledge of the first-century world (external evidence).

Many of the arguments used by those who argue for a pre–AD 70 date for Revelation are quite plausible at first glance. In the end, however, these arguments are supported neither by the majority of the external facts nor by the internal evidence. It also must be noted that arguments used for dating Revelation are strictly probabilistic in nature. To determine when this book was likely written requires a final judgment based upon a careful and objective weighing of the facts, with the outcome based upon the preponderance of the evidence. This question cannot be settled by creating a case to justify the predetermined outcome that our Lord returned in the clouds to judge Israel in AD 70—which is the sense I get from several preterist writers arguing for an early date for Revelation. In order to prove that the Lord returned in AD 70, preterists must prove that Revelation was written prior to AD 70. Therefore, having already made a determination about the date of the Lord's return, an argument is then constructed to argue for a pre–AD 70 date for the writing of Revelation. Such arguments may be internally plausible, but they are intrinsically circular and not necessarily supported by the facts at hand.

Arguments Favoring a Pre–AD 70 Date

Argument #1: In Revelation 11:1–12, John supposedly mentions the Jerusalem temple as though it is currently standing when he was given his vision.[7] If the temple was still standing when John recorded his vision, then the Book of Revelation must have been written before the temple's destruction at the hands of the Romans in AD 70. The passage reads as follows: "I was given a reed like a measuring rod and was told, 'Go and measure the temple of God and the altar, and count the worshipers there. But exclude the outer court; do not measure it, because it has been given to the Gentiles. They will trample on the holy city for 42 months'" (Rev. 11:1–2). If John is speaking of the temple in Jerusalem and it was still standing when John was given this vision, this demands a date of composition before the temple was destroyed.[8]

The post–AD 70 response to this interpretation is to simply notice the highly symbolic language throughout the passage that obviously points the reader in the direction away from that of the physical temple in Jerusalem. As G. B. Caird reminds us, "In a book in which all things are expressed in symbols, the very last things the temple and the holy city could mean would be the physical temple and earthly Jerusalem."[9] Caird points out that if John is referring to the Jerusalem temple, then a rather remarkable thing is said to occur—the Gentiles (who, according to the pre–AD 70 dating, would mean the armies of Titus—cf. Luke 21:24) occupy the outer court for three and a half years, but they leave the inner court (the altar) undefiled. This, of course, did not happen when the temple was destroyed and lacks any historical connection to the actual events of AD 70. This also ignores John's use of the metaphors of the outer court and the inner sanctuary where the altar is. However, the passage does make perfect sense if the temple had already been destroyed when John writes. The time of the Gentiles was already underway because the outer court was presently being trampled, while the true sanctuary (the heavenly temple) remains undefiled because it is protected by God.[10] The church on earth suffers while the church in heaven triumphs.

Revelation 11:3–11 tells of the two witnesses who prophesy for the same time period as the outer court is trampled by the Gentiles (1,260 days or 42 months), who exercise miracle power (which recalls to mind Moses and Elijah), and who then are slain by the beast in the great city called Sodom and Egypt (more on this below) only to be raised from the dead. Based on this account, the time period is very likely a symbolic description of the inter-advental period, not the time immediately before the temple is destroyed (the lifetime of the apostles until AD 70).[11] In fact, the measurements given John by the angel do not reflect the historical temple in Jerusalem at all. Instead they fit the heavenly temple depicted in Ezekiel 40–48[12] and which, as some have thought, may refer to "the spiritual building of the church."[13] It is also very important to recall that John is not instructed to measure a temple supposedly still standing in Jerusalem. John is instructed to measure the temple he sees before him in his heavenly vision. Therefore, the mention of "42 months" and the time of the Gentiles are much more likely references to that time between our Lord's first and second coming and not to that period of time immediately before AD 70 when Christians were warned to flee from Jerusalem when they saw that it had been surrounded by the armies of Titus.

Argument #2: In Revelation 17:9–11, John writes, "This calls for a mind with wisdom. The seven heads are seven hills on which the woman sits. They are also seven kings. Five have fallen, one is, the other has not yet come; but when he does come, he must remain for a little while. The beast who once was, and now is not, is an eighth king. He belongs to the seven and is going to his destruction." According to most commentators, this is a reference to the city of Rome and its seven hills.[14] The seven hills are also symbolic of seven kings. According to verse 10, the sixth king is in power when John writes. Therefore, if the first in this series of kings is either Augustus or Julius Caesar, then the sixth king is either Galba or Nero, both of whom reigned before AD 70.[15] If this is the case, then the chronology of the passage requires a pre–AD 70 date.

But as Beale and others have pointed out, there are a number of problems with such a historical identification. With what emperor does one begin counting? Are all emperors to be counted or only those who participated in the imperial cult? What about the short-term rulers who came between Nero and Vespasian? More importantly, how does one deal with Revelation 17:11? There we read of "the beast who once was, and now is not, [who] is an eighth king. He belongs to the seven and is going to his destruction."[16] How does this list of seven kings fit with the ten kings of Revelation 17:12?

Either John is teaching a literal resurrection of one of the earlier kings (hence the Nero myth) or else this is symbolic language that points us in the direction of a nonliteral interpretation of this succession of leaders. In fact, according to Beasley-Murray, "This whole procedure [of identifying emperors] should be viewed as misguided."[17] John is not giving his readers a history lesson, nor is he speaking to the question of the exact number of Roman emperors. As Sweet points out, John's readers "knew all about Nero, but were as unlikely to have known the succession of emperors as readers today know that of the Presidents of the United States."[18] The number seven is used throughout Revelation as the symbolic number of completeness,[19] therefore, as Caird wryly points out, John did not "arrive at the number [seven] by counting emperors."[20] John's point is that the church must face persecution throughout the entire present evil age (the completeness of this period symbolized by the seven emperors), and the church must suffer not only under the seventh king, but it must also face an eighth king, who will arise at the end of the age in conjunction with the final assault of the dragon, beast, and false prophet.[21] Therefore, the identification of the kings in this passage is far more difficult to prove than those who argue for an early date seem to indicate. The real issue for John's reader is not the chronology of emperors but the identity of the eighth king, who was yet to come.

Argument #3: Since the number 666 likely refers to Nero, this seems to indicate that Revelation was written during or shortly after Nero's reign (AD 68) and before AD 70.[22] As we have seen, since the number 666 is at least as theological in its significance as it is historical, what is symbolized by this number extends beyond Nero to all state leaders who oppose Christ and his kingdom. While Nero is certainly in the minds of John and his readers through the 666 imagery, Nero's reign of terror does not exhaust the prophecy of Revelation 13.

In fact, since the beast imitates the resurrection of Christ when his deadly wound is healed (Rev. 13:3), John is probably making the point that even though Nero was long dead, he had returned, in effect, in the person of Domitian, persecuting the church when John was given his vision.[23] This is the so-called "Nero myth," which held that after he died, Nero would miraculously return to life and lead a Parthian army against Rome. If Revelation 13:3–4 and 17:8–11 do indeed speak of a king who is a Nero *redivivus* (raised from the dead), then this requires a date much later than 68.[24] And since the beast is present (resurrected) when John writes Revelation, it is only natural to see John warning Christians across time of what to expect whenever they encounter what Bauckham calls "a deification of power."[25] This occurs whenever the state or its leader takes unto itself divine rights and privileges and, in doing so, mimics the death, resurrection, and parousia of Christ. This opposition from a series of such beasts will continue until an intensification of evil at the end of the age immediately before our Lord's second advent, when an eighth and final beast is manifest.

Argument #4: The reference to "Babylon" in the Book of Revelation is interpreted as symbolically referring to the city of Jerusalem and apostate Judaism. In Revelation 11:8 we read of the two witnesses, "Their bodies will lie in the street of the great city, which is figuratively called Sodom and Egypt, where also their Lord was crucified." It is argued that Jerusalem (the place where the Lord was crucified) is therefore to be identified as the great city. Then in Revelation 18:10–21, the great city is specifically identified as Babylon. This means that the destruction of Jerusalem in AD 70 fulfills the prophecy of the destruction of Babylon in Revelation 18.[26] In order for this to fit, Revelation must be written before AD 70.

The problem with this is that the same verse that is used to identify the "great city" as the place where Jesus is crucified is also called "Sodom and Egypt," suggesting that a nonliteral reading of the passage is in order, especially in light of the fact that throughout Revelation the reference to "Babylon" is clearly a reference to Rome (see Rev. 14:8; 17:18; 18:2, 10, 16, 18–19, 21).[27] According to John Sweet, "Like . . . Hiroshima for us, Sodom, Egypt, Babylon and Jerusalem were heavy with meaning. The 'great city', in whose street the witnesses lie, cannot any more than Vanity Fair be limited to one place and time."[28] In fact, as we will see, the identification of Rome as Babylon was made by virtually all Jewish writers *after* the Romans destroyed the temple in AD 70, but never before.[29] If this is indeed a reference to the city of Jerusalem in the apostolic period, it would be the only place where such identification is made.

Argument #5: In Revelation 1:7 John writes, "Look, he is coming with the clouds, and every eye will see him, even those who pierced him; and all the peoples of the earth will mourn because of him. So shall it be! Amen." Preterists argue that this is a prophetic reference to Jesus coming in judgment upon Israel in AD 70, which fulfills the prophecy in Zechariah 12:10–12. The earth is equated with Jerusalem, and the mention elsewhere in Revelation of the tribes is thought to be a reference to Israel. If true, this means Revelation must have been written before AD 70.[30]

There are two major problems with this interpretation. For one thing, the prophecy from Zechariah 12:10–12 is a reference to Israel's eschatological salvation, not her final judgment.[31] For another, the view that the "peoples of the earth" (literally, the "tribes of the earth") refers to Israel is a theological stretch at best. Nowhere (unless it is here) does the phrase "tribes of the earth" refer to just Israelite tribes. Whenever it is used in the Septuagint, it refers to "all nations," not to Israel.[32]

Arguments in Favor of a Post–AD 70 Date

Argument #1: The most important reason for dating Revelation after AD 70 is evidence of the presence of emperor worship and the imperial cult underlying much of what takes place throughout John's vision. A number of texts indicate that Christians were being forced to participate in the emperor cult in ways that violated their consciences (e.g., Rev. 13:4–8, 15–16; 14:9–11; 15:2; 16:2; 19:20; 20:4). As Moffatt once put it, whether persecution of Christians had already become widespread or not, "the few cases of repressive interference and of martyrdom in Asia Minor (and elsewhere) were enough to warn [John] of the storm rolling up on the horizon, though as yet only one or two drops had actually fallen."[33] While the persecution of Christians was already beginning during the reign of Nero, it was not widespread until the time of Domitian (AD 81–96) or even later. As several recent studies of Nero have demonstrated, the evidence shows that persecution of Christians in Rome (and not in Asia Minor, where John was) began under Nero because he used them as scapegoats for the great fire that destroyed much of Rome, not because they refused to worship him.[34]

Important studies of the historical background of Asia Minor during this time, such as S. R. F. Price's *Rituals and Power: The Roman Imperial Cult in Asia Minor* and Leonard Thompson's *The Book of Revelation: Apocalypse and Empire*, indicate that by the time of Domitian's reign the imperial cult and emperor worship was in full-flower.[35] Although Thompson admits that Roman sources depict Domitian as an evil tyrant without exception, nevertheless he proceeds to argue that persecution of Christians under Domitian's reign was actually quite isolated and Domitian may not be the monster Roman historians made him out to be. And yet as Thompson goes on to state, if the imperial cult preceded Domitian by "many reigns," it also continued long after Domitian was gone.[36]

The only truly firm date we have is AD 113, when Pliny (a Roman author and senator) wrote to Trajan (the emperor who came after Domitian) with a question about what to do with Christians who refuse to worship the emperor. Trajan replied that Christians were not to be sought out and executed, but if they did not worship the emperor and were convicted by a court, they were to be put to death.[37] This indicates that the conditions depicted in Revelation fit much better with a later date (the reign of Domitian in the midnineties) rather than an earlier one (before AD 70). What was then the practice (whether official or otherwise) in the time of Trajan (AD 113) most likely began in the time of Domitian, which many Romans considered the most volatile period in Roman history.[38] Sadly, Pliny's letter refers to Christians who had "apostatized" from the faith as long ago as twenty-five years—clear evidence of persecution of believers being quite intense about AD 90. The fact that people renounced their faith clearly points to a date in the time of Domitian, when the persecution of Christians was severe. That being said, surely the seeds of this persecution were sown during the reign of Nero, nearly thirty years earlier. As Beale puts it, "A date during the time of Nero is possible for Revelation, but the later setting under Domitian is more probable in the light of the evidence in the book for an expected escalation of emperor worship in the near future and especially the widespread, programmatic legal persecution portrayed as imminent or already occurring in Revelation 13."[39] The early date counterargument to this is that the evidence fits better with Nero (see above).

Argument #2: The historical situation facing the seven churches mentioned in Revelation 2–3 seems to fit much better with circumstances after AD 70 than does a date before the destruction of the temple. In Colin Hemer's important work, *The Letters to the Seven Churches of Asia in Their Local Setting*, he argues that the situation of the churches we see in Revelation chapters 2–3 most likely fits the time of Domitian. This includes evidence of persecution in particular provinces from local authorities—which explains why only three of the churches, Smyrna, Pergamum, and Philadelphia, were experiencing persecution. There is also evidence of Jews living in these areas who, in order to avoid the wrath of the imperial cult, were willing to pay high taxes and turn in Christians to local authorities. These were Jews who were no longer members of the synagogue and were debating other Jews about Christian truth claims.[40]

There are a number of other factors regarding the condition of the churches that support a later date as well. The spiritual lethargy of the church of Ephesus, which is depicted in Revelation 2:1–7 as losing its first love, seems to presuppose a time well after its establishment in the midfifties of the first century.[41] It is hard to imagine a church probably established in the fifties (see Acts 19:1–10)[42] so quickly losing its first love (i.e., if Revelation was written before AD 70) that it was in danger of losing its identity as a church if the people did not "repent and do the things [they] did at first" (Rev. 2:5). The church of Laodicea (Rev. 3:14–22) is described as wealthy—but a huge earthquake decimated the entire region in AD 61. A recovery to the wealthy conditions described by John and known to historians would seemingly take decades, not the three or four years required by a pre–AD 70 date.[43] The church in Pergamum (Rev. 2:12–17) had been home to a certain Antipas who, apparently, had been put to death as a martyr for Christ much earlier

(v. 13). That such persecution broke out years before, and that John speaks of Antipas's death as well in the past, certainly supports a later date.[44]

According to Beale there is no evidence that Nero's persecution of Christians after the great fire in the city of Rome was ever extended into Asia Minor (Turkey), where the seven churches of Revelation were located. This also fits better with John's exile to the island of Patmos.[45] It is much more likely for someone like John (who lived in Ephesus) to be exiled under Domitian than Nero.[46] As Price points out, the imperial cult of Domitian, which was well-established in Ephesus (along with the colossal statue), is probably what is in the background of Revelation 13 when John speaks of believers being put to death for not worshiping the beast or his image.[47] All of this supports a late date.

There is one other matter that relates to the historical situation of the churches. According to some commentators, the existence of a church at Smyrna itself points toward a later date, since it is likely that this church was not even founded until after AD 60.[48] We do need to note that Hemer, the leading authority on such matters, puts the date of founding of this congregation much earlier, circa 50–55.[49]

The early date response to the situation of the churches just set forth is to offer a number of alternative explanations, some of which are quite plausible, as Beale admits.[50] Ken Gentry contends that these arguments (even if true) do "not carry sufficient weight to serve as an anchor for the late date theory."[51] But given the state of the churches depicted in Revelation 2–3, especially in light of the known situation throughout the larger Roman Empire during the time of Domitian, the arguments for a later date are much more compelling, since so much of the evidence leads in this direction, confirming the evidence of a late date within the book itself.

Argument #3: As mentioned earlier, the reference to "Babylon" (the spiritual name for the city of Rome) in Revelation 18 is perhaps the strongest internal evidence of a later date. In all known Jewish literature written after AD 70 and the destruction of the temple, Rome is universally described as "Babylon" because, like the ancient Babylonians, Rome had sacked Jerusalem and destroyed the temple. Since John is writing to churches throughout Asia Minor, many of which had significant numbers of converted Jews among their members, this reference would make no sense whatsoever (without explanation) if John is using the term to refer to Jerusalem and not Rome.[52]

The response on the part of those who hold to an early date is to counter by trying to prove that Babylon was a reference to Jerusalem. This argument, which we have discussed previously, seems to be without much merit.

Argument #4: The testimony of the church fathers is virtually unanimous in affirming the later date. Clement, Eusebius, Origen, and Irenaeus (among others) all state that the book was written by John during the latter part of the reign of Domitian. Certainly, they all might be mistaken.[53] But there is no evidence for anyone arguing for a pre–AD 70 date of authorship. According to Irenaeus, the identity of the Antichrist "would have been announced by him who beheld the Apocalypse. For it was seen not very long ago in our day, toward the end of Domitian's reign."[54] This is most often taken to mean that John wrote Revelation as an old man exiled on Patmos before Domitian died in AD 96. The traditional post–AD 70 dating of Revelation largely stems from the comments of Irenaeus, although the internal and external evidence is now seen to support Irenaeus's contention.

Gentry, on the other hand, contends that the verb *was seen* refers to John, "who was seen" during Domitian's reign, not to the Apocalypse, which was written during the reign of Domitian.[55] But Robinson, who agrees with Gentry's dating, nevertheless accepts the traditional reading of Irenaeus's comments.[56] Beale points out that "the Apocalypse" (not John) is properly the subject of the verb *was seen*, which is why virtually all of Irenaeus's ancient readers agreed without question that Irenaeus was referring to the date of Revelation and not to the apostle. Furthermore, it is important to notice that when discussing the beast and his number, Irenaeus makes no reference to Nero but refers to Lateinos (an ancient king of the Latins) and the current Roman Empire. Therefore, both the internal and external evidence supports a late date for the writing of the Book of Revelation, and one wonders if preterist arguments for an early date are based more upon theological necessity than on the aggregate of the internal and external evidence.

JUST LIKE COVENANT THEOLOGY IS ----

8:20 a.m
APRIL 6, 2014

Notes

A Word of Thanks

1. Christopher Hill, *Antichrist in Seventeenth-Century England* (New York: Oxford University Press, 1971).

Introduction

1. I use the term *Antichrist* so many times in this book that I felt it would be wooden to include the definite article every time. I have used the lowercase when referring to anything other than the personal eschatological figure yet to come.

2. See the discussion of this matter in Keith A. Mathison, ed., *When Will These Things Be? A Reformed Response to Hyper-Preterism* (Phillipsburg, NJ: Presbyterian and Reformed, 2004).

3. See my treatment of this elsewhere: Kim Riddlebarger, *A Case for Amillennialism* (Grand Rapids: Baker, 2003). See also the books by Anthony Hoekema, *The Bible and the Future* (Grand Rapids: Eerdmans, 1979); and Cornelius P. Venema, *The Promise of the Future* (Carlisle, U.K.: Banner of Truth, 2000).

4. I am thinking of the excellent book by Bernard McGinn, *Antichrist: Two Thousand Years of the Human Fascination with Evil* (New York: Columbia University Press, 2000). McGinn believes that "the most important message of the Antichrist legend in Western history is what it has to tell us about our past, and perhaps even our present attitudes toward evil" (p. xx).

5. Robert Fuller contends that "the symbol of the Antichrist shapes an ontological reality congruent with our anxieties and in doing so satisfies the believer's need to interpret the surrounding world (e.g. humanistic education, rock music, ecumenical relations, hopes for world peace), as fraught with danger and deceit." See Robert Fuller, *Naming the Antichrist: The History of an American Obsession* (New York: Oxford University Press, 1995), 198–99.

Chapter 1: A Morbid Curiosity

1. See the discussion of the success of *Thief in the Night* and the fascinating background of its director/producer, Don Thompson, in Randall Balmer, *Mine Eyes Have Seen the Glory: A Journey into the Evangelical Subculture in America* (New York: Oxford University Press, 1989), 48–70.

2. The amazing success of Lindsey's book and many others in the same genre is described in Paul Boyer, *When Time Shall Be No More: Prophecy Belief in Modern American Culture* (Cambridge, MA: Belknap, 1999), 5–7; cf. McGinn, *Antichrist*, 258.

3. As Timothy P. Weber points out, the despair engendered by the horrors of World War I quashed much of the postmillennial optimism of the previous generations of American evangelicals and enabled dispensationalists to begin calling attention to the fact that world conditions were getting worse, not better. This theological mood swing underlies the pessimism of dispensational theology, popularized by Lindsey in the 1970s. See Timothy P. Weber, *Living in the Shadow of the Second Coming: American Premillennialism 1875–1982* (Grand Rapids: Zondervan, 1983), 103–27.

4. Hal Lindsey, *The Late Great Planet Earth* (Grand Rapids: Zondervan, 1970), 98–113.

5. Tim LaHaye and Jerry B. Jenkins, *Nicolae: The Rise of the Antichrist* (Wheaton: Tyndale, 1997).

6. Christopher Hill, *Antichrist in Seventeenth-Century England*.

7. See Neal Gabler, *Life: The Movie. How Entertainment Conquered Reality* (New York: Vintage Books, 1998).

8. According to Jeffrey Burton Russell, Christians were heavily dependent upon local folklore for much of their understanding of the activity of Satan. In this realm of folklore, "the most important of the Devil's many and varied accomplices is the Antichrist, whose influence permeates human affairs and who at the end of the world will come in the flesh to lead the forces of evil in a last, desperate battle against the good." See Jeffrey Burton Russell, *Lucifer: The Devil in the Middle Ages* (Ithaca, NY: Cornell University Press, 1986), 79.

9. The study of Alexander by Paul Cartledge makes this very point. The historian Arrian repeatedly speaks of Alexander's desire and craving (pothos) for more, which Cartledge argues is but one of the lenses through which Alexander wanted to be remembered. See Paul Cartledge, *Alexander the Great* (Woodstock, NY: Overlook, 2004), 221–22.

10. The view that Antichrist is Satan incarnate has been held by few Christians, the notable exception being the tenth-century writer Adso. See McGinn, *Antichrist*, 94–97; Wilhelm Bousset, *The Antichrist Legend: A Chapter in Christian and Jewish Folklore*, trans. A. H. Keane (London: Hutchison, 1896), 138–57; Russell, *Lucifer*, 103.

11. Peter Malone, *Movie Christs and Antichrists* (New York: Crossroad, 1990), 121–23.

12. Ibid., 122.

13. One thinks of more recent films loosely based on biblical eschatology such as *The Rapture* (1991), and the *End of Days* (1999), as well as the television series *Revelations* (2005).

14. As Bernard McGinn points out, however, in the absence of a clearly defined language to describe evil to a given culture, films like *Bram Stoker's Dracula* depict vampires ascending into heaven. McGinn, *Antichrist*, xiii.

15. Bernard McGinn, quoted in "The Way the World Ends," *Newsweek*, November 1, 1999, 69.

16. Fuller, *Naming the Antichrist*, 4.

17. Dave Hunt, *Global Peace and the Rise of Antichrist* (Eugene, OR: Harvest House, 1990), 55–64, 87–98.

18. Ibid., 5.

19. Hal Lindsey, *Planet Earth—2000 AD* (Palos Verde, CA: Western Front, 1994), 232–33.

20. Fuller, *Naming the Antichrist*, 3–4.

21. Ibid., 28.

22. Van Impe is the primary author and speaker for Jack Van Impe Ministries International (www.JVIM.org), which produces a weekly television program, publishes a newsletter, and maintains a ministry-based website. Van Impe is the author of numerous publications on biblical prophecy, including *The Great Escape*, *The Jack Van Impe Prophecy Bible*, and the DVD/video *Another Hitler Rising*.

23. Lindsey's website, the Hal Lindsey Oracle, is devoted to an analysis of current events through the lens of Lindsey's dispensationalism (www.hallindseyoracle.com).

24. See, for example, Barbara R. Rossing, *The Rapture Exposed* (Boulder, CO: Westview, 2004), 47–80.

25. Boyer, *When Time Shall Be No More*, especially 115–253.

26. Timothy P. Weber, *On the Road to Armageddon: How Evangelicals Became Israel's Best Friend* (Grand Rapids: Baker, 2004).

27. Michael D. Evans, *The American Prophecies: Ancient Scriptures Reveal Our Nation's Future* (New York: Warner Faith, 2004), 14–20.

28. Ibid., 34–36.

29. Influential treatments of this include: Sir Robert Anderson, *The Coming Prince* (repr., Grand Rapids: Kregel, 1957); and Alva J. McClain, *Daniel's Prophecy of the 70 Weeks* (Grand Rapids: Zondervan, 1969).

30. McClain, *Daniel's Prophecy of the 70 Weeks*, 10.

31. The idea that the Old Testament interprets the New Testament is not only the exact opposite of a proper Christian hermeneutic in which the New Testament interprets the Old, but the subject of verse 27 of Daniel's prophecy is not the Antichrist but the Messiah. See Meredith G. Kline, "The Covenant of the Seventieth Week," in *The Law and the Prophets: Old Testament Studies Prepared in Honor of Oswald Thompson Allis*, ed. John H. Skilton (Phillipsburg, NJ: Presbyterian and Reformed, 1974), 454–69.

32. See my discussion of this in Riddlebarger, *A Case for Amillennialism*, 149–56.

33. In a dispensational symposium dealing with the Antichrist, John Walvoord gives us a representative dispensational view of this text. "From his position of power, the man of sin will bring about the covenant of Daniel 9:27, which describes the last seven years leading up to the second coming of Christ. It is the final seven years of Israel's prophesied prophetic program, 483 years of which were completed before the crucifixion of Christ. The present age has intervened. The last seven years will be resumed when this covenant is signed. According to Daniel 9:27, the first 3 ½ years will be a period of relative peace, though it may include the invasion of Israel and the sneak attack by six nations as described in Ezekiel 38 and 39. In the middle of the seven years, however, the covenant will be broken and the leader of the ten countries will assume control over the entire world by proclamation. This will begin the world government of the end times, of which the Antichrist will be the head." John F. Walvoord, "Escape from Planet Earth," in *Foreshocks of Antichrist*, ed. William T. James (Eugene, OR: Harvest House, 1997), 376–77.

34. See the comprehensive discussions of the identification of 666 with Nero in Richard Bauckham, *The Climax of Prophecy* (Edinburgh: T & T Clark, 1993), 384–445; and G. K. Beale, *The Book of Revelation: A Commentary on the Greek Text* (Grand Rapids: Eerdmans, 1999), 718–28.

35. John F. Walvoord, *The Revelation of Jesus Christ* (Chicago: Moody, 1966), 204–12.

36. John F. Walvoord, *Major Bible Prophecies* (Grand Rapids: Zondervan, 1991), 344.

37. Hal Lindsey, *There's A New World Coming: A Prophetic Odyssey* (Santa Ana: Vision House, 1973), 193–95.

38. Hunt, *Global Peace and the Rise of Antichrist*, 43.

39. Chuck Smith, *What the World Is Coming To* (Costa Mesa, CA: Maranatha, 1977), 141–42.

40. David Webber, "Cyberspace: The Beast's Worldwide Spiderweb," in *Foreshocks of Antichrist*, ed. William T. James (Eugene, OR: Harvest House, 1997), 161.

41. Peter LaLonde and Paul LaLonde, *Racing toward the Mark of the Beast* (Eugene, OR: Harvest House, 1994), 148.

42. Weber, *On the Road to Armageddon*, 15.

43. See, for example, Hunt, *Global Peace and the Rise of Antichrist*, 55–64, 87–98; Lindsey, *Planet Earth—2000 AD*, 219–52; and Grant R. Jeffrey, *Armageddon: Appointment with Destiny* (New York: Bantam Books, 1990), 140–50.

44. Gary DeMar, *Last Days Madness* (Atlanta: American Vision, 1999), 36.

45. See, for example, W. G. Kummel, *Promise and Fulfillment* (London: SCM, 1957); George Eldon Ladd, *A Theology of the New Testament*, rev. ed. (Grand Rapids: Eerdmans, 1994); Herman Ridderbos, *The Coming of the Kingdom* (Philadelphia: Presbyterian and Reformed, 1962); and Ben Witherington, *Jesus, Paul and the End of the World* (Downers Grove, IL: InterVarsity, 1992).

Chapter 2: Forerunners of the Antichrist

1. McGinn, *Antichrist*, 9. I reject McGinn's view of this doctrine as a legend since I see the doctrine of Antichrist as part of biblical revelation. Nonetheless, McGinn's point is an important one.

2. The most influential work in this regard is Wilhelm Bousset, *The Antichrist Legend: A Chapter in Christian and Jewish Folklore*, trans. A. H. Keane (London: Hutchison, 1896). Geerhardus Vos takes issue with Bousset's thesis that the Antichrist legend is older than the messianic tradition and wryly notes that "the Antichrist has here eaten the young Christ-child after some such fashion as the Christian Apocalypse depicts in one of its visions." Geerhardus Vos, *The Pauline Eschatology* (Grand Rapids: Baker, 1982), 96–99.

3. For a discussion of the relationship between messianic expectation in various Jewish apocalyptic writings, see James C. VanderKam, "Messianism and Apocalypticism," in *The Continuum History of Apocalypticism*, ed. Bernard McGinn, John J. Collins, and Stephen J. Stein (New York: Continuum, 2003), 112–38.

4. D. F. Watson, "Antichrist," in *Dictionary of the Later New Testament and Its Developments*, ed. Ralph P. Martin and Peter H. Davids (Downers Grove, IL: InterVarsity, 1997), 50–53.

5. See H. C. Kee, "Testaments of the Twelve Patriarchs," in *Dictionary of New Testament Background*, ed. Craig A. Evans and Stanley E. Porter (Downers Grove, IL:

InterVarsity, 2000), 1200–1205. See also F. F. Bruce, "Excursus on Antichrist," in *1 & 2 Thessalonians*, Word Biblical Commentary, vol. 45 (Waco: Word, 1982), 179. In an early Christian writing—the *Ascension of Isaiah*, which includes the so-called *Testament of Hezekiah* (3:13–4:22)—the writer portrays Belial (or Beliar) as the "Prince of Demons," who is also a false Messiah and an end-times tyrant and persecutor of the faith. This anti-Messiah is Satan incarnate, who performs miracles and demands worship. The writers believe this to be fulfilled in the person of Nero (cf. Bruce, "Excursus on Antichrist," 182; Bauckham, *Climax of Prophecy*, 87–89).

6. Watson, "Antichrist," 50–53.

7. McGinn, *Antichrist*, 30.

8. Ralph P. Martin, *2 Corinthians*, Word Biblical Commentary, vol. 40 (Waco: Word, 1986), 199–201. But note Vos's dissent from this view in *Pauline Eschatology*, 100–101.

9. According to Vos, "There may be no exact resemblance in the behavior of the pagan tyrants to Antichrist's setting himself up in the temple of God as a self-deifier, but as between type and antitype, the correspondence is close enough." Thus we see in these rulers who proudly oppose the people of God and the messianic seed "types" of what a future Antichrist will be like. See Vos, *Pauline Eschatology*, 105–6.

10. Meredith Kline, *Kingdom Prologue* (South Hamilton, MA: Gordon-Conwell Theological Seminary, 1993), 132.

11. Ibid., 112–13. Augustine also regards Cain and Abel as "types" of two cities in his famous *City of God* (Books 15–18). See Augustine, "City of God," in *St. Augustin's City of God and Christian Doctrine*, vol. 2 of *Nicene and Post-Nicene Fathers*, ed. Philip Schaff (Grand Rapids: Eerdmans, 1979), 284–396.

12. See the discussion of this in Kline, *Kingdom Prologue*, 114–17.

13. Ibid., 114–15.

14. Ibid., 117.

15. Ibid., 169.

16. For discussions of the difficulties in identifying with precision which Pharaoh was in power and the date he was confronted by Moses, see R. K. Harrison, *Introduction to the Old Testament* (Grand Rapids: Eerdmans, 1979), 168–77. John Bright says the most common opinion "is quite plausible" that the Pharaoh was Ramses II and that the confrontation occurred in the latter part of his reign in the thirteenth century BC. John Bright, *A History of Israel* (Philadelphia: Westminster, 1981), 120–24.

17. Meredith G. Kline, *The Structure of Biblical Authority* (Grand Rapids: Eerdmans, 1981), 181–95; Geerhardus Vos, *Biblical Theology* (Grand Rapids: Eerdmans, 1977), 110–14.

18. See the discussion of the persecution of God's people in the City of Man (the "great city"), which is called Sodom and Egypt (Rev. 11:8), in Beale, *Book of Revelation*, 590–92. See also Bauckham, *Climax of Prophecy*, 169.

19. Bauckham, *Climax of Prophecy*, 187.

20. Kline, *Kingdom Prologue*, 170. According to Sweet, "These stories are frequently alluded to in Revelation, especially that of the furnace into which were thrown the Jews who refused to worship Nebuchadnezzar's image." See J. P. M. Sweet, *Revelation* (London: SCM, 1979), 17–18.

21. Irenaeus, *Against Heresies*, in *The Ante-Nicene Fathers*, vol. 1, ed. Alexander Roberts and James Donaldson (Grand Rapids: Eerdmans, 1979), 558. In his interpretation of the number of the beast (666), Irenaeus gets a bit creative. He reasons that Noah lived six hundred years before human sinfulness brought about the flood and

couples that with the dimensions of Nebuchadnezzar's gold statue (60 cubits high and 6 cubits wide), which he says are symbolic of the number of the final Antichrist, when apostasy and persecution will reach their zenith and human history will have run its course (6000 years).

22. Kline, *Kingdom Prologue*, 170.

23. See the discussion of Antiochus IV in Gregory C. Jenks, *The Origins and Development of the Antichrist Myth* (New York: Walter De Gruyter, 1991), 153–68.

24. McGinn, *Antichrist*, 13–16. See also John E. Goldingay, *Daniel*, Word Biblical Commentary, vol. 30 (Waco: Word, 1989), 326–29.

25. Harrison, *Introduction to the Old Testament*, 1110–27.

26. Watson, "Antichrist," 50.

27. Bruce, "Excursus on Antichrist," 180.

28. E. J. Young, *Daniel* (Carlisle, U.K.: Banner of Truth, 1978), 147–50. Young believes that the entire course of history is given here. The ten horns represent the time after the fall of the Roman Empire and refer to a series of nations who will arise (ten being a number that probably indicates completeness). After the ten kingdoms arise and have fallen, another kingdom symbolized by the little horn arises who is Antichrist.

29. Bruce, "Excursus on Antichrist," 180. Caird quips, "Though we cannot say that Caligula is the Antichrist, he undoubtedly sat for the portrait." G. B. Caird, *The Revelation of St. John* (Peabody, MA: Hendrickson, 1999), 166.

30. Vos, *Pauline Eschatology*, 123.

31. T. J. Geddert, "Apocalyptic," in *Dictionary of Jesus and the Gospels*, ed. Joel B. Green, Scot McKnight, and I. Howard Marshall (Downers Grove, IL: InterVarsity, 1992), 23.

32. Kline, "Covenant of the Seventieth Week," 463.

33. McClain, *Daniel's Prophecy of the 70 Weeks*, 10; John Walvoord, *Daniel: The Key to Prophetic Revelation* (Chicago: Moody, 1971), 231–37.

34. Young, *Daniel*, 197–201.

35. Ibid., 199.

36. Ibid., 201.

37. Kline, "Covenant of the Seventieth Week," 463.

38. Ibid.

39. Ibid., 465.

40. Ibid., 469.

41. Beale, *Book of Revelation*, 669.

42. According to Bousset, "The appearance of Gog and Magog is . . . intimately associated with the Antichrist in all traditions." See Bousset, *Antichrist Legend*, 195.

43. McGinn, *Antichrist*, 91, 96, 99, 140, 157, 178, 182.

44. Leslie C. Allen, *Ezekiel 20–48*, Word Biblical Commentary, vol. 29 (Dallas: Word, 1990), 210–11.

45. Lindsey, *Late Great Planet Earth*, 59–71. See the discussion of the role this interpretation of Ezekiel 38–39 has played in dispensational prophetic circles in Boyer, *When Time Shall Be No More*, 152–80.

46. See, for example, J. Dwight Pentecost, *Things to Come* (Grand Rapids: Zondervan, 1978), 326–31; Walvoord, *Major Bible Prophecies*, 328–37.

47. Edwin M. Yamauchi, *Foes from the Northern Frontier: Invading Hordes from the Russian Steppes* (Grand Rapids: Baker, 1982), 19–27. Rosh does not refer to Russia; it is a title, "prince." Meshech and Tubal are connected to the Hittites and were fierce warriors. Yamauchi describes the difficulties associated with identifying Gog with any

specific ancient empire or person and notes that there never has been any consensus about who or what is involved. Most commentators associate Gog with Gyges, king of Lydia in the seventh century BC. Compare Beale, *Book of Revelation*, 1025.

48. Allen, *Ezekiel 20–48*, 210–11; Beale, *Book of Revelation*, 1022–26.

49. Allen, *Ezekiel 20–48*, 202.

50. Charles Feinberg, *The Prophecy of Ezekiel* (Chicago: Moody, 1978), 218.

51. Allen, *Ezekiel 20–48*, 210.

52. Beale, *Book of Revelation*, 1025.

53. Ibid., 1022–23; Vos, *Pauline Eschatology*, 110–11.

Chapter 3: The Doctrine of Antichrist in the New Testament Era

1. According to Leon-Dufour, "the anti-God of the OT becomes the anti-Christ, who is already at work through his supporters before he reveals himself in the eschatological battle when he will finally be conquered." See Xavier Leon-Dufour, *Dictionary of Biblical Theology*, 2nd ed. (New York: Seabury, 1983), 23.

2. Erwin Kauder, "Antichrist," in *The New International Dictionary of New Testament Theology*, ed. Colin Brown (Grand Rapids: Zondervan, 1982), 1:125.

3. According to Victor Maag of the C. G. Jung Institute, "to those who molded the Antichrist conception, it signified all manner of ethical transgression, falsehood, seduction, violence. All these are evil, because they obstruct the good, that is, the cosmic order and everything that goes with it. Evil is a cosmic action. Evil belongs to the chaos." Victor Maag, "The Antichrist as a Symbol of Evil," in *Evil*, ed. James Hillman (Evanston, IL: Northwestern University Press, 1967), 79.

4. McGinn, *Antichrist*, 33.

5. Bousset, *Antichrist Legend*, 3–18.

6. Kauder, "Antichrist," 125.

7. Kline, *Structure of Biblical Authority*, 188–89.

8. Kauder, "Antichrist," 125; Kline, *Kingdom Prologue*, 132.

9. Donald A. Hagner, *Matthew 14–28*, Word Biblical Commentary, vol. 33b (Dallas: Word, 1995), 62.

10. See a more detailed discussion of this in Riddlebarger, *A Case for Amillennialism*, 81–99.

11. Geerhardus Vos sees this as a fundamental structure in Paul's thought, in Vos, *Pauline Eschatology*, 1–41. So does George Eldon Ladd, in Ladd, *Theology of the New Testament*, 66–67.

12. Kline writes of the manifestation of an "antichrist power of the messianic age, the little horn from the fourth beast (Dan 7:8 and 11:36ff.), the dragon-like agent of Satan that issues the final challenge against the city of God, evoking the day of wrath." Kline, *Kingdom Prologue*, 170.

13. Beale, *Book of Revelation*, 717–28.

14. J. Stuart Russell, *The Parousia: A Critical Inquiry into the New Testament Doctrine of Our Lord's Second Coming* (repr., Grand Rapids: Baker, 1983), 23.

15. The phrase "abomination of desolation" is drawn by Jesus from the Septuagint (Dan. 12:11), and is a technical term for an idolatrous act of sacrilege that renders the temple unclean or desolate. It refers to the actions of Antiochus IV in 167 BC, thereby serving as a foreshadowing of the events of AD 70. See the discussion in Hagner, *Matthew 14–28*, 699–701.

16. Ridderbos, *Coming of the Kingdom*, 523–25.

17. Ibid., 523.

18. Vos, *Pauline Eschatology*, 95.

19. According to Geddert, "the prophecy concerning the 'abomination of desolation' was fulfilled when the Jerusalem Temple was desecrated and destroyed in AD 70. This does not, however, rule out the possibility of another fulfillment in the future." Geddert, "Apocalyptic," 23.

20. Hagner, *Matthew 14–28*, 713–15.

21. D. A. Carson, "Matthew," in *The Expositor's Bible Commentary*, vol. 8, ed. Frank E. Gaebelein and J. D. Douglas (Grand Rapids: Zondervan, 1984), 499–502; Hagner, *Matthew 14–28*, 696–702.

22. C. E. B. Cranfield, *The Gospel according to St. Mark*, Cambridge Greek Testament (New York: Cambridge University Press, 1983), 401–2. Cf. Herman Ridderbos, *Matthew* (Grand Rapids: Zondervan, 1987), 442–43.

23. Vos, *Pauline Eschatology*, 96.

24. Hoekema, *The Bible and the Future*, 137–63.

25. G. B. Caird, *The Language and Imagery of the Bible* (Philadelphia: Westminster, 1980), 258–59.

26. Ibid., 259–60.

27. Dispensationalist Mark Hitchcock states that while possible double fulfillment is "an unacceptable method of interpretation." Mark Hitchcock, *What Jesus Says about Earth's Final Days* (Sisters, OR: Multnomah, 2003), 123n4.

28. Kenneth L. Gentry, *Perilous Times: A Study in Eschatological Evil* (Texarkana, AR: Covenant Media, 1999).

29. Beale, *Book of Revelation*, 48–49.

30. Gentry, *Perilous Times*, 133.

31. Ibid.

32. See the discussion of this in the appendix.

33. Bauckham, *Climax of Prophecy*, 450–52.

Chapter 4: Many Antichrists Have Already Come

1. But as Josef Ernst points out, "The basic idea is more widespread." J. Ernst, "ἀντίχριστος" in *Exegetical Dictionary of the New Testament*, vol. 1, ed. Horst Balz and Gerhard Schneider (Grand Rapids: Eerdmans, 1990), 111.

2. Raymond E. Brown, *The Epistles of John*, Anchor Bible, vol. 30 (Garden City, NY: Doubleday, 1983), 333.

3. Ibid., 331.

4. Stephen S. Smalley, *1, 2, 3 John*, Word Biblical Commentary, vol. 51 (Waco: Word, 1984), 80–81.

5. See Kauder, "Antichrist," 1:125; L. J. Lietaert Peerbolte, *The Antecedents of Antichrist: A Traditio-Historical Study of the Earliest Christian Views on Eschatological Opponents* (New York: E. J. Brill, 1996), 102.

6. Peerbolte, *Antecedents of Antichrist*, 102.

7. This essay was published in May 1921 and is one of Warfield's last publications before his death later that same year. B. B. Warfield, "Antichrist," in *Selected Shorter Writings of Benjamin B. Warfield*, vol. 1, ed. John E. Meeter (Phillipsburg, NJ: Presbyterian and Reformed, 1980), 356.

8. Warfield's Princeton Seminary colleague Geerhardus Vos is among them. See Vos, *Pauline Eschatology*, 94. For others who accept this connection, see Caird, *Reve-*

lation of St. John, 165–66; Beale, *Book of Revelation*, 680–81. According to Sweet, the beast can "be called Antichrist, which implies not just opposition to Christ, but to the claim to be Christ, as Satan claims to be God." Sweet, *Revelation*, 9.

9. Warfield, "Antichrist," 356. This is correct if Daniel 7:7–12 is not referring to an end-times Antichrist. But I think Daniel is doing just that! Indeed, as Smalley points out, while difficult to trace, there is a significant background to John's Antichrist teaching found in Jewish apocalyptic. See Smalley, *1, 2, 3 John*, 98. Brown believes that both Jewish and Christian traditions are in view here. See Brown, *Epistles of John*, 336.

10. Warfield, "Antichrist," 356–57.

11. Ibid., 358.

12. Brown notes that while some "have suggested that these Antichrists are meant by the author as the precursors of the great Antichrist still to come . . . that idea is refuted by the use of the Antichrists as a sign of the last hour, for that means he [John] is not thinking of them as precursors." Brown, *Epistles of John*, 337.

13. Warfield, "Antichrist," 358–59.

14. Ibid., 359–60. Warfield goes on to argue that this image of a multitude of antichrists supersedes the idea of an individual Antichrist altogether. I am not convinced, however, and will attempt to demonstrate that a connection exists between John's Antichrist and the other New Testament images of a personified persecutor of God's people.

15. Ibid., 360–61.

16. Smalley, *1, 2, 3 John*, xxiii.

17. Warfield, "Antichrist," 361.

18. Ibid., 358.

19. The following quote is from the Council of Trent: "Canon IX. If any one saith, that by faith alone the impious is justified; in such wise as to mean, that nothing else is required to co-operate in order to the obtaining the grace of Justification, and that it is not in any way necessary, that he be prepared and disposed by the movement of his own will; let him be anathema."

20. Henry Denzinger, *The Sources of Catholic Dogma*, trans. Roy J. Deferrari (St. Louis: Herder, 1957), secs. 496, 673. According to the Council of Constance (1414–18), heretics such as the followers of Wycliffe and Hus were to be asked, "whether he believes that blessed Peter was the vicar of Christ, possessing the power of binding and loosing on earth" (sec. 673).

Chapter 5: The Dragon, the Beast, and the False Prophet

1. Kline, *Kingdom Prologue*, 132.

2. Beale, *Book of Revelation*, 48.

3. Dennis E. Johnson, *Triumph of the Lamb* (Phillipsburg, NJ: Presbyterian and Reformed, 2001), 65.

4. See the discussion of the structure of Revelation in Bauckham, *Climax of Prophecy*, 1–37; Beale, *Book of Revelation*, 108–51; ibid., 25–48.

5. Beale, *Book of Revelation*, 50–69, 76–99.

6. The date of Revelation is discussed in the appendix.

7. Beale, *Book of Revelation*, 686.

8. Nero's depravity is described in great detail but then defended (to a degree) in the book by Edward Champlin, *Nero* (Cambridge, MA: Belknap, 2003). Champlin also discusses in detail the veracity of the traditional sources describing Nero's evil (Tacitus,

Suetonius, and Cassius Dio). Also see Miriam T. Griffin, *Nero: The End of a Dynasty* (New Haven: Yale University Press, 1984), 69, 75, 98–99, 169.

9. Joseph-Ernest Renan, *Antichrist*, trans. William G. Hutchinson (London: Walter Scott, 1899), 85.

10. Champlin, *Nero*, 143–77.

11. Renan, *Antichrist*, 75.

12. Champlin, *Nero*, 121–26.

13. F. F. Bruce, *New Testament History* (New York: Doubleday, 1980), 401.

14. The events surrounding Paul's and Peter's deaths during the Neronian persecution can be found in F. F. Bruce, *Paul: the Apostle of the Heart Set Free* (Grand Rapids: Eerdmans, 1979), 441–45.

15. The Greek term translated as "mark" is *charagma*, which is the technical term for imperial documents. See Caird, *Revelation of St. John*, 173; Sweet, *Revelation*, 217.

16. The circumstances surrounding Nero's death are discussed in Champlin, *Nero*, 1–6.

17. Ibid., 10–20.

18. Griffin, *Nero*, 214–15.

19. See the discussions in Bousset, *Antichrist Legend*, 95–117; Champlin, *Nero*, 10–20; J. J. Collins, "Sibylline Oracles," in *Dictionary of New Testament Background*, ed. Craig A. Evans and Stanley E. Porter (Downers Grove, IL: InterVarsity, 2000), 1107–12; J. M. Knight, "Ascension of Isaiah," in *Dictionary of New Testament Background*, ed. Craig A. Evans and Stanley E. Porter (Downers Grove, IL: InterVarsity, 2000), 129–30; McGinn, *Antichrist*, 45–54; Peerbolte, *Antecedents of Antichrist*, 326–39.

20. Milton S. Terry, trans., *Sibylline Oracles*, 4:154–60, www.sacred-texts.com/cla/sib/.

21. McGinn, *Antichrist*, 45–54.

22. For example, Kenneth L. Gentry, *Before Jerusalem Fell: Dating the Book of Revelation* (Atlanta: American Vision, 1998), 193–219; Martin Kiddle, *The Revelation of St. John* (New York: Harper and Brothers, 1940), 261; Renan, *Antichrist*, 221; Sweet, *Revelation*, 217.

23. For example, Bauckham, *Climax of Prophecy*, 384–452; Beale, *Book of Revelation*, 718–28; G. R. Beasley-Murray, *The Book of Revelation* (Grand Rapids: Eerdmans, 1974), 211; Johnson, *Triumph of the Lamb*, 192–98; Robert H. Mounce, *The Book of Revelation*, New International Commentary on the New Testament (Grand Rapids: Eerdmans, 1977), 253.

24. Henry Barclay Swete, *The Apocalypse of St. John* (New York: Macmillan, 1907), lxxxiv.

25. Bauckham, *Climax of Prophecy*, 451.

26. Beale, *Book of Revelation*, 695; Sweet, *Revelation*, 210–11.

27. Beale, *Book of Revelation*, 570.

28. Ibid., 695.

29. Ibid., 687–94; Caird, *Revelation of St. John*, 161–66; Sweet, *Revelation*, 206–9.

30. Caird, *Revelation of St. John*, 162.

31. Sweet, *Revelation*, 208.

32. Swete, *Apocalypse of St. John*, xc.

33. Caird, *Revelation of St. John*, 166.

34. Colin Hemer, *The Letters to the Seven Churches of Asia in Their Local Setting* (Grand Rapids: Eerdmans, 1989), 82–94.

35. Caird, *Revelation of St. John*, 177.

36. See, for example, ibid., 161–77; Renan, *Antichrist*, 206; Swete, *Apocalypse of St. John*, xci.

37. Walvoord, *Revelation of Jesus Christ*, 197.

38. George E. Ladd, *A Commentary on the Revelation of John* (Grand Rapids: Eerdmans, 1987), 176.

39. William Hendricksen, *More than Conquerors* (Grand Rapids: Baker, 1982), 144.

40. For further information on their positions, see Beale, *Book of Revelation*, and Johnson, *Triumph of the Lamb*.

41. Albert Barnes, "Revelation," in *Notes on the New Testament* (repr., Grand Rapids: Baker, 1965), 319–38.

42. David Chilton, *The Days of Vengeance: An Exposition of the Book of Revelation* (Fort Worth: Dominion, 1987), 326–29, 335–38; DeMar, *Last Days Madness*, 257–60.

43. E.g., Kenneth L. Gentry, *The Beast of Revelation* (Tyler, TX: Institute for Christian Economics, 1994), 9–77; and Gentry, *Perilous Times*, 126–33.

44. Chilton, *Days of Vengeance*, 344–52.

45. Although it must be noted that John believes a number of Jews have aided Rome in persecuting Christians (see Rev. 3:9).

46. Cf. Beale, *Book of Revelation*, 685; Johnson, *Triumph of the Lamb*, 187–94; Sweet, *Revelation*, 215.

47. Beale, *Book of Revelation*, 682.

48. Hendricksen, *More than Conquerors*, 177.

49. Young, *Daniel*, 159.

50. Johnson, *Triumph of the Lamb*, 188–89.

51. Isbon T. Beckwith, *The Apocalypse of John* (repr., Grand Rapids: Baker, 1967), 690–711; Caird, *Revelation of St. John*, 165; Kiddle, *Revelation of St. John*, 342; Ladd, *Commentary on the Revelation of John*, 231; Sweet, *Revelation*, 259.

52. Caird, *Revelation of St. John*, 219.

53. This means that the scene in Revelation 20 describes the present age (the interadvental period) and not a future millennium.

54. Beale, *Book of Revelation*, 865.

55. See the discussions in David E. Aune, *Revelation 17–22*, Word Biblical Commentary, vol. 52c (Nashville: Thomas Nelson, 1998), 945–49; Beckwith, *Apocalypse of John*, 704–8.

56. Caird, *Revelation of St. John*, 217; Johnson, *Triumph of the Lamb*, 249–50.

57. For example, Gentry, *Before Jerusalem Fell*, 146–64.

58. See the discussions of this in Caird, *Revelation of St. John*, 217–19; Johnson, *Triumph of the Lamb*, 248–53.

59. Beasley-Murray, *Book of Revelation*, 257.

60. Beale, *Book of Revelation*, 684.

61. Caird, *Revelation of St. John*, 215–16.

62. Chilton, *Days of Vengeance*, 424; DeMar, *Last Days Madness*, 359.

63. Barnes, "Revelation," 379–95.

64. Walvoord, *Revelation of Jesus Christ*, 244.

65. Dave Hunt, *Global Peace and the Rise of Antichrist*, 115; See also Dave Hunt's popular book, *A Woman Rides the Beast* (Eugene, OR: Harvest House, 1994).

66. Beale, *Book of Revelation*, 848.

67. Ibid.

68. Beasley-Murray, *Book of Revelation*, 261.

69. Beale, *Book of Revelation*, 850.

70. Caird, *Revelation of St. John*, 219.

71. Johnson, *Triumph of the Lamb*, 251.

72. LaLonde and LaLonde, *Racing toward the Mark of the Beast*, 148.

73. Tim LaHaye and Jerry B. Jenkins, *The Mark: The Beast Rules the World* (Wheaton: Tyndale, 2001).

74. S. R. F. Price, *Rituals and Power: The Roman Imperial Cult in Asia Minor* (New York: Cambridge University Press, 1984).

75. Caird, *Revelation of St. John*, 173.

76. Sweet, *Revelation*, 217.

77. Beale, *Book of Revelation*, 718–28.

78. See the discussions in Bauckham, *Climax of Prophecy*, 384–452; Caird, *Revelation of St. John*, 174–77; Gentry, *Before Jerusalem Fell*, 193–219.

79. Beale, *Book of Revelation*, 720.

80. Bauckham, *Climax of Prophecy*, 387. According to Bauckham, Suetonius lampooned Nero with a verse: "A new calculation: Nero killed his own mother" (ibid., 386).

81. Fuller, *Naming the Antichrist*, 28.

82. Beale, *Book of Revelation*, 721.

83. Ibid., 724–25.

84. Ibid., 724.

85. Ibid., 725.

86. Ibid. See the discussion in Bauckham, *Climax of Prophecy*, 384–452.

87. The Duke of Alba, for example, was responsible for the death of many thousands of Reformed Christians. See Henry Kamen, *The Duke of Alba* (New Haven: Yale University Press, 2004), 91–94. Kamen lists the dead in the range of just over one thousand, while Philip Schaff puts the number at 100,000, which is surely an exaggeration. See Philip Schaff, *Creeds of Christendom* (repr., Grand Rapids: Baker, 1983), 1:503n2.

88. Barnes, "Revelation," 383–84; Steve Gregg, *Revelation: Four Views, A Parallel Commentary* (Nashville: Thomas Nelson, 1997), 290–92.

Chapter 6: The Man of Lawlessness

1. F. F. Bruce, *1 and 2 Thessalonians*, Word Biblical Commentary, vol. 45 (Waco: Word, 1982), xxxiv–xxxv.

2. Flavius Josephus, "Wars of the Jews," in *Josephus: Complete Works*, trans. William Whitson (Grand Rapids: Kregel, 1960), 479–80.

3. Bruce, "Excursus on Antichrist," 180.

4. G. K. Beale, *The Temple and the Church's Mission: A Biblical Theology of the Dwelling Place of God* (Downers Grove, IL: InterVarsity, 2004), 273.

5. Gentry, *Perilous Times*, 95–114.

6. B. B. Warfield, "The Prophecies of St. Paul," in *Biblical Doctrines* (Grand Rapids: Baker, 1981), 610–11.

7. DeMar, *Last Days Madness*, 273–311.

8. Patrick Fairbairn, *The Interpretation of Prophecy* (repr., Carlisle, U.K.: Banner of Truth, 1993), 350–70.

9. Iain Murray, *The Puritan Hope* (Carlisle, U.K.: Banner of Truth, 1975), 41.

10. Walvoord, *Major Bible Prophecies*, 341. Walvoord writes, "Orthodox Jews will renew their ancient sacrificial worship in the rebuilt temple during the first three

and a half years of the seven years preceding the Second Coming. After this period the ruler will desecrate their temple and establish himself and Satan as the objects of worship." See also the popular book by Thomas S. McCall and Zola Levitt, *Satan in the Sanctuary* (Chicago: Moody, 1973).

11. George Eldon Ladd, *The Last Things* (Grand Rapids: Eerdmans, 1982), 58–72.

12. Vos, *Pauline Eschatology*, 94–135; cf. Herman Ridderbos, *Paul: An Outline of His Theology* (Grand Rapids: Eerdmans, 1982), 512–21.

13. Warfield, "Prophecies of St. Paul," 611. Leon Morris comments regarding Warfield's view, "Warfield was a great exegete and all his opinions must be carefully weighed, but this is one in which few have been able to follow him." See Leon Morris, *The First and Second Epistles to the Thessalonians*, New International Commentary on the New Testament (Grand Rapids: Eerdmans,1991), 226.

14. Bruce, "Excursus on Antichrist," 188; Sweet, *Revelation*, 4.

15. Beale, *The Temple and the Church's Mission*, 285–86.

16. See, for example, John Calvin, *The Epistles of Paul to the Romans and to the Thessalonians*, trans. Ross MacKenzie (Grand Rapids: Eerdmans, 1979), 403.

17. Pentecost, *Things to Come*, 204–5.

18. Jay Adams, *The Time Is At Hand* (Greenville, SC: A Press, 1987), 22ff.; Venema, *Promise of the Future*, 175.

19. Ridderbos, *Paul*, 521–26. Ridderbos sees the restrainer as a reference to the general providence of God, spoken of in apocalyptic terms; cf. Vos, *Pauline Eschatology*, 131–35.

20. Victor Maag, "The Antichrist as Symbol of Evil," in *Evil*, ed. James Hillman (Evanston, IL: Northwestern University Press, 1967), 60.

21. G. K. Beale, *1–2 Thessalonians*, IVP New Testament Commentary Series (Downers Grove, IL: InterVarsity, 2003), 29.

22. Ibid., 199–200.

23. Ibid., 201.

24. George Eldon Ladd, *The Presence of the Future* (Grand Rapids: Eerdmans, 1981), 327–28.

25. Beale, *The Temple and the Church's Mission*, 271–72; Beale, *1–2 Thessalonians*, 204; George Milligan, *Paul's Epistles to the Thessalonians* (repr., Old Tappan, NJ: Revell, n.d.), 98; Ridderbos, *Paul*, 526. Bruce, on the other hand, sees this as an abandonment of civil order. See Bruce, *1 and 2 Thessalonians*, 167.

26. See the discussion of this in Robert Gundry, *The Church and the Tribulation: A Biblical Examination of Posttribulationism* (Grand Rapids: Zondervan, 1981), 114–15.

27. Beale, *1–2 Thessalonians*, 207–9; cf. Ernest Best, *The 1ˢᵗ and 2ⁿᵈ Epistles to the Thessalonians* (London: Adam & Charles Black, 1972), 282.

28. Contra Best, who sees the apostasy as the Jewish rejection of the gospel. Cf. Best, *1ˢᵗ and 2ⁿᵈ Epistles to the Thessalonians*, 282.

29. Ibid., 283.

30. Beale, *1–2 Thessalonians*, 205; Ridderbos, *Paul*, 526–27.

31. Beale, *1–2 Thessalonians*, 206.

32. Milligan, *Paul's Epistles to the Thessalonians*, 98.

33. Vos, *Pauline Eschatology*, 111.

34. Beale, *1–2 Thessalonians*, 206–7; cf. Vos, *Pauline Eschatology*, 111–12.

35. Morris, *First and Second Epistles to the Thessalonians*, 221.

36. The verb here, *kathisai* "to sit," is in the aorist tense and has the sense of "taking his seat" rather than "sitting." It is, as Best says, "the minimum of respect and to make the maximum claim to deity, for God sits." See Best, *1ˢᵗ and 2ⁿᵈ Epistles to the Thessalonians*, 286.

37. Fairbairn, *Interpretation of Prophecy*, 361. Fairbairn writes, "Paul knows of no other temple but the church itself."

38. Beale, *1–2 Thessalonians*, 207–8.

39. Beale, *The Temple and the Church's Mission*, 245–68.

40. Beale, *Book of Revelation*, 557–71; Caird, *Revelation of St. John*, 130–32; Johnson, *Triumph of the Lamb*, 165–69; Sweet, *Revelation*, 183–84.

41. Beale, *1–2 Thessalonians*, 207–8.

42. Ibid., 208–9.

43. Ibid.

44. Gentry, *Perilous Times*, 103–4.

45. In Romans 11 Paul also speaks of the conversion of Israel after the fullness of the Gentiles has come (Rom. 11:25–26). Cf. Riddlebarger, *A Case for Amillennialism*, 180–94. Hodge believes the specific signs that precede the end of the age are the preaching of the gospel to the ends of the earth, the conversion of Israel, and the coming of Antichrist. See Charles Hodge, *Systematic Theology*, vol. 3 (repr., Grand Rapids: Eerdmans, 1979), 792–836.

46. Ridderbos, *Paul*, 527.

47. Beale, *1–2 Thessalonians*, 209–10.

48. Ibid., 214–17. See also the discussion of the history of interpretation of this text in Milligan, *Paul's Epistles to the Thessalonians*, 166–73.

49. See the lengthy discussion in Best, *1ˢᵗ and 2ⁿᵈ Epistles to the Thessalonians*, 290–302.

50. Ridderbos, *Paul*, 527.

51. Vos, *Pauline Eschatology*, 131–35.

52. Beale, *1–2 Thessalonians*, 216.

53. Ibid. Beale directs the reader to his commentary on Revelation (Beale, *Book of Revelation*, specifically pp. 973–1028) for additional parallels between Revelation 20 and 2 Thessalonians 2.

54. Morris, *First and Second Epistles to the Thessalonians*, 228.

55. Whether that be AD 70 or at the end of the age—both events are still future when Paul wrote this Epistle.

56. Beale, *1–2 Thessalonians*, 221–22.

57. Morris, *First and Second Epistles to the Thessalonians*, 230–31.

58. Gentry, *Perilous Times*, 112–13.

Chapter 7: Know Your Enemy

1. Bernard McGinn, *Antichrist: Two Thousand Years of the Human Fascination with Evil* (New York: Columbia University Press, 2000). See also the studies by Gregory C. Jenks, *The Origins and Development of the Antichrist Myth* (New York: Walter De Gruyter, 1991); and L. J. Lietaert Peerbolte, *The Antecedents of Antichrist: A Traditio-Historical Study of the Earliest Christian Views on Eschatological Opponents* (New York: E. J. Brill, 1996).

2. *Epistle of Barnabas* (4:1–5), quoted in J. B. Lightfoot and J. R. Harmer, *The Apostolic Fathers* (repr., Grand Rapids: Baker, 1984), 239–42.

3. Polycarp, *Epistle to the Philippians*, 7.1.

4. F. F. Bruce, "Excursus on Antichrist," 183–84.

5. Justin Martyr, *Dialogue with Trypho*, 110, quoted in *The Ante-Nicene Fathers*, vol. 1, ed. Roberts and Donaldson, 253–54.

6. See the surveys in Bruce, "Excursus on Antichrist," 184; McGinn, *Antichrist*, 58–60; Vincent Miceli, *The Antichrist* (Harrison, NY: Roman Catholic Books, 1981), 50–55; and Jeffrey Burton Russell, *Satan: The Early Christian Tradition* (Ithaca, NY: Cornell University Press, 1981), 80–88.

7. Irenaeus, *Against Heresies*, in *The Ante-Nicene Fathers*, vol. 1, ed. Roberts and Donaldson, 315–567.

8. Bruce, "Excursus on Antichrist," 184.

9. Irenaeus, *Against Heresies*, 5.30.1.

10. McGinn, *Antichrist*, 59.

11. Irenaeus, *Against Heresies*, 5.30.2.

12. Ibid., 5.28.3.

13. Ibid., 5.30.3–4.

14. Ibid., 5.25.4.

15. A. Cleveland Coxe, "Introductory Notice to Hippolytus," in *The Ante-Nicene Fathers*, vol. 5, ed. Roberts and Donaldson, 3–7.

16. Hippolytus, "Treatise on Christ and Antichrist," in *The Ante-Nicene Fathers*, vol. 5, ed. Roberts and Donaldson, 204–19.

17. Bruce, "Excursus on Antichrist," 184; McGinn, *Antichrist*, 60–62; Johannes Quasten, *Patrology*, in *The Ante-Nicene Literature after Irenaeus*, vol. 2 (Westminster, MD: Christian Classics, 1990), 170–71.

18. Hippolytus, "Treatise on Christ and Antichrist," 207.

19. Ibid., 206.

20. Hippolytus, *Commentary on Daniel*, 2.39, quoted in "Fragments from Commentaries," in *The Ante-Nicene Fathers*, vol. 5, ed. Roberts and Donaldson, 184.

21. Hippolytus, "Treatise on Christ and Antichrist," 212–14.

22. Hippolytus, *Commentary on Daniel*, 2.4–6, quoted in "Fragments from Commentaries," in *The Ante-Nicene Fathers*, vol. 5, ed. Roberts and Donaldson.

23. McGinn, *Antichrist*, 62.

24. Charles E. Hill, *Regnum Caelorum: Patterns of Millennial Thought in Early Christianity*, 2nd ed. (Grand Rapids: Eerdmans, 2001), 160–69.

25. Bousset, *Antichrist Legend*, 186.

26. Norman Cohn, *The Pursuit of the Millennium* (New York: Oxford University Press, 1970), 79; McGinn, *Antichrist*, 100–103.

27. Christopher Hill, *Antichrist in Seventeenth-Century England*, 179.

28. Origen, "De Principiis," in *The Ante-Nicene Fathers*, vol. 4, ed. Roberts and Donaldson, 239–382.

29. Origin, *On First Principles*, 2.11. See the discussion of this section of *On First Principles* in Charles E. Hill, *Regnum Caelorum*, 176–80.

30. Origen, "Against Celsus," 6.45, in *The Ante-Nicene Fathers*, vol. 4, ed. Roberts and Donaldson, 395–669.

31. Origen, "Commentary on John," 2.4, in *The Ante-Nicene Fathers*, vol. 10, ed. Allan Menzies (Grand Rapids: Eerdmans, 1979), 297–408.

32. McGinn, *Antichrist*, 64.

33. Ibid., 76.

34. Ibid., 76–77.

35. Augustine, "City of God," 18.53, 20.12, in *St. Augustine's City of God and Christian Doctrine*, vol. 2 of *Nicene and Post-Nicene Fathers*, ed. Schaff, 1–511.

36. Ibid., 20.19, 20.23.

37. Miceli, *Antichrist*, 71–72.

38. Augustine, "Homilies on the First Epistle of John," 3.4, 3.8, in *St. Augustin: Homilies on the Gospel of John; Homilies on the First Epistle of John; Soliloquies*, vol. 7 of *Nicene and Post-Nicene Fathers*, ed. Philip Schaff (Grand Rapids: Eerdmans, 1979), 460–529.

39. McGinn, *Antichrist*, 77.

40. Augustine, "City of God," 19.19, in *St. Augustin's City of God and Christian Doctrine*, vol. 2 of *Nicene and Post-Nicene Fathers*, ed. Schaff.

41. Brian E. Daley, "Apocalypticism in Early Christian Theology," in *The Continuum History of Apocalypticism*, ed. Bernard McGinn, John J. Collins, and Stephen J. Stein (New York: Continuum, 2003), 221–53; McGinn, *Antichrist*, 63.

42. See the discussion and chart of Antichrist's physical characteristics in McGinn, *Antichrist*, 68–74, 103–6.

43. Miceli, *Antichrist*, 85.

44. McGinn, *Antichrist*, 80–82.

45. Daley, "Apocalypticism in Early Christian Theology," 249. See the helpful discussion of Gregory I in Miceli, *Antichrist*, 75–80.

46. Selections from Adso's letter along with an introductory essay can be found in Bernard McGinn, *Visions of the End: Apocalyptic Traditions in the Middle Ages* (New York: Columbia University Press, 1998), 82–87.

47. E. Ann Matter, "The Apocalypse in Early Medieval Exegesis," in *The Apocalypse in the Middle Ages*, ed. Richard K. Emmerson and Bernard McGinn (Ithaca, NY: Cornell University Press, 1992), 50.

48. McGinn, *Antichrist*, 101.

49. McGinn, *Visions of the End*, 83.

50. Cited in Miceli, *Antichrist*, 86.

51. Much of this art is depicted in Emmerson and McGinn, *The Apocalypse in the Middle Ages*, 105–289.

52. Miceli, *Antichrist*, 89–92.

53. Emmerson and McGinn, *The Apocalypse in the Middle Ages*, 293–413.

54. Christopher Hill, *Antichrist in Seventeenth-Century England*, 7; cited in Miceli, *Antichrist*, 84.

55. Christopher Hill, *Antichrist in Seventeenth-Century England*, 7.

56. McGinn, *Antichrist*, 115.

57. Ibid., 121.

58. Ibid.

59. See the discussions of this in ibid., 114–35.

60. McGinn, *Visions of the End*, 35.

61. See the essays by McGinn, *Visions of the End*, 126–41; and E. Randolph Daniel, "Joachim of Fiore: Patterns of History in the Apocalypse," in *The Apocalypse in the Middle Ages*, ed. Emmerson and McGinn, 27–88.

62. McGinn, *Visions of the End*, 127.

63. Daniel, "Joachim of Fiore," 77–78, 85.

64. As Cohn points out, Joachim's "idea of the third age could not really be reconciled with the Augustinian view that the Kingdom of God had been realized, so far as it ever could be realized on this earth, at the moment when the church came into

being, and that there would never be any Millennium but this." See Cohn, *The Pursuit of the Millennium*, 109.

65. McGinn, *Antichrist*, 138.

66. Ibid., 138–39.

67. Ibid., 140.

68. Ibid., 142; McGinn, *Vision of the End*, 135.

69. McGinn, *Antichrist*, 142.

70. Ibid., 143–81.

71. Christopher Hill, *Antichrist in Seventeenth-Century England*, 9.

72. McGinn, *Antichrist*, 207–8; Heiko A. Oberman, *Luther: Man between God and the Devil* (New York: Image Books, 1992), 67–72.

73. Oberman, *Luther*, 42–44.

74. Ibid., 71.

75. Julius Kostlin, *The Theology of Luther*, trans. Charles Hay (Philadelphia: Lutheran Publication Society, 1897), 1:410.

76. Ewald M. Plass, *What Luther Says* (Saint Louis: Concordia, 1959), vol. 1, 35–36n17.

77. Ibid., 1:95.

78. Ibid., 1:100.

79. Ibid., 2:1937.

80. Luther, "Table Talk," in *Luther's Works*, vol. 54, ed. Theodore G. Tappert (Philadelphia: Fortress, 1957), 101.

81. Ibid., 346–47.

82. Plass, *What Luther Says*, 1:84.

83. Ibid., 1:103

84. Ibid., 1:104.

85. "Apology" of the Augsburg Confession, 15.18.

86. According to Berkouwer, "The difference between Luther and Calvin was that the latter tended to identify the antichrist not so much with an individual pope, but with the ecclesiastical kingdom that would allegedly be sustained throughout all ages. In principle, however, there was a good deal of agreement between the two Reformers here." G. C. Berkouwer, *The Return of Christ* (Grand Rapids: Eerdmans, 1981), 263.

87. Calvin, *Epistles of Paul*, 398–99.

88. Ibid., 401.

89. John Calvin, "Prefatory Address," in *Institutes of the Christian Religion*, ed. John T. McNeill, trans. Ford Lewis Battles (Philadelphia: Westminster, 1960), 6.

90. Calvin, *Epistles of Paul*, 402.

91. Ibid., 403.

92. Ibid., 403–4.

93. Calvin, *Institutes*, 4.2.12; cf. 4.7.25.

94. John Calvin, *The Gospel according to St. John 11–21 and the First Epistle of John*, trans. T. H. L. Parker (Grand Rapids: Eerdmans, 1979), 257.

95. Ibid., 256.

96. Calvin, *Epistles of Paul*, 404–5.

97. Berkouwer is citing from Calvin, *Institutes*, 4.7.25. See Berkouwer, *Return of Christ*, 268.

98. Christopher Hill's fascinating work capably discusses and documents this point in *Antichrist in Seventeenth-Century England*, 1–40.

99. Ibid., 9. Bucer writes, "for the Antichrists, the pseudobishops and clergy, following their head, the supreme Roman Antichrist." Martin Bucer, *De Regno Christi*, in *Melanchthon and Bucer*, Library of Christian Classics, ed. Wilhelm Pauck (Philadelphia: Westminster, 1969), 209.

100. Christopher Hill, *Antichrist in Seventeenth-Century England*, 16.

101. Ibid., 9–11, 20, 22–24, 31.

102. Westminster Confession of Faith (1643), 25.6.

103. Ladd, *Commentary on the Revelation of John*, 11.

104. Gregg, *Revelation*, 34–37.

105. Christopher Hill, *Antichrist in Seventeenth-Century England*, 25.

106. Ibid., 25–26.

107. McGinn gives a date of 1695 and goes on to point out that Brightman also believed these events would be followed by a millennial reign of Christ over the earth, through his saints. McGinn, *Antichrist*, 222.

108. Christopher Hill, *Antichrist in Seventeenth-Century England*, 26–27. Cf. Peter Toon, "Puritan Eschatology, 1600–1648," in the *Evangelical Magazine* (1969): 6.

109. W. Robert Godfrey, "Millennial Views of the Seventeenth Century and Beyond," unpublished paper, 1.

110. Christopher Hill, *Antichrist in Seventeenth-Century England*, 111.

111. Ibid., 62–63.

112. Nicholas Tyacke, *Anti-Calvinists: The Rise of English Arminianism* (Oxford: Clarendon, 1991), 70–71, 266–70.

113. Christopher Hill, *Antichrist in Seventeenth-Century England*, 69–70.

114. Ibid., 98–110.

115. Godfrey, "Millennial Views of the Seventeenth Century and Beyond," 1–2; Christopher Hill, *The Experience of Defeat* (New York: Penguin Books, 1984), 54.

116. Christopher Hill, *Antichrist in Seventeenth-Century England*, 183–84.

117. McGinn, *Antichrist*, 238–40.

118. Ibid., 239–40.

119. Daniel Whitby (1638–1726), an eccentric Anglican writer, is the author of the two-volume work *Paraphrase and Commentary on the New Testament* (1703), which contained an eighteen-page treatise discussing the millennial reign of Christ. Whitby believed that the world would be converted by the gospel, the Jews would return to Palestine, and both the papacy and Islam would be defeated. This would lead to a thousand years of righteousness on earth. See Weber, *Living in the Shadow of the Second Coming*, 13. Also see Stephen J. Stein, "Introduction" to Jonathan Edwards, *Apocalyptic Writings* (New Haven: Yale University Press, 1977), 7. According to Stein, Edwards assimilated Whitby's views indirectly through the writings of Moses Lowman (1680–1752), who was, in turn, heavily influenced by Whitby. Edwards left behind a series of notes entitled "Extracts from Mr. Lowman" and refers to them throughout his discussion of Antichrist in "An Humble Attempt." See *Apocalyptic Writings*, 219–21. Also see C. C. Goen's essay, "Jonathan Edwards: A New Departure in Eschatology," *Church History* 28, no. 1 (March 1959): 25–41. Goen points out that while Whitby was Edwards's archenemy in the Arminian controversy, nevertheless, he did influence Edwards's overall eschatological outlook (37).

120. Goen, "Jonathan Edwards," 38.

121. Fuller, *Naming the Antichrist*, 65–68.

122. Robert W. Jenson, *America's Theologian: A Recommendation of Jonathan Edwards* (New York: Oxford University Press, 1988), 132.

123. Jonathan Edwards, "A History of the Work of Redemption," in *The Works of Jonathan Edwards*, vol. 1 (Carlisle, U.K.: Banner of Truth, 1979), 604–5.

124. Ibid., 595.

125. Jonathan Edwards, *Apocalyptic Writings*, in *Works of Jonathan Edwards*, vol. 5, ed. Stephen Stein (New Haven: Yale University Press, 1977), 129. Cf. George M. Marsden, *Jonathan Edwards: A Life* (New Haven: Yale University Press, 2003), 87–89; McGinn, *Antichrist*, 239–40.

126. Edwards, "A History of the Work of Redemption," 595.

127. Jonathan Edwards, "An Humble Attempt," in *The Works of Jonathan Edwards*, vol. 2 (Carlisle, U.K.: Banner of Truth, 1979), 306, 309. See also, Edwards, *Apocalyptic Writings*, 99, 116.

128. McGinn, *Antichrist*, 242–49.

129. Ernest R. Sandeen, *The Roots of Fundamentalism: British and American Millenarianism 1800–1930* (Grand Rapids: Baker, 1979), 42.

130. This is part of the general thesis set forth by McGinn, although I disagree with McGinn's attempt to explain this transition from a personal Antichrist to an institutional Antichrist in terms of the mythological "Antichrist's symbolizing of ultimate human evil." See McGinn, *Antichrist*, 245–49.

131. Hodge, *Systematic Theology*, 3:800–36, specifically 814–15, 822, 824–25, and 830.

132. Ibid., 3:836.

133. Louis Berkhof, *Systematic Theology* (Grand Rapids: Eerdmans, 1986), 702–3.

134. McGinn, *Antichrist*, 226.

135. Miceli, *Antichrist*, 126.

136. Ibid., 125–28; McGinn, *Antichrist*, 227.

137. McGinn, *Antichrist*, 226. For a summary of Bellarmine's and Suarez's views, see P. Huchede, *History of Antichrist* (Rockford, IL: Tan Books and Publishers, 1976).

138. Miceli, *Antichrist*, 131–32.

139. *Catechism of the Catholic Church* (New York: Image Books, 1995), 675–76.

Chapter 8: The Antichrist

1. S. P. Tregelles, *The Man of Sin* (Chiswick, U.K.: Sovereign Grace Advent Testimony, 1850), 3.

2. Warfield, *Antichrist*, 361. This is a conflict, Warfield, will necessarily end in victory. Surely this reflects Warfield's postmillenialism.

3. Morris, *First and Second Epistles to the Thessalonians*, 220–21.

4. Berkhof, *Systematic Theology*, 702.

5. McGinn, *Antichrist*, xx.

6. Hoekema, *The Bible and the Future*, 162.

7. Vos, *Pauline Eschatology*, 133–35.

Appendix

1. Gentry, *Before Jerusalem Fell*; see also Gentry, *Beast of Revelation*.

2. See John A. T. Robinson, *Redating the New Testament* (Philadelphia: Westminster, 1976), 221–53; J. M. Ford, *Revelation*, in the Anchor Bible, vol. 38 (Garden City, NY: Doubleday, 1975), 21–46. For an assessment of the influence of Lightfoot, Westcott, and Hort, see Stephen Neill and Tom Wright, *The Interpretation of the New Testament:*

1861–1986 (New York: Oxford University Press, 1988), 34–40. The important volumes from the famed threesome are: F. J. A. Hort, *The Apocalypse of St. John, 1–3* (London: Macmillan, 1908), xi–xxxiii; J. B. Lightfoot, *Biblical Essays* (repr., Grand Rapids: Baker, 1979), 51–70; Lightfoot and Harmer, *Apostolic Fathers*, 3; B. F. Westcott, *The Gospel according to St. John* (Grand Rapids: Eerdmans, 1962), lxxxiv–lxxxvii.

3. See, for example, D. A. Carson, Douglas J. Moo, and Leon Morris, *An Introduction to the New Testament* (Grand Rapids: Zondervan, 1992), 476. See also Beale, *Book of Revelation*, 4. While Carson, Moo, Morris, and Beale all acknowledge that the earlier dating is possible, both volumes affirm that the cumulative weight of the evidence is clearly on the side of the later dating.

4. Beale writes, "The consensus among twentieth-century scholars is that the Apocalypse was written during the reign of Domitian around AD 95. A minority of commentators have dated it immediately prior to the destruction of Jerusalem in AD 70." Beale, *Book of Revelation*, 4.

5. Sweet, *Revelation*, 27.

6. So-called critical scholars include the commentaries from R. H. Charles, H. B. Swete, G. B. Caird, Martin Kiddle, and J. P. M. Sweet, while conservative evangelical scholars include George Ladd, John Walvoord, G. R. Beasley-Murray, Alan Johnson, Robert Thomas, and Robert Mounce.

7. Robinson, *Redating the New Testament*, 238–42. Robinson says, "It is clear from what follows that this is the old temple of the earthly city" (p. 239).

8. Gentry, *Before Jerusalem Fell*, 169–74.

9. Caird, *Revelation of St. John*, 131.

10. Bauckham, *Climax of Prophecy*, 272; Johnson, *Triumph of the Lamb*, 165–69; Sweet, *Revelation*, 8.

11. See, for example, the discussion in Kiddle, *Revelation of St. John*, 174–97.

12. Beale, *Book of Revelation*, 21, 559–65.

13. Swete, *Apocalypse of St. John*, 132.

14. See the summation of these issues in Beckwith, *Apocalypse of John*, 704–9. Futurists tend to see this as a reference to a succession of kingdoms. See Ladd, *Commentary on the Revelation of John*, 229; and Joseph A. Seiss, *The Apocalypse* (repr., Grand Rapids: Zondervan, 1957), 391–94.

15. Gentry, *Before Jerusalem Fell*, 153–59; Robinson, *Redating the New Testament*, 242–52.

16. Beale, *Book of Revelation*, 21–24.

17. Beasley-Murray, *Book of Revelation*, 257.

18. Sweet, *Revelation*, 257.

19. Beale, *Book of Revelation*, 870–76; Beasley-Murray, *Book of Revelation*, 257; Caird, *Revelation of St. John*, 216–18; Johnson, *Triumph of the Lamb*, 250–51.

20. Caird, *Revelation of St. John*, 218.

21. Beasley-Murray, *Book of Revelation*; Johnson, *Triumph of the Lamb*, 251.

22. Gentry, *Before Jerusalem Fell*, 193–219.

23. Swete, *Apocalypse of St. John*, lxxxiv.

24. Beale, *Book of Revelation*, 17–18; Bauckham, *Climax of Prophecy*, 429–31.

25. Bauckham, *Climax of Prophecy*, 451. Sweet puts it this way: "In a world which was accepting a deified state under a deified head as the source of all salvation, and in a church which was accepting this valuation at the expense of its proper witness to the rule of God, Revelation uncovered the missing dimension, so that Christians should act according to the will of the God they could not see, rather than that of the

Caesar they could—so that at whatever cost, they should put eternal destiny before apparent security and prosperity in the present." Sweet, *Revelation*, 2.

26. DeMar, *Last Days Madness*, 359.

27. Bauckham, *Climax of Prophecy*, 172; Caird, *Revelation of St. John*, 138.

28. Sweet, *Revelation*, 15.

29. Beale, *Book of Revelation*, 25.

30. Chilton, *Days of Vengeance*, 64–67; cf. Gentry, *Before Jerusalem Fell*, 121–32.

31. See, for example, Gerard Van Groningen, *Messianic Revelation in the Old Testament* (Grand Rapids: Baker, 1990), 905–7; Beale, *Book of Revelation*, 26; Caird, *Revelation of St. John*, 18.

32. Beale, *Book of Revelation*, 26.

33. Cited in Kiddle, *Revelation of St. John*, xxxvii.

34. Griffin, *Nero*, 15; Champlin, *Nero*, 121.

35. S. R. F. Price, *Rituals and Power: The Roman Imperial Cult in Asia Minor* (New York: Cambridge University Press, 1984), 196–98; Leonard L. Thompson, *The Book of Revelation, Apocalypse and Empire* (New York: Oxford University Press, 1990), 13–17. Thompson writes that "some scholars still argue for dating the book shortly after Nero's death when several people were vying to be emperor; but when the weight of internal and external evidence is taken together, we may conclude with most scholars that Revelation was written sometime in the latter years of Domitian's reign, that is, 92–96 CE" (p. 15).

36. Thompson, *Book of Revelation*, 97, 104.

37. Pliny the Younger, *Letters*, 10.96–97, www.earlychristianwriting.com/text/pliny.html.

38. Thompson, *Book of Revelation*, 96–101.

39. Beale, *Book of Revelation*, 9.

40. Hemer, *The Letters to the Seven Churches of Asia in Their Local Setting* (Grand Rapids: Eerdmans, 1989), 11.

41. Ibid., 35–56.

42. See the discussion in Bruce, *Paul, the Apostle of the Heart Set Free*, 286–99.

43. Hemer, *Letters to the Seven Churches of Asia*, 178–209.

44. Ibid., 78–105.

45. Swete, *Apocalypse of St. John*, 12.

46. Beale, *Book of Revelation*, 12.

47. Price, *Rituals and Power*, 197–98. See also, Hemer, *Letters to the Seven Churches of Asia*, 35–56.

48. Beale, *Book of Revelation*, 17.

49. Hemer, *Letters to the Seven Churches of Asia*, 66.

50. Beale, *Book of Revelation*, 17n89.

51. Gentry, *Before Jerusalem Fell*, 320.

52. Beale, *Book of Revelation*, 18–19.

53. Early date defenders point out that Irenaeus's position regarding John's authorship of both Revelation and the Gospel is self-contradictory. See Robinson, *Redating the New Testament*, 222.

54. Irenaeus, *Against Heresies*, 5.30.3.

55. Gentry, *Before Jerusalem Fell*, 48–57.

56. Robinson, *Redating the New Testament*, 221.

SELECTED BIBLIOGRAPHY

Adams, Jay. *The Time Is At Hand*. Greenville, SC: A Press, 1987.

Allen, Leslie C. *Ezekiel 20–48*. Word Biblical Commentary. Vol. 29. Dallas: Word, 1990.

Anderson, Sir Robert. *The Coming Prince*. Reprint, Grand Rapids: Kregel, 1957.

Augustine. "City of God." In *St. Augustin's City of God and Christian Doctrine*. Vol. 2 of *Nicene and Post-Nicene Fathers*. Edited by Philip Schaff. Grand Rapids: Eerdmans, 1979.

———. "Homilies on the First Epistle of John." In *St. Augustin: Homilies on the Gospel of John; Homilies on the First Epistle of John; Soliloquies*. Vol. 7 of *Nicene and Post-Nicene Fathers*. Edited by Philip Schaff. Grand Rapids: Eerdmans, 1979.

Aune, David E. *Revelation 17–22*. Word Biblical Commentary. Vol. 52c. Nashville: Thomas Nelson, 1998.

Balmer, Randall. *Mine Eyes Have Seen the Glory: A Journey into the Evangelical Subculture in America*. New York: Oxford University Press, 1989.

Barnes, Albert. "Revelation." In *Notes on the New Testament*. Reprint, Grand Rapids: Baker, 1954.

Bauckham, Richard. *The Climax of Prophecy*. Edinburgh: T & T Clark, 1993.

Beale, G. K. *The Book of Revelation: A Commentary on the Greek Text*. Grand Rapids: Eerdmans, 1999.

———. *1–2 Thessalonians*. IVP New Testament Commentary Series. Downers Grove, IL: InterVarsity, 2003.

———. *The Temple and the Church's Mission: A Biblical Theology of the Dwelling Place of God*. Downers Grove, IL: InterVarsity, 2004.

Beasley-Murray, G. R. *The Book of Revelation*. Grand Rapids: Eerdmans, 1974.

Beckwith, Isbon T. *The Apocalypse of John*. Reprint, Grand Rapids: Baker, 1967.

Berkouwer, G. C. *The Return of Christ*. Grand Rapids: Eerdmans, 1981.

215

Best, Ernest. *The 1st and 2nd Epistles to the Thessalonians*. London: Adam & Charles Black, 1972.

Bousset, Wilhelm. *The Antichrist Legend: A Chapter in Christian and Jewish Folklore*. Translated by A. H. Keane. London: Hutchison, 1896.

Boyer, Paul. *When Time Shall Be No More: Prophecy Belief in Modern American Culture*. Cambridge, MA: Belknap, 1999.

Bright, John. *A History of Israel*. Philadelphia: Westminster, 1981.

Brown, Raymond E. *The Epistles of John*. Vol. 30 of the Anchor Bible. Garden City, NY: Doubleday, 1983.

Bruce, F. F. "Excursus on Antichrist." In *1 & 2 Thessalonians*. Word Biblical Commentary. Vol. 45. Waco: Word, 1982.

———. *New Testament History*. New York: Doubleday, 1980.

———. *Paul: the Apostle of the Heart Set Free*. Grand Rapids: Eerdmans, 1979.

Bucer, Martin. *De Regno Christi*. In *Melanchthon and Bucer*. Library of Christian Classics. Edited by Wilhelm Pauck. Philadelphia: Westminster, 1969.

Caird, G. B. *The Language and Imagery of the Bible*. Philadelphia: Westminster, 1980.

———. *The Revelation of St. John*. Peabody, MA: Hendrickson, 1999.

Calvin, John. *The Epistles of Paul to the Romans and to the Thessalonians*. Translated by Ross MacKenzie. Grand Rapids: Eerdmans, 1979.

———. *The Gospel according to St. John 11–21 and the First Epistle of John*. Translated by T. H. L. Parker. Grand Rapids: Eerdmans, 1979.

———. *Institutes of the Christian Religion*. Edited by John T. McNeill. Translated by Ford Lewis Battles. Philadelphia: Westminster, 1960.

Carson, D. A. "Matthew." In *The Expositor's Bible Commentary*. Vol. 8. Edited by Frank E. Gaebelein and J. D. Douglas. Grand Rapids: Zondervan, 1984.

Carson, D. A., Douglas J. Moo, and Leon Morris. *An Introduction to the New Testament*. Grand Rapids: Zondervan, 1992.

Cartledge, Paul. *Alexander the Great*. Woodstock, NY: Overlook, 2004.

Champlin, Edward. *Nero*. Cambridge, MA: Belknap, 2003.

Chilton, David. *The Days of Vengeance: An Exposition of the Book of Revelation*. Fort Worth: Dominion, 1987.

Cohn, Norman. *The Pursuit of the Millennium*. New York: Oxford University Press, 1970.

Collins, J. J. "Sibylline Oracles." In *Dictionary of New Testament Background*. Edited by Craig A. Evans and Stanley E. Porter. Downers Grove, IL: InterVarsity, 2000.

Coxe, A. Cleveland. "Introductory Notice to Hippolytus." In *The Ante-Nicene Fathers*. Vol. 5. Edited by Alexander Roberts and James Donaldson. Grand Rapids: Eerdmans, 1979.

Cranfield, C. E. B. *The Gospel according to St. Mark*. Cambridge Greek Testament. New York: Cambridge University Press, 1983.

Daley, Brian E. "Apocalypticism in Early Christian Theology." In *The Continuum History of Apocalypticism*. Edited by Bernard McGinn, John J. Collins, and Stephen J. Stein. New York: Continuum, 2003.

Daniel, E. Randolph. "Joachim of Fiore: Patterns of History in the Apocalypse." In *The Apocalypse in the Middle Ages*. Edited by Richard K. Emmerson and Bernard McGinn. Ithaca, NY: Cornell University Press, 1992.

DeMar, Gary. *Last Days Madness*. Atlanta: American Vision, 1999.

Denzinger, Henry. *The Sources of Catholic Dogma*. Translated by Roy J. Deferrari. St. Louis: Herder, 1957.

Edwards, Jonathan. *Apocalyptic Writings*. In *Works of Jonathan Edwards*. Vol. 5. Edited by Stephen Stein. New Haven: Yale University Press, 1977.

———. "A History of the Work of Redemption." In *The Works of Jonathan Edwards*. Vol. 1. Carlisle, U.K.: Banner of Truth, 1979.

Ernst, J. "ἀντίχριστος." In *Exegetical Dictionary of the New Testament*. Vol. 1. Edited by Horst Balz and Gerhard Schneider. Grand Rapids: Eerdmans, 1990.

Evans, Michael D. *The American Prophecies: Ancient Scriptures Reveal Our Nation's Future*. New York: Warner Faith, 2004.

Fairbairn, Patrick. *The Interpretation of Prophecy*. Reprint, Carlisle, U.K.: Banner of Truth, 1993.

Feinberg, Charles. *The Prophecy of Ezekiel*. Chicago: Moody, 1978.

Ford, J. M. *Revelation*. Anchor Bible. Vol. 38. Garden City, NY: Doubleday, 1975.

Fuller, Robert. *Naming the Antichrist: The History of an American Obsession*. New York: Oxford University Press, 1995.

Gabler, Neal. *Life: The Movie. How Entertainment Conquered Reality*. New York: Vintage Books, 1998.

Geddert, T. J. "Apocalyptic." In *Dictionary of Jesus and the Gospels*. Edited by Joel B. Green, Scot McKnight, and I. Howard Marshall. Downers Grove, IL: InterVarsity, 1992.

Gentry, Kenneth L. *The Beast of Revelation*. Tyler, TX: Institute for Christian Economics, 1994.

———. *Before Jerusalem Fell: Dating the Book of Revelation*. Atlanta: American Vision, 1998.

———. *Perilous Times: A Study in Eschatological Evil*. Texarkana, AR: Covenant Media Foundation, 1999.

Godfrey, W. Robert. "Millennial Views of the Seventeenth Century and Beyond." Unpublished paper.

Goen, C. C. "Jonathan Edwards: A New Departure in Eschatology." *Church History* 28, no. 1 (March 1959).

Goldingay, John E. *Daniel*. Word Biblical Commentary. Vol. 30. Waco: Word, 1989.

Gregg, Steve. *Revelation: Four Views, a Parallel Commentary*. Nashville: Thomas Nelson, 1997.

Griffin, Miriam T. *Nero: The End of a Dynasty*. New Haven: Yale University Press, 1984.

Gundry, Robert. *The Church and the Tribulation: A Biblical Examination of Posttribulationism*. Grand Rapids: Zondervan, 1981.

Hagner, Donald A. *Matthew 14–28*. Word Biblical Commentary. Vol. 33b. Dallas: Word, 1995.

Harrison, R. K. *Introduction to the Old Testament*. Grand Rapids: Eerdmans, 1979.

Hemer, Colin. *The Letters to the Seven Churches of Asia in Their Local Setting*. Grand Rapids: Eerdmans, 1989.

Hendricksen, William. *More than Conquerors*. Grand Rapids: Baker, 1982.

Hill, Christopher. *Antichrist in Seventeenth-Century England*. New York: Oxford University Press, 1971.

———. *The Experience of Defeat*. New York: Penguin Books, 1984.

Hippolytus. "Fragments from Commentaries." In *The Ante-Nicene Fathers*. Vol. 5. Edited by Alexander Roberts and James Donaldson. Grand Rapids: Eerdmans, 1979.

———. "Treatise on Christ and Antichrist." In *The Ante-Nicene Fathers*. Vol. 5. Edited by Alexander Roberts and James Donaldson. Grand Rapids: Eerdmans, 1979.

Hitchcock, Mark. *What Jesus Says about Earth's Final Days*. Sisters, OR: Multnomah, 2003.

Hodge, Charles. *Systematic Theology*. 3 Vols. Reprint, Grand Rapids: Eerdmans, 1979.

Hoekema, Anthony. *The Bible and the Future*. Grand Rapids: Eerdmans, 1979.

Hort, F. J. A. *The Apocalypse of St. John, I-III*. London: Macmillan, 1908.

Huchede, P. *History of Antichrist*. Rockford, IL: Tan Books and Publishers, 1976.

Hunt, Dave. *Global Peace and the Rise of Antichrist*. Eugene, OR: Harvest House, 1990.

———. *A Woman Rides the Beast*. Eugene, OR: Harvest House, 1994.

Irenaeus. *Against Heresies*. In *The Ante-Nicene Fathers*. Vol. 1. Edited by Alexander Roberts and James Donaldson. Grand Rapids: Eerdmans, 1979.

Jeffrey, Grant R. *Armageddon: Appointment with Destiny*. New York: Bantam Books, 1990.

Jenks, Gregory C. *The Origins and Development of the Antichrist Myth*. New York: Walter De Gruyter, 1991.

Jenson, Robert W. *America's Theologian: A Recommendation of Jonathan Edwards*. New York: Oxford University Press, 1988.

Johnson, Dennis E. *Triumph of the Lamb*. Phillipsburg, NJ: Presbyterian and Reformed, 2001.

Josephus, Flavius. "Wars of the Jews." In *Josephus: Complete Works*. Translated by William Whitson. Grand Rapids: Kregel, 1960.

Kamen, Henry. *The Duke of Alba*. New Haven: Yale University Press, 2004.

Kauder, Erwin. "Antichrist." In *The New International Dictionary of New Testament Theology*. Edited by Colin Brown. Grand Rapids: Zondervan, 1982.

Kee, Howard Clark. "Testaments of the Twelve Patriarchs." In *Dictionary of New Testament Background*. Edited by Craig A. Evans and Stanley E. Porter. Downers Grove, IL: InterVarsity, 2000.

Kiddle, Martin. *The Revelation of St. John*. New York: Harper and Brothers, 1940.

Kline, Meredith G. "The Covenant of the Seventieth Week." In *The Law and the Prophets: Old Testament Studies Prepared in Honor of Oswald Thompson Allis*. Edited by John H. Skilton. Phillipsburg, NJ: Presbyterian and Reformed, 1974.

———. *Kingdom Prologue*. South Hamilton, MA: Gordon-Conwell Theological Seminary, 1993.

———. *The Structure of Biblical Authority*. Grand Rapids: Eerdmans, 1981.

Knight, J. M. "Ascension of Isaiah." In *Dictionary of New Testament Background*. Edited by Craig A. Evans and Stanley E. Porter. Downers Grove, IL: InterVarsity, 2000.

Kostlin, Julius. *The Theology of Luther*. Translated by Charles Hay. Philadelphia: Lutheran Publication Society, 1897.

Kummel, W. G. *Promise and Fulfillment*. London: SCM, 1957.

Ladd, George E. *A Commentary on the Revelation of John*. Grand Rapids: Eerdmans, 1987.

———. *The Last Things*. Grand Rapids: Eerdmans, 1982.

———. *The Presence of the Future*. Grand Rapids: Eerdmans, 1981.

———. *A Theology of the New Testament*. Revised edition. Grand Rapids: Eerdmans, 1994.

LaHaye, Tim, and Jerry B. Jenkins. *The Mark: The Beast Rules the World*. Wheaton: Tyndale, 2001.

———. *Nicolae: The Rise of the Antichrist*. Wheaton: Tyndale, 1997.

LaLonde, Peter, and Paul LaLonde. *Racing toward the Mark of the Beast*. Eugene, OR: Harvest House, 1994.

Leon-Dufour, Xavier. *Dictionary of Biblical Theology*. 2nd edition. New York: Seabury, 1983.

Lightfoot, J. B. *Biblical Essays*. Reprint, Grand Rapids: Baker, 1979.

Lightfoot, J. B., and J. R. Harmer. *The Apostolic Fathers*. Reprint, Grand Rapids: Baker, 1984.

Lindsey, Hal. *The Late Great Planet Earth*. Grand Rapids: Zondervan, 1970.

———. *Planet Earth—2000 AD*. Palos Verde, CA: Western Front, 1994.

———. *There's a New World Coming: A Prophetic Odyssey*. Santa Ana: Vision House, 1973.

Luther, Martin. "Table Talk." In *Luther's Works*. Vol. 54. Edited by Theodore G. Tappert. Philadelphia: Fortress, 1957.

Maag, Victor. "The Antichrist as a Symbol of Evil." In *Evil*. Edited by James Hillman. Evanston, IL: Northwestern University Press, 1967.

Malone, Peter. *Movie Christs and Antichrists*. New York: Crossroad, 1990.

Marsden, George M. *Jonathan Edwards: A Life*. New Haven: Yale University Press, 2003.

Martin, Ralph P. *2 Corinthians*. Word Biblical Commentary. Vol. 40. Waco: Word, 1986.

Martyr, Justin. "Dialogue with Trypho." In *The Ante-Nicene Fathers*. Vol. 1. Edited by Alexander Roberts and James Donaldson. Grand Rapids: Eerdmans, 1979.

Mathison, Keith A., ed. *When Will These Things Be? A Reformed Response to Hyper-Preterism*. Phillipsburg, NJ: Presbyterian and Reformed, 2004.

Matter, E. Ann. "The Apocalypse in Early Medieval Exegesis." In *The Apocalypse in the Middle Ages*. Edited by Richard K. Emmerson and Bernard McGinn. Ithaca, NY: Cornell University Press, 1992.

McCall, Thomas S., and Zola Levitt. *Satan in the Sanctuary*. Chicago: Moody, 1973.

McClain, Alva J. *Daniel's Prophecy of the 70 Weeks*. Grand Rapids: Zondervan, 1969.

McGinn, Bernard. *Antichrist: Two Thousand Years of the Human Fascination with Evil*. New York: Columbia University Press, 2000.

———. *Visions of the End: Apocalyptic Traditions in the Middle Ages*. New York: Columbia University Press, 1998.

Miceli, Vincent. *The Antichrist*. Harrison, NY: Roman Catholic Books, 1981.

Milligan, George. *Paul's Epistles to the Thessalonians*. Reprint, Old Tappan, NJ: Revell, n.d.

Morris, Leon. *The First and Second Epistles to the Thessalonians*. New International Commentary on the New Testament. Grand Rapids: Eerdmans, 1991.

Mounce, Robert H. *The Book of Revelation*. New International Commentary on the New Testament. Grand Rapids: Eerdmans, 1977.

Murray, Iain H. *The Puritan Hope*. Carlisle, U.K.: Banner of Truth, 1975.

Neill, Stephen, and Tom Wright. *The Interpretation of the New Testament: 1861–1986*. New York: Oxford University Press, 1988.

Oberman, Heiko A. *Luther: Man between God and the Devil*. New York: Image Books, 1992.

Origen. "Against Celsus." In *The Ante-Nicene Fathers*. Vol. 4. Edited by Alexander Roberts and James Donaldson. Grand Rapids: Eerdmans, 1979.

———. "Commentary on John." In *The Ante-Nicene Fathers*. Vol. 10. Edited by Allan Menzies. Grand Rapids: Eerdmans, 1979.

———. "De Principiis." In *The Ante-Nicene Fathers*. Vol. 4. Edited by Alexander Roberts and James Donaldson. Grand Rapids: Eerdmans, 1979.

Peerbolte, L. J. Lietaert. *The Antecedents of Antichrist: A Traditio-Historical Study of the Earliest Christian Views on Eschatological Opponents*. New York: E. J. Brill, 1996.

Pentecost, J. Dwight. *Things to Come*. Grand Rapids: Zondervan, 1978.

Plass, Ewald M. *What Luther Says*. St. Louis: Concordia, 1959.

Price, S. R. F. *Rituals and Power: The Roman Imperial Cult in Asia Minor*. New York: Cambridge University Press, 1984.

Quasten, Johannes. *Patrology*. In *The Ante-Nicene Literature after Ireneaus*. Vol. 2. Westminster, MD: Christian Classics, 1990.

Renan, Joseph-Ernest. *Antichrist*. Translated by William G. Hutchinson. London: Walter Scott, 1899.

Ridderbos, Herman. *The Coming of the Kingdom*. Philadelphia: Presbyterian and Reformed, 1962.

———. *Matthew*. Grand Rapids: Zondervan, 1987.

———. *Paul: An Outline of His Theology*. Grand Rapids: Eerdmans, 1982.

Riddlebarger, Kim. *A Case for Amillennialism*. Grand Rapids: Baker, 2003.

Robinson, John A. T. *Redating the New Testament*. Philadelphia: Westminster, 1976.

Rossing, Barbara R. *The Rapture Exposed*. Boulder, CO: Westview, 2004.

Russell, Jeffrey Burton. *Lucifer: The Devil in the Middle Ages*. Ithaca, NY: Cornell University Press, 1986.

———. *Satan: The Early Christian Tradition*. Ithaca, NY: Cornell University Press, 1981.

Russell, J. Stuart. *The Parousia: A Critical Inquiry into the New Testament Doctrine of Our Lord's Second Coming*. Reprint, Grand Rapids: Baker, 1983.

Sandeen, Ernest R. *The Roots of Fundamentalism: British and American Millenarianism 1800–1930*. Grand Rapids: Baker, 1979.

Schaff, Philip. *Creeds of Christendom*. Reprint, Grand Rapids: Baker, 1983.

Seiss, Joseph A. *The Apocalypse*. Reprint, Grand Rapids: Zondervan, 1957.

Smalley, Stephen S. *1, 2, 3 John*. Word Biblical Commentary. Vol. 51. Waco: Word, 1984.

Smith, Chuck. *What the World Is Coming To*. Costa Mesa, CA: Maranatha, 1977.

Stein, Stephen J. "Introduction" to Jonathan Edwards. In *Apocalyptic Writings*. New Haven: Yale University Press, 1977.

Sweet, J. P. M. *Revelation*. London: SCM, 1979.

Swete, Henry Barclay. *The Apocalypse of St. John*. New York: Macmillan, 1907.

Thompson, Leonard L. *The Book of Revelation, Apocalypse and Empire*. New York: Oxford University Press, 1990.

Toon, Peter. "Puritan Eschatology, 1600–1648." In the *Evangelical Magazine*. 1969.

Tregelles, S. P. *The Man of Sin*. Chiswick, U.K.: Sovereign Grace Advent Testimony, 1850.

Tyacke, Nicholas. *Anti-Calvinists: The Rise of English Arminianism*. Oxford: Clarendon, 1991.

VanderKam, James C. "Messianism and Apocalypticism." In *The Continuum History of Apocalypticism*. Edited by Bernard McGinn, John J. Collins, and Stephen J. Stein. New York: Continuum, 2003.

Van Groningen, Gerard. *Messianic Revelation in the Old Testament*. Grand Rapids: Baker, 1990.

Venema, Cornelius P. *The Promise of the Future*. Carlisle, U.K.: Banner of Truth, 2000.

Vos, Geerhardus. *Biblical Theology*. Grand Rapids: Eerdmans, 1977.

———. *The Pauline Eschatology*. Grand Rapids: Baker, 1982.

Walvoord, John F. *Daniel: The Key to Prophetic Revelation*. Chicago: Moody, 1971.

———. "Escape from Planet Earth." In *Foreshocks of Antichrist*. Edited by William T. James. Eugene, OR: Harvest House, 1997.

———. *Major Bible Prophecies*. Grand Rapids: Zondervan, 1991.

———. *The Revelation of Jesus Christ*. Chicago: Moody, 1966.

Warfield, B. B. "Antichrist." In *Selected Shorter Writings of Benjamin B. Warfield*. Vol. 1. Edited by John E. Meeter. Phillipsburg, NJ: Presbyterian and Reformed, 1980.

———. "The Prophecies of St. Paul." In *Biblical Doctrines*. Grand Rapids: Baker, 1981.

Watson, D. F. "Antichrist." In *Dictionary of the Later New Testament and Its Developments*. Edited by Ralph P. Martin and Peter H. Davids. Downers Grove, IL: InterVarsity, 1997.

Webber, David. "Cyberspace: The Beast's Worldwide Spiderweb." In *Foreshocks of Antichrist*. Edited by William T. James. Eugene, OR: Harvest House, 1997.

Weber, Timothy P. *Living in the Shadow of the Second Coming: American Premillennialism 1875–1982*. Grand Rapids: Zondervan, 1983.

———. *On the Road to Armageddon: How Evangelicals Became Israel's Best Friend*. Grand Rapids: Baker, 2004.

Westcott, B. F. *The Gospel according to St. John*. Grand Rapids: Eerdmans, 1962.

Witherington, Ben. *Jesus, Paul and the End of the World*. Downers Grove, IL: InterVarsity, 1992.

Yamauchi, Edwin M. *Foes from the Northern Frontier: Invading Hordes from the Russian Steppes*. Grand Rapids: Baker, 1982.

Young, E. J. *Daniel*. Carlisle, U.K.: Banner of Truth, 1978.

SCRIPTURE INDEX

Subject Index

Abel, 41, 197n11
abomination of desolation, 49, 68, 70–72, 139, 199n15
Adam and Eve, 40
Adso, 138, 142–43, 147, 164
Albertus Magnus, 138
Albigenses, 165
Alexander the Great, 22, 23, 194n9
already/not yet, 35–36, 64, 123–24
American culture, Antichrist speculation in, 26, 33, 160–61
American Revolution, 160
amillennialism, 13, 15, 119, 121, 131
Ancient of Days, 50, 103
angel of Revelation 20, 131
Anointed One, 54–55
Antichrist (as eschatological individual), 14, 36, 85, 170–71
in Daniel, 48–51
as evil personified, 23
in film and fiction, 17–25
as final heretic, 175–76
as Jew, 136–38, 143
in John's epistles, 77
in medieval art, 143
as myth, 62, 161, 211n130
as Satan with human face, 23–24
antichrist(s)
as contrary to Christ, 140–41
as internal threat, 85–87
in New Testament, 38, 39

as one who denies Jesus Christ, 21
as present reality, 78–80, 82–83, 85
as series of foes, 36, 122, 134, 175
as spiritual principle, 139
used in two senses, 169–70
Antichrist speculation, 20
in American culture, 26, 33, 160–61
among Puritans, 154–57
in Middle Ages, 144
Antichristus (play), 143
anti-Messiah, 197n5
Antiochus IV Epiphanes, 40, 48–50, 70, 73, 92, 104, 118, 127, 130, 161, 169, 199n15
Antipas, 100, 188–89
antipope, 145, 165
antitype, 69, 197n9
apocalyptic genre, 38–40, 91
apostasy, 67, 78, 85, 86, 90, 124, 125–26, 134, 136, 165, 170, 171, 174, 176
Arians, 164
Armageddon, 19, 26
Arminianism, 156
Arrian, 194n9
art, depiction of Antichrist, 143
Ascension of Isaiah, 95, 197n5
Assyria, 92
Attila the Hun, 23
Augsburg Confession, 150
Augustine, 140–41, 143, 146, 197n11

229

Kim Riddlebarger (Ph.D., Fuller Theological Seminary) is senior pastor of Christ Reformed Church in Anaheim, California, a visiting professor of systematic theology at Westminster Seminary California, and author of *A Case for Amillennialism: Understanding the End Times*. He is cohost of the popular *White Horse Inn* weekly radio program.